The Big6™ Collection

The Best of the

Big6 eNewsletter

Volume 2

Edited by
Michael B. Eisenberg
and
Laura I. Robinson

Linworth Books

Professional Development Resources for
K-12 Library Media and Technology Specialists

Editors: Michael B. Eisenberg and Laura I. Robinson

Linworth Books:
Carol Simpson, Editorial Director
Judi Repman, Associate Editor

Published by Linworth Publishing, Inc.
480 East Wilson Bridge Road, Suite L
Worthington, Ohio 43085

ISBN: 1-58683-194-1

5 4 3 2 1

Table of Contents

Introduction

Notes from Mike and Laura

*W*elcome again, Big6ers! We're back with our second compilation of articles from the *Big6™ Newsletter*. The content is brand new—including the very best from the last three years of the *Big6 eNewsletter*. This new collection is jam-packed with even more Big6 useful tips and ideas, comprehensive articles, and practical lesson plans that are ready for implementation in classrooms at all levels. This time around, we solicited articles and lessons that span the full range—kindergarten through the college level—and focus on key educational issues such as standards, technology, special needs, and learning styles.

We all know that the Big6 makes a vast difference in kids' learning, and increasingly, there's proof of its effectiveness:

> *Data collected from thousands of students showed that students who were taught informative nonfiction using the Big6 approach with a combination of analytical, creative, and practical activities, outperformed students who were taught two alternative approaches (see materials at: www.yale.edu/pace).*

> — **Linda Jarvin, Ph.D., Associate Director, PACE Center, Yale University**

The Big6 has helped educators to integrate information and technology literacy as well as critical thinking into student learning, particularly the past few years. This book presents the latest Big6 thinking, tools, and strategies from dozens of Big6 authors—classroom teachers and teacher-librarians on the frontlines in addition to researchers and academics from around the globe. Combined, they offer valuable resources that are ready for your immediate use.

The Big6

If you're new to the world of Big6, here's a quick overview:

The Big6 Skills, developed by Mike Eisenberg and Bob Berkowitz, is the most widely-known and widely-used approach to teaching information and technology skills in the world. Used in thousands of K-12 schools, higher education institutions, and corporate and adult training programs, the Big6 information problem-solving model is applicable whenever people need and use information. The Big6 integrates information search and use skills along with technology tools in a systematic process to find, use, apply, and evaluate information to specific needs and tasks. The Big6 is a process model of problem solving that encompasses six stages and two sub-stages under each. People go through these Big6 stages—consciously or not—when they seek or apply information to solve a problem or make a decision. It's not necessary to complete these stages in a linear order, and a given stage doesn't have to take a lot of time. In almost all successful problem-solving situations, all stages are addressed at some point in time.

In addition to considering the Big6 as a process, another useful way to view the Big6 is as a set of basic, essential life skills. These skills can be applied across situations—to school, personal, and work settings. The Big6 Skills are applicable to all subject areas across the full range of grade levels. Students and adults can use the Big6 Skills whenever they need information to solve a problem, make a decision, or complete a task—whether on a personal or work/school related level.

Why Big6?

We all suffer from information overload. There's just too much "stuff" out there, and it's not easy to keep up. At the same time, there's an irony—yes, we are surrounded by information, but we can never seem to find what we want, when we want it, and in a form we want it so that we can use it effectively.

One solution to the information problem—the one that seems to be most often adopted in schools (as well as in business and society in general)—is to speed things up. We try to pack in more and more content, to work faster to get more done. But, this is a losing proposition. Speeding things up can only work for so long. Instead, we need to think about helping students to work smarter, not faster. There is an alternative to speeding things up. It's the smarter solution—one that helps students develop the skills and understandings they need to find, process, and use information effectively. This smarter solution focuses on process as well as content. Some people call this smarter solution "information literacy." An increasingly popular term is information, communication, and technology literacy or ICT skills. All of these—processes, critical thinking, computers and more—are included in the Big6 approach. The Big6 offers a process model of how people of all ages solve an information problem. Twenty-first century tools, technologies, and resources all make sense in a Big6 context.

One of the things we hear over and over is just how busy teachers and students are. "There's just no time. That's why we can't do even one more thing, even something that seems as valuable as the Big6."

Well, it's true about everyone being so busy. With more and more content packed into curriculum, state and local standards, and required tests, the time demands on teachers and students are overwhelming. That's why it's so important that the Big6 must not be an add-on. We don't **add** the Big6; we **integrate** by focusing Big6 learning on assignments and tasks in the classroom curriculum. The Big6 helps students achieve curriculum goals and objectives, and as students improve their Task Definition, Information Seeking, Use of Information and other Big6 abilities, they can actually save time and effort. That's why we talk about efficiency as well as effectiveness in Big6 stage #6—Evaluation.

This Book: Contents

We compiled the contents for this book into five topic categories. Each part offers articles, ideas, tips, or lessons that focus on issues in today's education world. Throughout the book, you will find a diverse and varied range of material about technology, learning and teaching, standards, and of course, the Big6.

Part I: The Big6 Skills

This section is organized by the six stages of the Big6 Skills. Each chapter begins with an explanation of that stage and is followed with practical tips, lessons, and articles for teaching and learning the Big6. Part I ends with *Big6 for All*, a chapter that shares and celebrates Big6 success stories!

Part II: Big6 in Action: K-Higher Education

Part II is divided into chapters according to grade level. Here you will find a wealth of ready-to-use ideas, strategies, lesson plans, and graphic organizers for classroom use. Further topics include working with students with diverse learning needs as well as using music and art as the context for Big6 teaching and learning.

Part III: Big6 and Technology

Technology is an integral part of every Big6 stage; it is not an add on or an enhancement. This part will explore new technologies of the 21st century and includes articles that discuss the relationship of technology and the Internet to the information problem-solving process. Authors relate the latest technology developments to the Big6 and share ideas about how technology can be used to enhance learning and teaching.

Part IV: Teaching Information Problem Solving

Part IV contains various "TIPS"—Teaching Information Problem Solving—all centered around the Big6 Skills. Highlights include suggestions on how to write a grant application, quick and easy Big6 reinforcements, and an explanation of how Big6 joined with *NewsBank* to create a curriculum resource focused around the Big6 Skills.

Part V: Big6 and Content Standards in the Curriculum

State and district learning standards have become an integral part of the educational landscape across the U.S. In Part V, we see how learning standards are directly related to the Big6 Skills and how they are incorporated into different curriculum areas.

As you can see, this book is filled with conceptual explanations of the Big6 approach, connections to standards and other key educational issues, and practical, easy-to-implement activities and lessons. We thank all the authors who contributed and everyone who helped in the production, especially Sue Wurster, Executive Manager of Big6 Associates and Donna King and Wendy Medvetz from Linworth Publishing.

We hope you find this book to be helpful—immediately and for many years to come. Think big—Big6, that is.

Mike Eisenberg and Laura (Eisenberg) Robinson
January 30, 2005

The Big6™ Skills

The Big6 is a process model of how people of all ages solve an information problem.

1. **Task Definition**
1.1 Define the information problem
1.2 Identify information needed to complete the task (to solve the information problem)
   - What's the task?
   - What types of information do I need?

2. **Information Seeking Strategies**
2.1 Determine the range of possible sources (brainstorm)
2.2 Evaluate the different possible sources to determine priorities (select the best sources)
   - What are possible sources?
   - Which are the best?

3. **Location and Access**
3.1 Locate sources (intellectually and physically)
3.2 Find information within sources
   - Where is each source?
   - Where is the information in each source?

4. **Use of Information**
4.1 Engage (e.g., read, hear, view, touch) the information in a source
4.2 Extract relevant information from a source
   - How can I best use each source?
   - What information in each source is useful?

5. **Synthesis**
5.1 Organize information from multiple sources
5.2 Present the information
   - How can I organize all the information?
   - How can I present the result?

6. **Evaluation**
6.1 Judge the product (effectiveness)
6.2 Judge the information problem-solving program (efficiency)
   - Is the task completed?
   - How can I do things better?

Handout created by: Barbara J. Shoemaker, School Media Specialist, Mill Road Elementary, K-2, Red Hook Central School District, Red Hook, NY

The Super3

Contains the same basic elements as the Big6, but is written for younger students to understand.

1. Plan—(Beginning)

When students get an assignment or a task, BEFORE they start doing anything, they should think:

- What am I supposed to do?
- What will it look like if I do a really good job?
- What do I need to find out to do the job?

Big6 Steps:

- Task Definition
- Information Seeking Strategies

2. Do—(Middle)

In the Middle the students DO the activity. This is where they read, view, tell, make a picture and so forth.

Big6 Steps:

- Location and Access
- Use of Information
- Synthesis

3. Review—(End)

Before finishing the product and turning it in, students should stop and think—Is this done?

- Did I do what I was supposed to do?
- Do I feel ok about this?
- Should I do something else before I turn it in?

Big6 Steps:

- Evaluation

The "Big6" is copyright © (1987) Michael B. Eisenberg and Robert E. Berkowitz. For more information, visit: www.big6.com

Super3 information from http://academic.wsc.edu/redl/classes/tami/super3.html. Created by Tami J. Little. Handout created by: Barbara J. Shoemaker, School Media Specialist, Mill Road Elementary, K-2, Red Hook Central School District, Red Hook, NY

Part I:
The Big6™ Skills

CHAPTER 1

Task Definition

A Good Way to Get Started: Task Definition

By Mary Cooper / From the Big6 website: www.big6.com

1.1 Define the information problem

- What does your teacher want you to do? Make sure you understand the requirements of the assignment.
- Ask your teacher to explain the assignment if it seems vague or confusing.
- Restate the assignment in your own words and ask if you are correct

1.2 Identify the information you need in order to complete the task (to solve the information problem)

- What information do you need in order to do the assignment?
- Your teacher will often tell you what information you need.
- If he or she does not, it will help to write a list of questions that you need to look up.

Let's say your assignment is to do a report on a foreign country, and you choose Portugal.

- What information do you need to create your report?
- What kind of things do you think you should learn about?
- Do you want to learn about the history, the food, the festivals and traditions, the economy, local crops, folk tales, language, religion, geography (rivers, mountains, landscape, etc.), climate, government, art or music?
  - What is Portugal's form of government?
  - What language(s) do people speak in Portugal?
  - What is the official language?

- What is the geography of Portugal? Are there rivers? Mountains? Is it near the ocean? How big is the country?

- What do the farmers grow in Portugal?

- What kind of food do people eat in Portugal?

- What are the traditional celebrations and holidays?

- What does the flag of Portugal look like?

- Where is Portugal located?

- What are the major cities in Portugal?

- Are there states or regions in Portugal?

- These questions can be used as a place to start. You may find additional information that is not included in your original question.

Use Task Definition to Achieve Standards

By Janet Murray / vE4, no4

As a librarian, I used to think (and even wrote) that my primary responsibility in Big6 research projects was to facilitate seeking, accessing and using information (Big6 stages 2, 3 and 4). But when students come to the library looking for information, they often say, "I need a book about..." a topic that is so broad that we have a vast number of books from which to choose, or so narrow that no school library would have a whole book on that topic. More frequently, they go to a computer, enter one or two words on a topic in a search engine, and expect everything they need to magically appear. When pressed to describe the classroom teacher's assignment, they are often unable to re-state it in their own words. That tells me that they haven't really understood what they are to do. Classroom teachers and library media specialists can help student comprehension simply by requiring them to re-write the assignment in their own words. Learning to paraphrase is an essential skill that applies not only to Use of Information but to Task Definition as well.

I also like the strategy Mike and Bob suggest in *Teaching Information & Technology Skills* (secondary and elementary versions, Linworth, 2000): "to help the students assume responsibility for their own tasks" by deliberately providing a minimum of information about an assignment, thus encouraging the students to ask appropriate questions. Another way to encourage students to take responsibility is to give them meaningful choices in an assignment, not only in Task Definition but in Synthesis as well.

Since I've been teaching the Big6 online course, I've realized that I need to get involved with teachers' research plans from the very beginning. I need to encourage them to define their research tasks in a way that will help students achieve content, information literacy and national technology standards. In order for students to develop higher order thinking skills, teachers (and their library media teacher colleagues) need to re-examine their traditional research projects in light of those standards; here are a few to stimulate your thinking:

From the National Information Literacy Standards:

http://www.ala.org/aaslTemplate.cfm?Section=Information_Power&Template=/ContentManagement/ContentDisplay.cfm&ContentID=19937

1.1 recognizes the need for information
1.3 formulates a question based on information needs

From ISTE's National Educational Technology Standards for Students (NETS-S):

http://cnets.iste.org/students/s_stands.html

6.1 Students use technology resources for solving problems and making informed decisions

From ISTE's compilation of content area standards:

http://cnets.iste.org/currstands/

English/Language Arts:
"Students conduct research on issues and interests by generating ideas and questions, and by posing problems."

Mathematics:
Students "apply a wide variety of strategies to solve problems and adapt the strategies to new situations."

Science:
"Scientific investigations involve asking and answering a question and comparing the answer with what scientists already know about the world."

Social Studies:
Students can "locate, access, organize, and apply information about an issue of public concern from multiple points of view."

Assembling a collection of facts gleaned from a variety of resources does not necessarily improve students' ability to apply information literacy skills to solve problems. Notice the emphasis on "generating ideas and questions" and "asking and answering a question." We know we can apply the Big6 to information problems in life and work as well as in school, but how will the students learn to generate their own questions if we never give them the opportunity to do that in school? And how much more motivated will they be if the assignment is derived from a real question for which they want an answer? For example, Judy Greenfield (Information Specialist, The Dahlgren School, Dahlgren, VA) commented, "I used the Big6 last week with the third and fourth graders. We solved the 'problem' about how to select just the right book to read. They loved it! And it was a much better approach than the way I used to do things."

One way to challenge classroom teachers designing research project assignments is to encourage them to ask essential questions that will result in enduring understandings. "In Mapping the Big Picture Integrating Curriculum & Assessment K-12, Heidi Hayes Jacobs defines an essential question as the essence of what your students will examine and learn in the course of their study (Jacobs, 1997). Essential questions promote deep and enduring understanding. They cannot be answered in one sentence." The Web page Transforming Standards to Understandings gives examples of essential questions and relates them to a selection of California state standards.

Students in the Big6 online course have really struggled with this concept. As they begin to create a Big6 Unit Plan that incorporates standards, their task definitions are often phrased in traditional terms: "study a state" or "study an animal." We challenge them to rephrase their Task Definition as an essential question. This is significantly more difficult if you've already decided on the activities you want to use, or are trying to impose an "essential question" on top of an existing unit. In a workshop where I was first exposed to the concept of "backward design," I heard a teacher describe his students' task as "collecting stamps from other countries." That's an activity-based Task Definition; it doesn't require the students to ask and answer a question that will lead them to understand (and remember) the reasons why cultures are so different.

In Joyce Valenza's article "For the Best Answers, Ask Tough Questions," (http://www.joycevalenza.com/questions.html) she observes that students can easily deduce that there's no point to recompiling a bunch of facts that already appear in an encyclopedia. "With basic information so easy to access, shouldn't we now focus our students' attention on questions that will challenge them to use information meaningfully - to think, analyze, evaluate and invent?" She also refers her readers to other sites that illuminate the nature of essential questions.

How can we adapt the study of a state, a country or an animal (traditional content area topics) to help students develop higher order thinking skills and achieve standards like those listed in ISTE's compilation of Social Studies standards for global connections (http://cnets.iste.org/currstands/cstands-ss_ix.html)?

   a. give examples of conflict, cooperation, and interdependence among individuals, groups, and nations;

   b. examine the effects of changing technologies on the global community;

   c. explore causes, consequences, and possible solutions to persistent, contemporary, and emerging global issues, such as pollution and endangered species;
   What do we want the students to understand <u>about</u> the topic and <u>beyond</u> the topic? At the elementary level, what if we asked them to choose the state or country they'd most like to live in or animal they'd most like to adopt as a pet? Asking why the state capitol is located where it is promotes some understanding about geography and history. At the secondary level, essential questions will be phrased in more global terms: Why are some states growing in population while others are declining? Why do people move from rural to urban areas? Why are some countries involved in conflicts with their neighbors? Why are some animals endangered? What can we do about it?

First, the students would need to explore their own values: what's important to them about where they live? What animal they'd want to join their family or save from extinction? Now we've made an important connection to their prior knowledge and supplied some personal motivation. With high school students, I often use the example of choosing which college to attend.

What information would they need to make this type of decision? Where can they find the information? Where can they find the <u>best</u> information? Now we're back in familiar territory: the Big6 Skills guide us to seek, access and use information efficiently and effectively.

Nearing the completion of the Big6 online course, Daurene Jerome (Librarian, Mount Ararat Middle School, Topsham, ME) observed that one "thing that has evolved in my thinking about Big6 is I now place much more importance on stage #1, Task Definition. I used to think that Task Definition was just a quick step before you went on to the 'real' steps. I now realize how important it is for students to have a clearly defined task, and to be part of the process of 'defining the task'. I really like the sample exercise where students generate questions about their topics rather than having the questions spoon-fed to them. 'Task Definition' is another opportunity for students to develop their questioning skills."

How To Impress Your Teachers by Asking Good Questions!

By Barbara A. Jansen / From the Big6 website: www.big6.com

Based on the work of Angelo Ciardiello*

*I*s this for a grade? When is it due? How long does it have to be? Can I go to the bathroom? These are the questions that most kids ask in class and most teachers expect to hear. You can be smarter than your classmates, impress your teachers, and learn a lot, too, if you ask better questions.

Basically, there are four kinds of questions.

Fact Questions

Usually these questions start with the words
- Who…
- What…
- Where…
- When…

Some examples of Fact Questions are:
- Who is the president of the United States?
- What do sea turtles eat?
- Where is the Pecos River?
- When were most fossils formed in this area?

Why Questions

Usually these questions start with the words
- Why…
- How…
- In what ways…

Some examples of Why Questions are:
- How do insects differ from reptiles?
- How do plants use the sun?
- Why do you need to learn to use a map?
- Why should you eat from the food pyramid?
- In what ways do scientists think dinosaurs became extinct?
- In what ways are life cycles of the chicken and frog similar?

Idea Questions

Usually these questions start with the words
- Imagine...
- Suppose...
- Predict...
- If..., then...
- How might...
- Can you create...

- What are some possible consequences...

Some examples of Idea Questions are:
- Imagine that you could travel to another planet. Can you tell about that planet and why you would like to go?
- Suppose that you lived in Mexico. Can you tell about which holiday you would enjoy the most?
- If (name a European explorer) came back today, what would he think about the changes?
- How might people from Alaska adapt to life in a southern state such as Florida?
- What are some possible consequences if people do not recycle?
- Can you create a new animal that has some of the characteristics of a mammal, a fish, a reptile, an amphibian and a bird? How might it live in our habitat?

Opinion Questions

Usually these questions start with the words
- Defend...
- Judge...
- Justify...
- What do you think about...
- What is your opinion about...

Some examples of Opinion Questions are:
- What do you think about native people destroying the rain forest so they can farm?
- How do you feel about the different styles of music we have studied?
- What is your opinion about having rules in the cafeteria during lunch? Justify your opinion. (Justify means to tell why you think so.)

If you will learn to ask questions from all four categories, then you will know more about the subjects you are taking in school. Your teachers will know that you care about your school work and are interested in your own learning.

Try it! You may find that asking good questions is actually fun!

*This article is based on: Ciardiello, Angelo. (1998). Did you ask a good question today? "Alternative cognitive and metacognitive strategies." *Journal of Adolescent & Adult Literacy*. 42, 210-219.

The BIG 6

CHAPTER 2

Information Seeking Strategies

A Good Way to Get Started: Information Seeking Strategies

By Barbara Jansen / From the Big6 website: www.big6.com

2.1 Determine the range of possible sources (brainstorm)

This means that you need to make a list of all the **possible sources** of information that will help you answer the questions you wrote in Task Definition. Consider library books, encyclopedias, and web sites to which your library subscribes (ask your librarian!), people who are experts in your subject, observation of your subject, free web sites and survey.

2.2 Evaluate the different possible sources to determine priorities (select the best sources)

Now, look carefully at your list. Which ones are actually **available** to you and are **easy** for you to use? Circle these. If there are some that you need help using, ask your teacher, librarian, mom or dad.

Coping with Information Overload: Narrowing a Topic that Is Too Broad

By Mary Cooper / vE1, no2

A common challenge for information processors is tackling a topic that is too broad for the scope of the project. The challenge can become overwhelming for middle school students because often there isn't time to consult with teachers and library media specialists about defining a topic. As Eisenberg and Berkowitz suggest, Task Definition often becomes a problem because students don't spend enough time on it. And, as teachers and library media specialists are aware, students who have not defined the task will not be successful in solving their information problem.

"Coping with Information Overload: Narrowing a Topic That is Too Broad" is a two-session lesson. It is designed for students in a combined 4th and 5th grade class to work together to develop a protocol for narrowing a topic that is too broad. The students document their findings by posting the protocol on the school's website. (See "Advice from Room 12—Narrowing a Topic that is Too Broad") (http://www.seattleschools.org/schools/ae2/classrooms/room12/room12.htm) Students will be able to access their recommendations from the website whenever they need to refer to them.

The 5th graders participated in a year-long interdisciplinary unit about World War II. They studied what life was like for men, women, and children around the world during the war. These 5th graders became experts about this very broad topic. As experts, they led a panel discussion about how this large topic could be broken into manageable sub-topics.

During the first session of the lesson, the 5th grade expert panel was seated in front of the class. The panel responded to the question: "If you, your friend, or your sibling were given an assignment to do a report or project about World War II, what would you suggest?" Members of the panel responded that the topic was too broad. They suggested that it would take a year (or more) to finish such a project. The panel brainstormed a list of manageable topics. The list included:

- A timeline
- One person
- One country or place
- One battle
- The Holocaust
- Japanese-American internment
- Resistance movements
- A description of what caused World War II
- A description of what happened because of World War II
- Personal stories related to World War II

During session two, the 5th grade expert panel, with help from the audience of 4th graders, brainstormed a list of strategies to use to deal with any assignment that is too broad. The results are posted (See "Advice from Room 12—Narrowing a Topic That is Too Broad" http://www.seattleschools.org/schools/ae2/classrooms/room12/room12.htm)

The students in Room 12 are preparing to start a unit about the civil rights movement. Before they choose topics for individual projects, a class session in the library will be devoted to reviewing the protocol on the website and generating a list of manageable topics for this unit. When the students finish their projects about the civil rights movement, a class session will be devoted to reviewing the published protocol, and revising it if necessary.

A "Narrowing the Topic" protocol lesson could be useful when launching and concluding an information-processing unit or project. If students collaborate at the beginning to create a list of strategies and manageable topics, they can feel more confident as they start a project. If students review and document these strategies at the close of a unit, they will be able to refer to the protocol when needed. A class list of strategies could become a "work in progress," posted in the classroom and on the website. Classes could review and revise the lists in the context of each applicable Big6 project throughout the year.

Coping with Information Overload: Selecting the Best Search Engine

By Mary E. Cooper / vE1, no2

"Several general situations are likely to induce information anxiety: not understanding information; feeling overwhelmed by the amount of information to be understood; not knowing if certain information exists; not knowing where to find information; and, perhaps the most frustrating, knowing exactly where to find the information, but not having the key to access it." (Wurman, 1989, p. 44). As troubling as these situations may be for adults, they can be overwhelming for fourth and fifth grade students.

Compounding the problem, many fourth and fifth graders are inexperienced or struggling readers. In his research with competent readers, Smith (1971) found that readers may experience a loss of comprehension when they are concerned about missing information or when they are expected to put too much visual information into memory. The brain can handle incoming visual information at a limited rate. The amount of visual information that a reader's brain can process is related to the reader's previous amounts of non-visual related information (i.e. reading experience and prior knowledge about the topic). In addition, the brain can store only a limited amount of information in short-term memory. Smith concluded:

> One final point about reading. In any situation where an individual is anxious, or unsure, or has experienced an unhappy succession of "failures," his behavior exhibits an inevitable consequence— he demands far more information before he makes a decision. His very hesitancy aggravates his difficulties. A similar dilemma confronts anyone trying to read in a condition of anxiety, regardless of the material he is reading or his underlying reading ability. The more anxious he is, the less likely he is to rely on non-visual information. The ironic consequence is that such demanding behavior makes the possibility of error and misunderstanding greater rather than less. Where the relaxed individual sees order, tenseness creates visual confusion. Whether the source of the unrealistic demand lies in the student or the teacher, over-dependence on visual information will overload the otherwise competent reader (p. 11).

It is apparent, therefore, that fourth and fifth grade students are at great risk for information anxiety, and that when confronted with information overload, the less proficient readers among them may find themselves in a double bind if they try to rely on inadequate non-visual information. Wurman (1989) also suggests that interest in a subject and the ability to make connections to prior information are two safeguards against information anxiety.

The following lesson, "Coping with Information Overload: Selecting the Best Search Engine," was designed to help fourth and fifth grade students develop strategies to alleviate the burden of too much or inappropriate information. To foster connections to prior knowledge and to ensure that the interest level is high, this lesson was embedded into the class' yearlong integrated thematic unit and was part of ongoing Big6 instruction.

This lesson creates opportunities for students to develop information literacy skills as defined in the "Information Literacy Standards for Student Learning." These standards, developed by the American Association of School Librarians (AASL) and the Association for Educational Communications and Technology (AECT), were published by the American Library Association (ALA) in 1999 in the monograph *Information Power: Building Partnerships for Learning* (See http://www.ala.org/aasl/ip_toc.html). "Information Literacy

Standards for Student Learning" (Standard 9) states that students will "collaborate with others, both in person and through technologies, to identify information problems and to seek their solutions. They lead, facilitate, negotiate, and otherwise participate in defining the information needs of a group" (AASL/AECT, 1998, p. 41).

Coping with Information Overload: Selecting the Best Search Engine

This year, the fourth and fifth grade students in one class at AEII/Decatur Elementary School (Seattle, Washington) are working on an integrated thematic unit about railroads and public policy. As part of a Big6 information-based project, each student chose a topic or question of personal interest about trains. When the students began to locate information for this project (Big6 #3—Location & Access), they realized they would need to search the Web. In previous years, the sites for student projects had been bookmarked on the library computers, or students were assisted with searches in the library on an individual basis. Over the summer, however, the school was wired to provide Internet access in the classrooms, and students were no longer required to use the library computers exclusively for searching the Web. Many students had limited Web searching experience and some students had trouble when they tried to find websites that were appropriate for their projects.

How could a lesson be designed to help students locate appropriate Web sites for their projects? Some findings relevant to the design of the project are as follows:

- To prevent information overload, Hopkins (1995) recommends that reference librarians not only help users identify multiple sources, but also provide guidance in choosing which sources might be most relevant.

- Akin (1998) suggests that it helps to guide students to develop strategies for reducing information overload, and it helps if students adopt a pro-active response to information inundation. She found that fourth grade students often were hesitant to express anxiety about information overload, and suggested that school library media specialists need to monitor students to gauge, document, and alleviate their anxieties about being overwhelmed by information-processing tasks.

- Hess (1998) recommends that librarians instruct students so that they learn how to filter and manage information taken from the Web. He admonishes that there will be a disruption in the processing cycle if these skills aren't learned.

Eisenberg and Berkowitz (1999) noted that Big6 information problem-solving steps don't necessarily proceed in a sequential order, and that looping may be necessary. It was apparent that the students attempting to locate information about trains needed to loop back to Big6 #2.2, Select the Best Sources, to discover the patterns in responses from search engines.

The "Selecting the Best Search Engine" lesson was designed to help students analyze the strengths and weaknesses of the search engines recommended by the school library's website (http://www.seattleschools.org/schools/ae2/library/library.htm), and to document the patterns they found. The student responses about patterns were then combined and posted to the school's Web site (See "Advice from Room 13 About Using the Search Engines on the AEII/Decatur Elementary School Library Website" at http://www.seattleschools.org/schools/ae2/classrooms/room13/room13.htm).

In addition, a questionnaire was designed to give students a forum for discussing their attitudes about using the Web as a source. Since the questionnaire was administered before and after the lesson, students had the opportunity to recognize changes in their attitudes as they gained skill in Web searching. By sharing and comparing their levels of confidence and anxiety, as suggested by Akin (1998), students were reminded that they are not alone when feeling overwhelmed by information.

The lesson was divided into two sessions. For the first session, students completed a search results worksheet (see Worksheet 1) featuring a pre-lesson questionnaire. The questionnaire asked students to respond, using a scale of 1 to 5, to rate how nervous, excited, and confident they would feel if they were told to research their train questions using only the Internet.

The students then worked in groups of four and used the search engines on the AEII/Decatur Library "Searching the Web" page to search for "trains," "locomotives," "rattlesnake," "Utah (or any state)," and "transcontinental railroad." These search engines include KidsClick!, Yahooligans, and Metacrawler. Students completed the worksheet to record how many sites each search engine found for each topic.

For the second session, students completed another worksheet that included the same pre-lesson questionnaire. The worksheet also asked students to compare and contrast the three search engines in relation to the topics that they researched. On the back of the worksheet, students wrote advice about using these search engines. The synthesis of the students' advice can be found on the Room 13 Web page (See "Advice from Room 13 About Using the Search Engines on the AEII/Decatur Elementary School Library Website" at http://www.seattleschools.org/schools/ae2/classrooms/room13/room13.htm).

Worksheet 1

	Yahooligans	Metacrawler	Kids
Click!			
Railroads			
Trains			
Locomotives			
Rattlesnake			
Utah (or any state)			
Transcontinental Railroad			

Note: The term **"rattlesnake"** was included because students were studying the impact of railroads on the U.S. West, and rattlesnake was a topic of interest. In addition, the term was included so that students could compare how the search engines could be used to search in this category in the future.

An Analysis of the "Select the Best Sources Lesson"

An analysis of the responses (see Results 1) to the pre- and post-lesson questionnaires shows that in the first session, five students reported that they were nervous about using the Web for research; in the second session, no student reported being nervous. In the first session, eight students reported feeling confident about using the Web for research; in the second session, 17 students reported feeling confident.

When the students compared and contrasted the search engines, most of them reported that Metacrawler listed the highest number of results for each search, and KidsClick! yielded the fewest number of results. In response to the question about which search engine they would choose to search for information about a state, most of them reported that they would try KidsClick! first because it listed fewer sites. Most of the students responded that they would use Metacrawler to find information about an unfamiliar animal or train because it would be more likely to list more sites.

Many students recommended using KidsClick! or Yahooligans before trying Metacrawler. With Metacrawler, they wrote, too many sites may be listed, and many sites are written at an adult reading level. Some students suggested starting a search with the search engine that is likely to list the fewest number of sites.

Results 1

Response to the Pre- and Post-Lesson Questionnaire

Question 1: How nervous are you?	1 Non Nervous	2	3	4	5 Very Nervous
Number of responses Pre-Lesson	11	5	5	1	5
Number of responses Post-Lesson	11	5	11	0	0
Question 2: How excited are you?	1 Not excited (ho-hum)	2	3	4	5 Very excited
Number of responses Pre-Lesson	4	0	12	5	6
Number of responses Post-Lesson	4	0	12	5	6
Question 3: How confident are you?	1 Not confident (I need help)	2	3	4	5 Very confident (I can help others)
Number of responses Pre-Lesson	5	3	4	5	3
Number of responses Post-Lesson	0	2	11	12	2

Total number of respondents = 27

Conclusion

Upper elementary students, who may be inexperienced or struggling readers, are at great risk for overload and anxiety in information-processing environments. With guidance, these students can develop and practice pro-active strategies for preventing information overload. Developing readers can be further protected from information anxiety if they have interest in and background knowledge about the topic before beginning information problem-solving activities.

Bibliography:

Akin, L. (1998). Information overload and children: A survey of Texas elementary school students. *SLMQ Online: School Library Media Quarterly Online* [Online]. Available: http://www.ala.org/aasl/SLMQ/overload.html

American Association of School Librarians and the Association for Educational Communications and Technology. (1998). *Information power: Building partnerships for learning*. Chicago, IL: American Library Association.

Eisenberg, M. B., & Berkowitz, R. E. (1999). *Teaching information and technology skills: The Big6 in elementary schools*. Worthington, OH: Linworth Publishing, Inc.

Hess, B. (1998). *Graduate student cognition during information retrieval using the WWW: A pilot study.* Paper presented at the Annual Conference of the American Educational Research Association (Montreal, Canada, April 14-23, 1999). Department of Educational Psychology, University of Georgia, Athens, Georgia. (ED 429 118)

Hopkins, R. L. (1995). Countering information overload: The role of the librarian. *Reference Librarian*, n 49-50, 305-333.

Smith, F. (1971). *Overloading the competent reader*. Paper presented at the annual meeting of the National Council of Teachers of English (61st, Las Vegas, Nov. 1971). (ED 085 674)

Wurman, R. S. (1989). *Information anxiety*. New York: Doubleday.

Know Your Information Sources

By Susan McMullen / vE4, no1

Related Information Literacy Skills: Big6 #2 - Information Seeking Strategies

Purpose: To help students recognize various information sources and to apply appropriate criteria for selecting the best information source(s) for their particular research need.

Learning Contexts: The lesson is applicable for tasks that involve any type of information seeking, research, or report writing in secondary and higher education settings.

Discussion: When confronted with a research project, students are frequently either overwhelmed by or uninformed about their information source choices. Today's students frequently equate information seeking with the World Wide Web. They do not realize that there are a wide variety of information choices available to them, each requiring different finding methods. This exercise will help students identify different sources of information, their quality and content, and understand how they are organized. By understanding the various types of information and where information comes from, students will recognize appropriate sources for specific seeking or research topics.

Sample in Context: This lesson begins with a brainstorming activity in which the instructor asks the students to identify different information sources. If the class is small, each student may be asked to give one source. The instructor and students then review the "Know Your Information Sources" handout to get familiar with the major resources. Once familiar with these major resources, students are asked to complete the "What Source Would You Use" exercise. After this initial preparation, students are then asked to apply appropriate selection criteria to their information task.

Item: Know Your Information Sources

Using the "Know Your Information Sources" handout, determine the best information source(s) to use in the situations presented in the "What Source Would You Use" exercise. Upon completing the exercise, think about your own information task. As you prepare for research, think about the questions on the bottom half of the exercise sheet. Your answers will help you determine the most useful sources for locating information on your topic.

What Source Would You Use?

N = Newspaper, PM = Popular Magazine, SJ = Scholarly Journal,
R = Reference Book, B = Book, W = Web, P = Person
Hint: you may select more than one source

_____ to find statistics on the number of working mothers with children under the age of five

_____ to locate an in-depth article about the level of absenteeism among working mothers
     with children under the age of five

_____ to find out information about the day care center that XYZ corporation opened in your
     hometown

_____ to learn about presentations offered at the National Association for Family Child Care
     Conference in July 2001

_____ to find a current analysis of how working mothers in the 21st century are coping with
     child care issues

_____ to find out how much families are paying for child care

_____ to read a detailed analysis of child-care options in the workplace

_____ to learn about companies that are offering child care at the workplace

Apply Your Skill:

Now let's apply what we have learned about information sources to a specific research need.

Task Definition: As your company's personnel director, your employer has asked you to
make a recommendation on whether or not to provide a day care center at your workplace.
Included in your recommendation will be a report about the current workplace situation, an
examination of other case studies, and information about the advantages and disadvantages
for providing day care at the workplace.

   As you prepare to research, think about these questions. Your answers will help you
determine the most useful sources of information on your topic.

1. Q: Who is your audience?
   A: Your employer.

2. Q: What types of information do you need?
   A: Case studies, statistics, information about whether or not day care has worked at other
   workplaces, survey of employee attitude.

3. Q: Has this subject been studied for a long time or is it new?
   A: This topic has been studied for the last 10 – 20 years.

4. Q: Who is doing research on this topic? Is there a special interest group or organization?
   A: Organizations of working mothers or personnel directors

5. What do you already know about this topic? Not too much, only that employees have
   been missing work lately due to childcare problems.

Sources to use for this information task: books, articles from both popular magazines and
scholarly journals, web to find organizations and their research, human sources.

The BIG6™ CHAPTER 3
Location and Access

A Good Way to Get Started: Location & Access

By Anna Bajer Sievers Olson and Lola Cowling /
From the Big6 website: www.big6.com

3.1 Locate sources

Figure out **where** you will get these sources. Beside each source, write its location. If it is a web site, list its web address. Try to use those that your teacher or librarian have linked or bookmarked. This will save you time. If your source is a person, figure out how you will contact him or her and make a note of this.

Now, you will actually **get the sources**. You may have to get and use them one at a time. If so, come back to this step to locate each source.

3.2 Find information within sources

Now that you have the source in hand, how will you **get to the information** that you need? (Remember the questions you wrote in Task Definition?) This all depends on the source.

A. First make a list of words that will help you find information in all of your sources. These are called **keywords**. They are like synonyms and related words to your topic. You can find many of these in the questions you wrote in Big6 Task Definition. Here is an easy way to create keywords (http://www.big6.com/showarticle.php?id=136). (see Handout 1)

B. Now make a **list of the sources** of information you will use. Beside each, note how you will access the information you need.

- **Book:** Look at the **index** or **table of contents** for your topic and keywords
- **Encyclopedia:** Use the **index volume** (usually the last volume in the set) for the topic and keywords.
- **Web sites** that are subscribed to by your library (such as Gale, Worldbook Online, etc.): type **topic and keywords** in the search box. Try them separately and some together. Ask your librarian for help if needed.
- **Free web sites:** use **topic and keywords** in subject directories.

Handout 1 / Creating Keywords

Look at the keyword builder below. Notice where the major topic, subtopics and synonyms/related words are placed.

To give you an idea for how to fill in your keyword builder, look at the example on the next page.

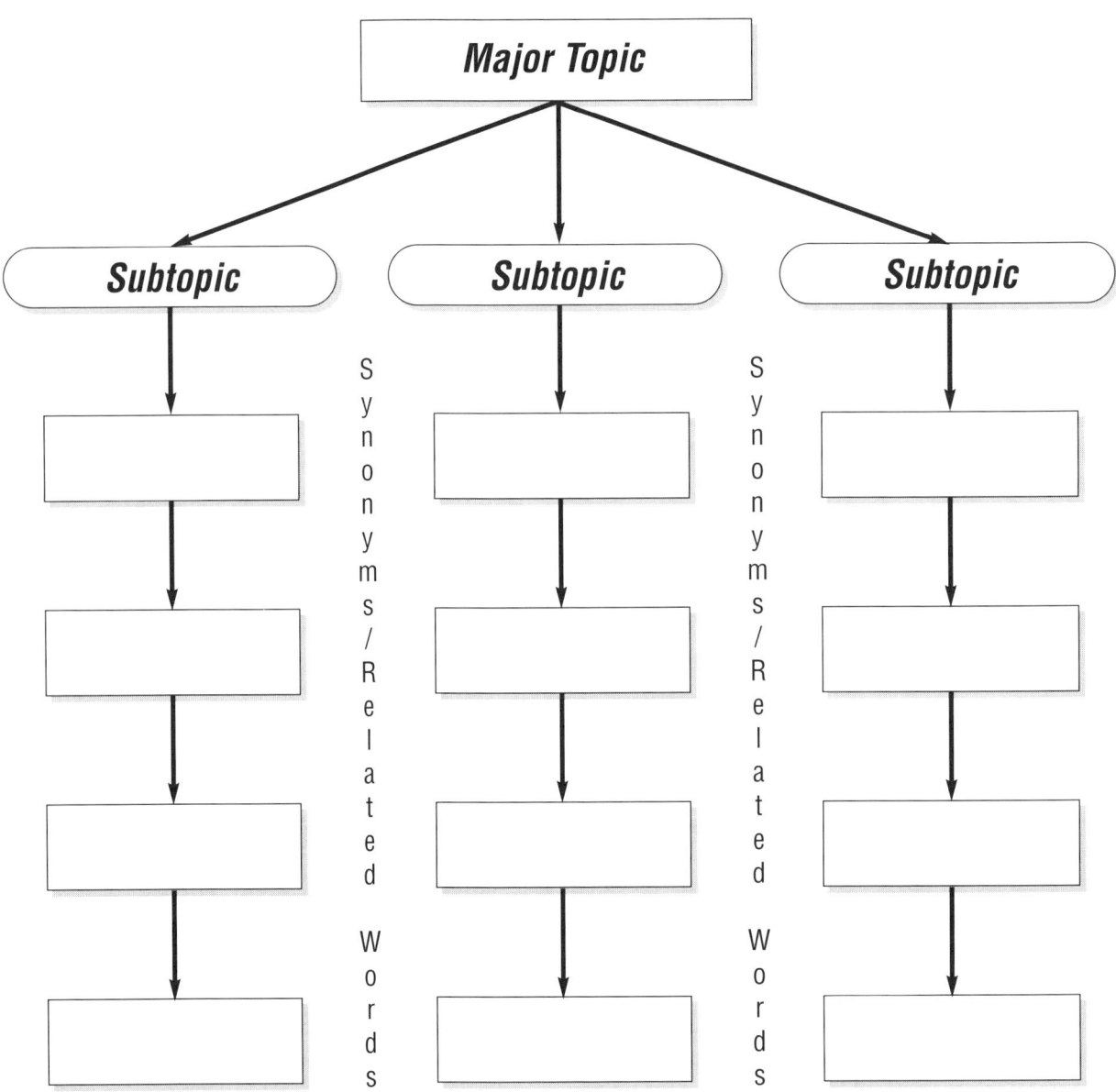

Look at the keyword builder below. Notice where the major topic, subtopics and synonyms/related words are placed.

To give you an idea for how to fill in your keyword builder, look at the example at the below.

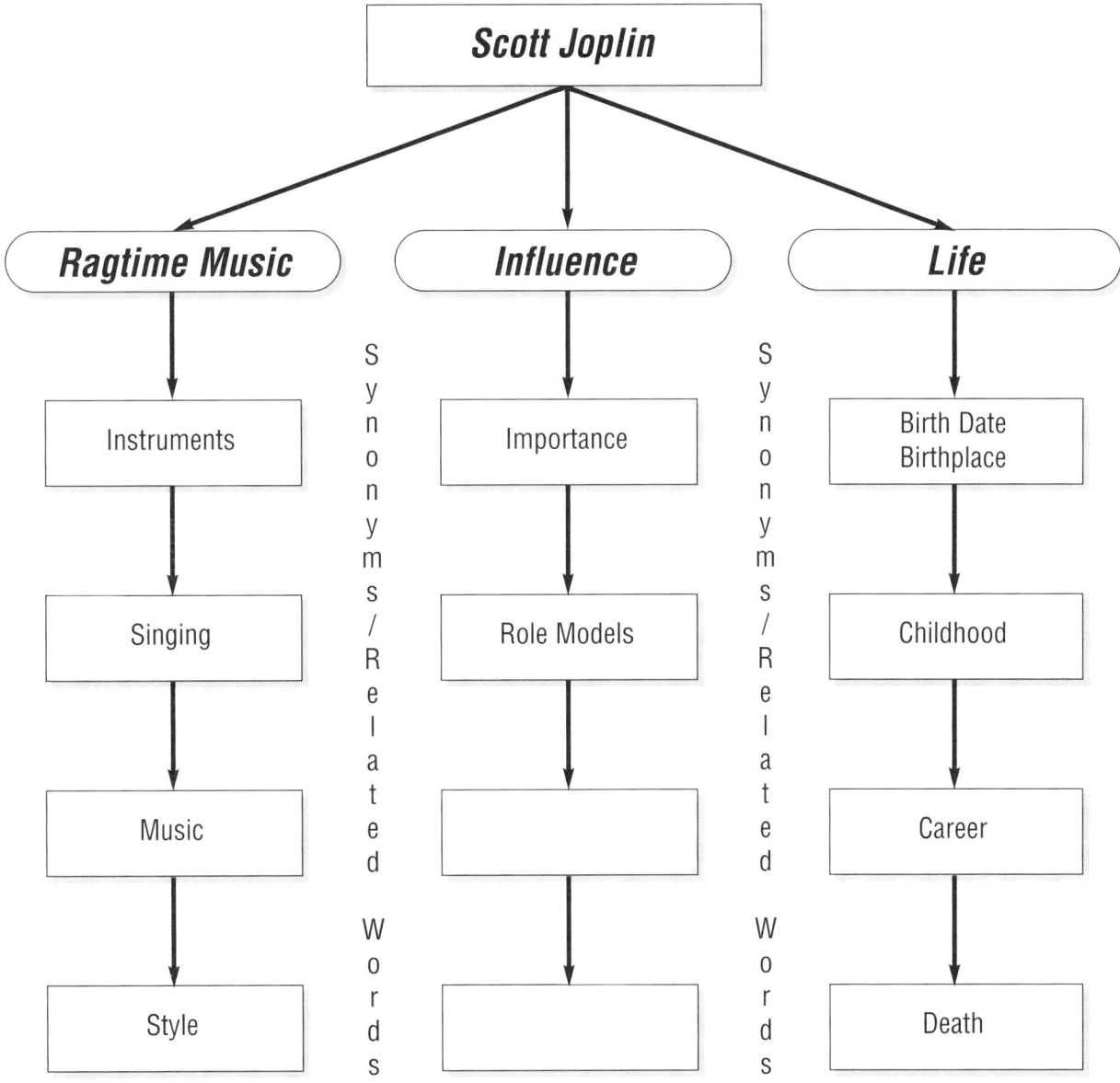

Eisenberg, Michael B. and Berkowitz, Robert E. Information Problem-Solving: The Big Six Skills Approach to Library & Information Skills Instruction. Norwood, NJ: Ablex Publishing Company, 1990, p. 119.

Selecting and Locating the Best Sources

By Barbara Jansen / From the Big6 website: www.big6.com

W here do I start? Which source is best? I did a Web search and got 1,346,896 web sites! Help!!

Where DO you start to find information on your topic? Breaking down the task makes it much more manageable. Here's a good way to start:

1. Decide which types of resources will best meet your needs. Consider print (both paper and online) and human resources:

   ■ Print (paper and online) Books, encyclopedias, magazines, professional journals, primary sources such as diaries, newspapers, personal journals, maps, photographs.

   ■ Human sources: Practitioners and researchers such as doctors, teachers, university professors, other professionals and any other expert in the field of study. Laymen (ordinary people) can be useful when you are conducting a survey, just need opinions, or if you are finding oral history of an area. You may be a resource if you are conducting an experiment or making observation.

2. Choose the best and most authoritative sources.
   How do you know which are best? Here are considerations:

   ■ Answer this question: "Which sources would the leading academics (researchers and university professors) use?"

   ■ Look at the bibliographies and additional readings in the back of textbooks and other books on the subject.

   ■ Use academic, refereed journals, read the bibliographies in articles that pertain to your subject.

   ■ Ask your teacher or other knowledgeable people for ideas on the best sources.

   ■ Read reviews of books if you are not sure. Ask your librarian where you can obtain these reviews.

   ■ Which titles appear in several sources? Those will be most likely be the best and most authoritative.

3. Choosing the best human resources (people who are experts in the subject you are studying):

   ■ Devise interview questions before you contact your human sources.

   Find people at the following places:
   ■ Institutions of higher education
   ■ Businesses
   ■ Professional agencies such as law and accounting offices
   ■ Nonprofit organizations such as Red Cross and United Way
   ■ Service agencies such as hospitals, clinics, and police stations, and so forth.

Sample Lesson Plan: Location and Access

By Robert E. Berkowitz and Michael B. Eisenberg /
From the Big6 website: www.big6.com

Title: Keyword Generator: A Tool to Boost Use of Keywords

Author: Robert E. Berkowitz and Michael B. Eisenberg

Related Big6 Skills: Big6 #3—Location & Access

Purpose: Students will learn to brainstorm and organize keywords.

Learning Contexts: This lesson is appropriate for middle, secondary, or college age students who need to further develop their research skills.

Discussion: The Keyword Generator is a tool for Location & Access—to use when teaching students how to conduct better searches. Often students have trouble when generating vocabulary terms for searching. And even when they do come up with some key terms, they may not consider how various terms relate to each other. The Keyword Organizer provides a framework for helping students to think through their topics, relevant keywords, and connections among the words. Optimizing vocabulary is especially important when using the Web, because many search engines do not have a controlled vocabulary for more precise searching.

Teaching keyword searching (or any other Big6 Skill) should only take place in the context of an assignment. Here's a tool to use when working with a group about to look for information in electronic and print resources.

Potential situations might be:

- 8th graders searching the Web for information to write biographies of current newsmakers
- 11th graders working on a unit about "war"—using a variety of print, electronic, and online resources to study the causes, nature, and effects of particular wars
- High school economics students looking for strategic intelligence on various corporations
- A community college course social issues class studying "intellectual property in the information age" and looking for copyright regulations across types of media.

Sample in Context: One major unit in Mr. Robinson's economics class focuses on the stock market and making good investment decisions. The unit spans the entire year and focuses on competitive intelligence and the use of quality information.

In the beginning of the school year, Mr. Robinson helps the students to determine the major aspects for investigation related to various companies and industries, e.g., products, finances, markets, competitors, etc.

The students enter these aspects as "subtopics" in the Keyword Generator and brainstorm synonyms that also describe each subtopic. For example, for the keyword subtopic "finances," they generate:

- Budget
- Income and expenses
- Balance sheet
- Assets
- Sales

- Funds.

After trying some of these terms in searching the Web and the full-text magazine and newspaper databases, the students reflect on which terms were most useful. If students need to continue searching, they can revise their Keyword Generator or add subtopics that further focus their searching.

Figure 1. Example for Secondary Level Lesson

Access: Keyword Searching

The key to access within a resource is the **vocabulary**. The following exercise will help to develop a rich vocabulary for searching on a particular topic.

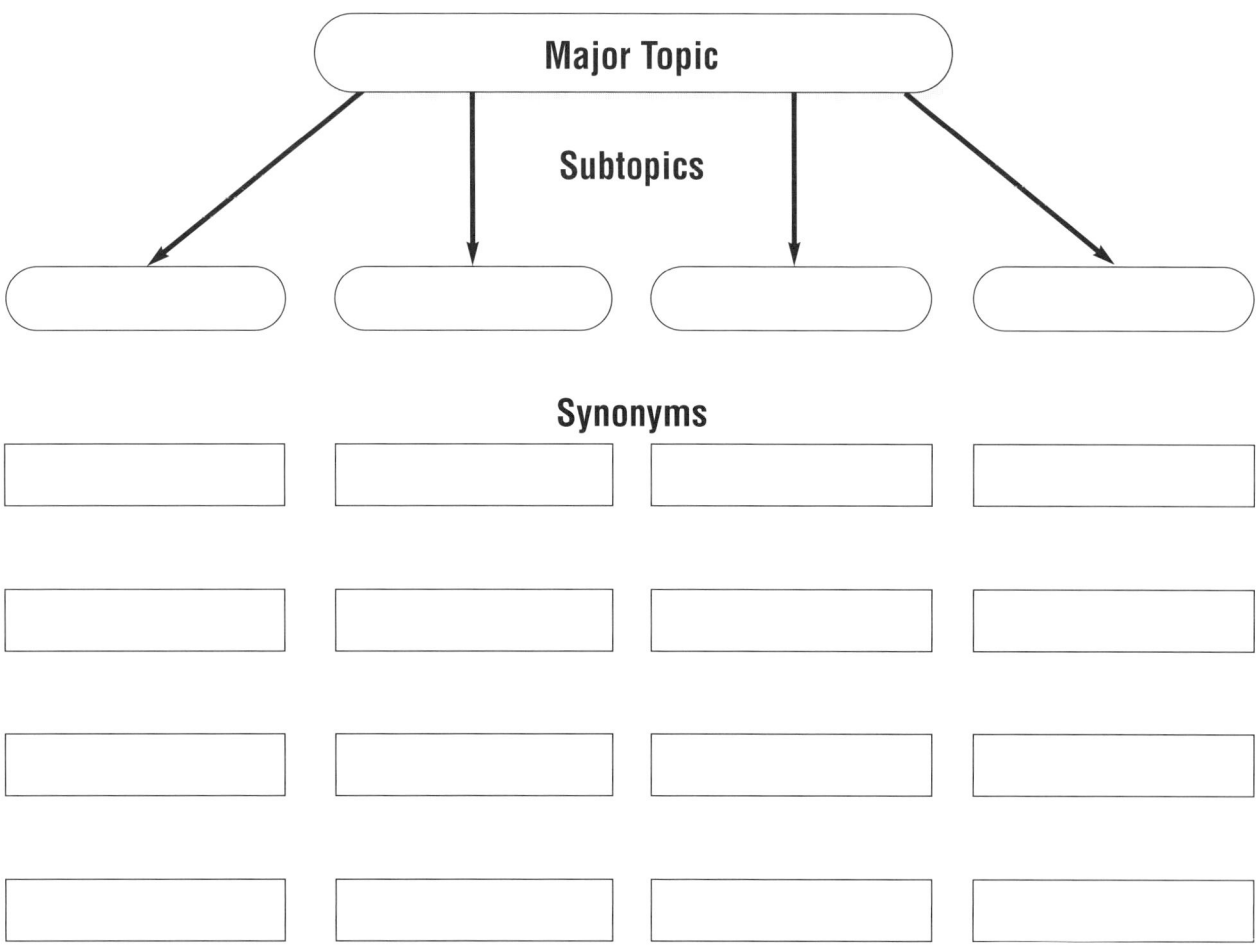

CHAPTER 4

Use of Information

A Good Way to Get Started: Use of Information

By Barbara Jansen / From the Big6 website: www.big6.com

4.1 Engage in the source (read, listen, view, touch)

Most likely you will need to **read, listen or view** your source. If you can't understand any of it, be sure to ask an adult to help you. **It's OK not to understand, it's not OK not to ask for help.** You are looking for the information you need. You may not need to read, listen to, or view all of your source. You may be able to skip around, finding subheadings and topic sentences (read the first sentences in each paragraph) that will take you to your information.

4.2 Take out the relevant information from a source

It's time to take some notes. We have help available on note taking and citing your sources. (http://www.big6.com/kidsshowarticle.php?id=78)

Expository Text: The Choice for Some, a Challenge for Others

By Joyce Melton Pagés, Ed.D / vE1, no2

*S*tories. Children love them. The charm of the characters, the relevance of the character's problem, and the spark of the language invite children into literature. The lure of an interesting plot can keep children reading and listening to literature for hours. That's the focus of this article—Big6 #4—Use of Information—how students interact with written material.

Fascinating facts and puzzling possibilities draw some children into informational writing. They love learning about the world around them. They ask many questions and dive into tradebooks, encyclopedias, and informational Web sites to satisfy their "need to know." They, too, don't want to put that book down when they are reading about topics that intrigue them.

Unfortunately, most children do not enjoy reading expository text. Some children become bored with expository style writing. Others become very frustrated. While most of them can read stories successfully, many of them lack the strategies to read expository writing. This affects their learning in content area subjects, their confidence, and their attitude toward reading. Further, in a world of abundant, ever-increasing information, the inability to read expository text greatly affects the child's development of information literacy skills and lifelong learning strategies.

Factors Affecting Student Success with Expository Text

Reading is a complex process that involves the reader in strategically using his or her knowledge and experiences to construct meaning. Because narrative and expository style text are so different, the ability to read narrative text does not ensure success with expository text. In fact, there are many factors that affect the way children read expository text. These factors can be classified in three categories:

- Text Factors
- Reader Factors
- Instructional Factors

Text Factors

Text factors relate primarily to the differences between narrative and expository style writing. Some of these factors relate to how the author has explained the information while other factors involve how the publisher has chosen to present the information. Internal text factors include the clarity and cohesion of the author's style, language, and explanation. External text factors include the format, typographical aids, and graphic features that affect the layout and presentation of the ideas. The following table characterizes some of the key differences between narrative and expository text.

As authors and publishers make decisions about how they will support the reader's comprehension of a selection, they often manipulate text factors to make the writing more "readable." One of the most common ways is to lower the readability level as measured by a readability formula. This is typically done through reducing word length and sentence length. Unfortunately, using this strategy to make text easier often makes it more difficult for readers to comprehend. Shorter words are often more vague and less descriptive. For example, "big" is easier to identify and pronounce than "massive," but "massive" does a

Narrative Text	Expository Text
Tells a story.	Delivers information.
Invites children into the story through characters to which children can relate.	Invites children into text through explaining information but has no characters or situations that draw the child into the selection.
Has a relatively predictable storyline starting with a "once upon a time" setting, character, or event and generally finishing with an ending which aligns with "and they all lived happily ever after." Stands alone as a complete piece	Reflects a variety of text patterns. Authors of expository text have a wider variety of options available to them (i.e. enumeration, time order, comparison-contrast, question-answer, cause-effect, problem-solution). Expository text authors can even change text patterns several times within a selection.
Uses illustrations to support a student's comprehension of the selection.	Often relies on the use of other resources to support an understanding of the selection.
	Uses graphic aids, illustrations, photographs all aids to deliver information. Depending on how they're integrated with the text and whether the reader knows how to use them, they may support or inhibit understanding.
Includes fewer new words.	Includes more unfamiliar words.
Includes common usage with which students may have had some experience.	Includes technical vocabulary related to the content and words which have both technical meanings and common usage meanings. Students experience difficulty when they transfer a common usage meaning to a situation in which the technical meaning is intended.
Provides more content to support an understanding of new vocabulary words. In addition, narrative writing sometimes provides the child with multiple opportunities to experience the new words.	Typically provides one exposure to a new vocabulary word with varying degrees of context support. Some expository selections have several new words in close proximity; thus significantly reducing context.

much better job of conveying to the reader the vast, commanding nature of the ocean. As a result, when words are less descriptive, the reader must do more to construct the meaning that the author is trying to communicate. Further, when reducing sentence length, authors often omit conjunctions and signal words that help the reader anticipate the writer's direction and construct the relationships between ideas. When these signals are not provided, the reader must construct that relationship or surmise the author's direction with somewhat choppy writing. In this paragraph, without "unfortunately," "for example," "but," "as a result," and "further" to signal transition and direction, the reader would be left to create his/her own understanding of the relationships among the ideas. Opting for brevity in word length and sentence length instead of clarity and cohesion makes the text more difficult and less interesting.

Reader Factors

While text factors are visible and may be readily changed and manipulated, reader factors are much more complex. They reside in the reader and can only be changed through experience and instruction. Further, they more greatly affect a reader's success with a reading selection than text factors. They affect how the reader will respond to text features. Reader factors include the learner's:

- Vocabulary, language, and life experiences
- Experience with reading and writing expository text
- Understanding of reading processes and his/her ability to employ them (These processes include altering reading rate to purpose and material, monitoring comprehension and using fix-up strategies to support comprehension, using text structure to cognitively organize information, asking questions and reading for answers, reading like a writer, etc.)
- Silent reading experience
- Ability to use a variety of strategies to recognize and assign meaning to unfamiliar words.

All of these factors depend on the reader's experiences. Since parents who read to their children in the early years typically choose fiction, most children enter school with limited, if any, experience with expository writing. Their familiarity with the style and structure of narrative writing gives them story grammar to support their reading of stories, but the "here's the information" style of much expository text is unfamiliar and challenging. This affects the strategies that a child can employ while cognitively organizing information. Without an understanding of how expository text "works," readers don't know how to use internal and external text organizational aids to support their construction of meaning. In fact, Duthie (1994) states that if we do not offer young students many experiences with informational texts we are contributing to future difficulties.

Since readers comprehend by relating new information to what they already know, prior knowledge and experiences are essential for successful reading of information. Readers who lack the necessary prior knowledge must have instructional support to prepare them for a selection. In addition, students must develop an understanding of the role of prior knowledge in their comprehension. They must develop strategies for using context to support understanding and for building their own background when they are reading expository text independently. Since narrative selections usually stand alone, many students do not understand that they may have to use other materials to supplement their comprehension of expository selections.

Since so many children experience difficulty reading expository writing, many teachers have children read their textbook content orally in class. This significantly limits students' development as effective silent readers of expository writing. Further, it affects their development as independent, information literate learners. In most real-world situations, oral reading of information is not an option; even when it is an option, it is not the most efficient, effective way to read information. Students must develop the strategies to read informational writing silently. With experience and appropriate instructional strategies, silent reading supports independent learning across the curriculum.

Instructional Factors

Through instruction and the provision of meaningful experiences, teachers can bridge the gap between readers and authors of expository text. In supporting children's success with expository writing, teachers should employ strategies which:

- Engage children in processes that get them to do what good readers do.

- Use authentic, well-written texts that support the reader through clear, cohesive writing and well-designed illustrations, photographs, graphic aids, and typographical features.
- Provide children with real reasons to read expository text—answer questions, research topics, develop projects, solve problems, participate in debates, tutor younger children, etc.
- Teach skills and strategies within the context of approaches such as the Big6 or Super3.

The following strategies can support children's development of effective, strategic expository text reading strategies.

1. Read expository text to children. Help them develop an understanding of how writers of expository text explain their ideas. Point out signals and aids that the author or publisher provides to support their learning.

2. Introduce young children to informational text through alphabet books. Yopp and Yopp (2000) suggest strategies for using informational alphabet books in primary-grade classrooms.

3. Take advantage of students' natural curiosity. Use their questions to provide experience with expository writing. One way to do this is to record a child's question on an overhead transparency or chalkboard and model how you would locate the information. Show how you would find a reference that might include the information. Have the students listen for the answer to the question while you read the information aloud.

4. Provide the students with successful silent reading experiences. Use well-written tradebooks that supply the reader with appropriate signals and aids to support meaning-making. Encourage the child to read informational writing about his or her interests and hobbies. Pages (1999) recommends strategies for motivating reluctant silent readers to read meaningfully at http://www.kidbibs.com/learningtips/lt50.htm

5. Encourage students to ask questions and read to answer those questions. Students can write their questions on medium stick-on notes and mount them in their book. They can read to answer their questions and record the information on the stick-on note under the question.

6. Encourage students to write while they read. Taking reading notes, summarizing, and mapping are excellent strategies to strengthen student comprehension. Pages (1999) has included summarizing and mapping strategies at http://www.kidbibs.com/learningtips/lt33.htm and http://www.kidbibs.com/learningtips/lt38.htm respectively.

7. Support comprehension by building background. By activating prior knowledge, building background, and linking the reading selection to that background, teachers support student reading and teach children about their reading and learning processes. Children who understand their own cognitive processes develop efficient, effective lifelong learning strategies.

8. Teach children about expository text patterns and the signals authors use to provide direction for the reader. Use strategies to help children identify expository text patterns. Pages (1999) has included some strategies at http://www.kidbibs.com/learningtips/lt39.htm.

9. Use graphic tools such as Venn Diagrams (for comparison-contrast pattern), timelines (for time order), semantic maps for main topic with details, cause-effect chains (for cause-effect pattern), etc. When these tools are used with children instructionally, students learn to mentally organize information in meaningful ways. They learn to analyze the information, consider organizational strategies, and choose a strategy that supports his or her learning of the information. With time and experience, this will help the learner take control of his or her own learning. (See http://www.kidbibs.com/learningtips/ lt26.htm for comparison-contrast graphic tools.)

10. Use think-alouds to support comprehension. Starting with the first heading, model the use of typographical aids, graphic aids, text patterns, etc. The teacher may do this by reading the text/aid aloud and by telling what it makes her or him think of (prior knowledge, a question, a prediction, how s/he will use the information, etc.). This continues throughout the designated portion of text.

11. Provide children with opportunities to write expository text. When children write, they develop an understanding of authors' writing options. Reading like a writer helps them develop the flexibility and strategies to support active construction of meaning. Tremendous growth occurs when writing supports reading and reading supports writing. Wray and Lewis (1999) recommend an approach to factual writing at http://www.readingonline.org/articles/writing/index.html

12. Monitor student progress in relation to their research, projects, and learning. Use conferencing and mini-lessons to supplement their learning as needed.

13. Provide children with opportunities to work with buddies and small groups to research topics and work on projects, etc. Students can promote thinking, solve problems, respond creatively, and support each other's growth in meaningful ways.

14. Encourage parents to read expository text to their children. Help them understand how this benefits their child.

15. Introduce children to favorite writers of nonfiction. The young child who enjoys Gail Gibbons' simple illustrations and explanations or the older child who is fascinated by the incredible photography and writing of Seymour Simon may start to broaden his or her knowledge base by reading other books by these authors. In addition, discovering informational series such as Eyewitness Visual Dictionaries can draw children into information in motivating and meaningful ways.

Conclusion

Independence! That's the goal. It involves giving children the tools, power, and confidence to ask questions and seek answers. It's what learning is all about. The Big6 approach gives students the guidance they need to ultimately take charge of their own learning. Further, the processes involved in implementing the Big6 approach support children's development as readers, writers, and learners. Without question, this approach gives them the skills they need to develop their lifetime learning strategies.

But, when learners lack experience with expository text, they often need instructional support to benefit from the Big6 approach. Reading-writing instruction that engages children in reading like writers and writing like readers can help them develop as effective, efficient silent readers of information. This reading-writing instruction supports the development of Big6 Skills; at the same time, Big6 Skills support student development of reading and writing strategies.

From the preschool years on, teachers and parents can inspire curiosity, feed students' hunger for knowledge, and engage children in processes that shape their learning for a lifetime. Coupling effective reading-writing instruction with Big6 Skills helps students of the 21st century spell success "I-N-D-E-P-E-N-D-E-N-C-E!"

References:

Duthie, C. (1994). A genre study for the primary classroom. *Language Arts,* 71, 588-595.

Pagés, J. M. (1999). *LearningTip #50: Strategies help reluctant silent readers read to learn.* [Online]. Available: http://www.kidbibs.com/learningtips/lt50.htm. (Current Feb. 3, 2000).

Pagés, J. M. (1999). *LearningTip #39: Using an author's style and text patterns to support the reading of information.* [Online]. Available: http://www.kidbibs.com/learningtips/lt39.htm. (Current Feb. 3, 2000).

Pagés, J. M. (1999). *LearningTip #38: Getting the details to fit together while reading, writing, and studying.* [Online]. Available: http://www.kidbibs.com/learningtips/lt38.htm (Current Feb. 3, 2000).

Pagés, J. M. (1998). *LearningTip #33: Summarizing helps students monitor understanding, clarify thinking, and strengthen learning.* [Online]. Available: http://www.kidbibs.com/learningtips/lt33.htm (Current Feb. 3, 2000).

Pagés, J. M. (1998). *LearningTip #26: Comparison strategies support reading, writing, and learning.* [Online]. Available: http://www.kidbibs.com/learningtips/lt26.htm (Current Feb. 3, 2000).

Wray, D., & Lewis, M. (1999). *An approach to factual writing.* [Online]. Available: http://www.readingonline.org/articles/writing/index.html (Current at Feb. 8, 2000)

Yopp, R. H., & Yopp, H. K. (2000, February). *Sharing informational text with young children, The Reading Teacher,* 53, 410-423.

Ideas About Note Taking and Citing Sources

By Barbara Jansen / *From the Big6 website: www.big6.com*

Note Taking

Taking notes in middle school and high school should be more than just copying common knowledge, facts or ideas from others. In addition to the note taking from sources such as books, web sites, journals and texts, you should add your own ideas and opinions about the information. Jamie McKenzie calls this "green ink" or fresh thinking (McKenzie, 2000). You should also use electronic means whenever possible to take and store notes. This makes notes easily accessible and searchable, as well as allowing for ease of revising, amending, and creating a final product or paper. (McKenzie, 2000)

Note taking tips:

1. **Paraphrase:** Don't copy and paste huge blocks of text. If you need the information from a large amount of text, paraphrase it. Paraphrasing is appropriate for supporting information, biographical information, predictions, hypothesis, and drawing conclusions. You will put the information into your own words. This type of note taking must be cited (giving credit to its source).

2. **Summarize** (read a large section for overall meaning and summarize it into one or two sentences). Summarizing is typically used for beginning research, i.e., general explanatory material. It must be cited unless the information contains common facts and knowledge.

3. **Copy and paste** small portions of text such as specific details, facts, definitions, and statistics. Typically you don't need to cite this kind of information if it is common knowledge, unless it is a new or unique perspective on the knowledge.

4. **Direct quotes.** Quotations are reserved for one or two sentence statements that prove a point or reveal an attitude. Don't use quotations to make your point, just to back it up. They are especially appropriate for primary sources such as diaries, journals, speeches, interviews, letters, memos, manuscripts, memoirs, and autobiographies. You need to use quotation marks and footnotes. (Stripling and Pitts, 1988)

Tip to avoid plagiarism: Add quotation marks around text that is extracted directly from the source, and add brackets or some other notation to information that you summarize or paraphrase as soon as you write, type or paste the notes in the note taking form (see page 36). Do this so you won't forget whether or not it is a direct quote or paraphrased when you are using the information in a paper. You will include the quotation marks around a direct quote in your final paper. You do not need to put quotation marks around a paraphrase or summary, but you do need to cite either.

Possible electronic organizers for note taking:

Word processed.

Create your own template or use the one provided.

Suggested fields: Name, date, source (title, author, publication, date, URL, etc.), subject of that information, abstract (pertinent information-paraphrase, avoid copying and pasting huge blocks of text), ideas (record your ideas and reactions to the information, ways to use it in the paper, your opinions, or further research you need to do on the information). You should save each with a descriptive title or sequential number (McKenzie, 2000)

Instructions for saving the note taking form as a template in Microsoft Word:

1. Download this form (see Handout 1 on page 37) (http://www4.adhost.com/big6/files/NoteTakingForm.doc) created in Microsoft Word.

2. Click on File > Save As

3. Title it with a short descriptive name such as NoteForm

4. Choose Document Template for Save as type. Notice that the folder that it will save into has changed to Templates. This will save it as a template. Click OK
   Every time you choose New Office Document, there is an icon for that form. When selected, it comes up as an untitled Word document, but it has the form fields for you to fill in.

Here is the same note taking form template (in PDF format) (http://www4.adhost.com/big6/files/NoteForm.pdf). This one is used to record notes by hand. You will need Acrobat Reader (www.adobe.com) to view or print this file. However, to save time and effort you are strongly encouraged to take notes in digital form whenever possible.

Create a database.

- Use Microsoft Access or another database application. Use the suggested fields above.

Citing Sources

Do it! Check with your teacher to see if he or she prefers parenthetical citation or footnotes. Here is what you need to know:

1. To create parenthetical citations you will create a Works Cited list on a separate page at the end of your paper. It is alphabetized by author (or title if there is no author). Use this page for information on writing the citations (http://www.standrews.austin.tx.us/library/WorksCited.htm).

2. If you are using footnotes, you will cite your sources on the page on which they appear. Microsoft Word does this automatically:

   Type the text that you wish to cite. After the period insert the footnote (don't put a space). Here's how:

   - Click on Insert on the menu bar.
   - Click Footnote...
   - Click OK at the dialog box (unless you need to customize it).
   - Word will put your cursor at the bottom of the page with the footnote number. Type in the citation. The author's name will appear in normal order (not reversed), separated

from the other information with a comma. Publication data (City: Publisher, year) appears in parentheses, and no period is used until the very end of the citation.

- Continue typing text in the body of the paper above.
- Note: You can put more than one footnote on a page.

References

McKenzie, Jamie. (2000) *Beyond Technology: Questioning, Research and the Information Literate School.* Bellingham, WA: FNO Press.

Note taking tips modified from: Stripling, Barbara K. and Judy M. Pitts. (1988). *Brainstorms and Blueprints: Teaching Library Research as a Thinking Process.* Englewood, CO: Libraries Unlimited, Inc.

Handout 1

Your name:_____ **Today's date:**_____

Source (title, author, publication, date, URL, etc.)	
Subject	
Abstract (pertinent information— paraphrase, avoid copying and pasting huge blocks of text)	
Ideas (record here your ideas and reactions to the information, ways to use it in your paper, your opinions, or further research you need to do on the information)	

Save with a descriptive title or a sequential number.

Diamond Thinking

By Robert E. Berkowitz / vE1, no4

Related Big6 Skills: Big6 #4—Use of Information

Purpose: In this activity, students associate their ideas with the information they find.

Learning Contexts: Grades 6-12. Diamond Thinking is an Information Use strategy that helps students become divergent thinkers. This activity encourages students to expand their ideas as they engage and extract information from material they read, hear, or view.

Discussion: Ask students to list information from their research in the "Information" diamond (left diamond). Students then respond to that information by writing their thoughts in the "My Thoughts" diamond (right diamond). Information in the "My Thoughts" diamond may be based upon personal opinion or experience. In addition, students may fill in the "My Thoughts" with questions that were not answered by information they read, heard, or viewed.

Variation: One variation is to switch the headings and make "My Thoughts" in the left diamond, and "Information" in the right column. Using this variation, students begin by listing their ideas and opinions, and through research, complete the right diamond with information that validates or disputes their opinion.

Item: Diamond Thinking handout

Sample in Context: Students in Mr. Lake's 12th grade health class are working on a communicable diseases unit. Mr. Lake's assignment includes accessing and locating information on the Web about communicable diseases. To help students personalize the experience, he uses the "Diamond Thinking" strategy.

As students locate and read web-based information on their topics from the pre-selected sites, they complete the left diamond with four facts that relate to how the disease is transmitted. These facts are placed in the "Information" diamonds.

Students respond with their opinion or personal experience in the corresponding right "My Thoughts" diamond. In this way, students are able to provide their own strategies about preventing the spread of communicable diseases.

As an extension of this assignment, students may continue their research to determine the effectiveness or viability of their recommendations. Students proceed down the Diamond Thinking handout until they've completed their assignment. It is easy to see how Diamond Thinking can act as a springboard for a variety of extension activities.

Diamond Thinking Handout

By Robert E. Berkowitz

While you're researching your topic, use the graphic organizer below to record and think about what you've read, heard, or viewed. This exercise will help you become a divergent thinker and will help you expand your ideas as you gather (engage and extract) information from sources.

1. In the "Information" diamond below, list facts you've read, heard, or viewed about your topic.

2. In the "My Thoughts" diamond, list your thoughts, feelings, experiences, or unanswered questions that relate to your facts in the "Information" diamond.

Topic:_____

Information   **My Thoughts**

Information   **My Thoughts**

Information   **My Thoughts**

Big6 Stage 4 - Use of Information: Where the Rubber Meets the Road

By Janet Murray / vE5, no3

Teaching students to "extract relevant information" and "organize information from multiple sources" is a challenge, and yet, what skill could be more important to their ability to make informed decisions in the future? When students either print or cut and paste whole articles or pages from the World Wide Web, what have they accomplished? They haven't truly "engaged" with the information in a source; they've just amassed a collection of material from which they hope the "right stuff" will pop out at them the night before the assignment is due. Stages 4 and 5 of the Big6 Skills are the ones that determine whether or not significant new learning will occur: using and synthesizing information is where the rubber meets the road. This article focuses on Big6 #4: Use of Information.

4.1 Engage (e.g. read, hear, view, touch) the information in a source.

Read: Traditionally, we have taught students to interact with printed information by emphasizing guide words, bold-faced subheadings, indexes, tables of contents, topic sentences, and skimming and scanning. Textbooks may provide pre-reading questions at the ends of chapters. Some of these same strategies apply to web pages, most of which have bold-faced subheadings. Many have site maps that serve as indexes, and some information-rich sources have top-level pages that serve as tables of contents. Maps, graphs, and tables organize information in visual formats that students learn to interpret to satisfy content standards in social studies, science, and math.

Hear: Have we also taught students how to listen and take notes during a teacher's presentation of significant content material? Some students in the Big6 online course have incorporated interviews in their project designs. They take advantage of community resources (people!) to enhance students' understanding of the immigrant experience or local history. Students practice writing interview questions that will elicit the information they need before they conduct the interview, and learn to take notes while someone is speaking.

View: According to the National Information Literacy Standards for Student Learning (http://www.ala.org/aaslTemplate.cfm?Section=Information_Power&Template=/ ContentManagement/ContentDisplay.cfm&ContentID=19937), the student who is information literate "...derives meaning from information presented creatively in a variety of formats." [Standard 5.2] Media literacy emphasizes the importance of engaging and extracting information from video and other multimedia presentations. In today's world, it is far too easy for filmmakers and videographers to create images that imply a reality that simply does not exist. It is no longer true to say "the camera never lies."

A number of organizations that are dedicated to media literacy offer websites with sample lessons and guidance for educators. The Alliance for a Media Literate America (http://www.amlainfo.org/medialit/index.php) "is committed to promoting media literacy education that is focused on critical inquiry, learning, and skill-building." In its definition of media literacy, the AMLA concludes: "Today's information and entertainment technologies communicate to us through a powerful combination of words, images and sounds. As such we need to develop a wider set of literacy skills helping us to both comprehend the messages we receive, and to effectively utilize these tools to design and distribute our own messages." The Media Awareness Network "is based on the belief that to be functionally literate in the world today – to be able to read the messages that inform, entertain and sell to us daily – young people need critical thinking skills."

Touch: Finally, students can engage information by touching it. Science museums with hands-on exhibits designed for children are the most obvious example. My twin grandsons explored principles of physics at the Oregon Museum of Science and Industry this summer. Laboratory experiments in the typical science classroom provide another example. Field trips to outdoor sites often offer students the opportunity to engage by touching what they've learned about in the classroom.

4.2 Extract relevant information from a source.

I use the Big6 as a scaffold or framework to help students achieve the National Information Literacy Standards for Student Learning. Standard 2 states that "the student who is information literate evaluates information critically and competently," and 2.1 determines accuracy, relevance, and comprehensiveness.

Barbara Jansen's "Trash-N-Treasure" (http://www.big6.com/showarticle.php?id=45) method of teaching students how to take notes provides a valuable model that is well worth re-reading. Students in the Big6 online course have adapted Jansen's strategy to meet the needs of their students and teachers by creating note-taking templates. I've noticed that my middle school students tend to underline or highlight whole sentences or paragraphs rather than pertinent phrases, and that is the real jewel in the concept of "treasure" words—the ones that most efficiently and effectively answer the research question.

Of course, success in taking notes will also depend upon the quality of the question(s). Students must reevaluate their understanding of *Task Definition* (Big6 #1) and generate pertinent questions. When we are *seeking information* (Big6 #2), we need to consider whether or not the potential source is reliable, accurate, and meets our needs. When we begin to extract information, we need to reconsider our earlier conclusions. The Big6 Skills is recursive!

Facts, point of view, opinion

According to the AASL standards, the student who is information literate "evaluates information critically and competently" and
2.2 distinguishes among facts, point of view, and opinion;
2.3 identifies inaccurate and misleading information.

The World Wide Web is a particularly challenging source of information from this perspective. We know that people create Web sites to support their opinions, and may be selective in the information they present, but how can we persuade students to be more critical in their selection of information sources? A Presidential election year provides great opportunities to analyze and compare articles that use information selectively to support a point of view.

It can be difficult to find examples of biased Web sites on controversial issues that will not offend the standards of your community. In the past, I have used topics like abortion (a disastrous choice in a Texas presentation) and gun control (not a great choice on a military base) to demonstrate how web sites use information selectively to support a point of view. Cloning and the new laws pertaining to the identification and treatment of terrorists are current issues about which people have strong opinions reflected in the news media and on web sites.

Recently, I've been using a single site (http://whyfiles.org/165video_violence/index.html) that offers conflicting views about the influence of violent television and video games on behavior. It's an issue to which students can relate (and one about which they probably already have an opinion of their own)!

Responsible use: citation, citation, and citation

The information literate student "practices ethical behavior" and "respects intellectual property rights." (National Information Literacy Standards 8.2) From ISTE's National Educational Technology Standards for Students (NETS-S) (http://cnets.iste.org/students/s_stands.html): 2.2 Students practice responsible use of technology systems, information, and software

With the advent of the World Wide Web, copying and pasting information is so easy that some teachers won't even allow their students to use the Internet for research. Personally, I think that teaching responsible use is a better idea. First, I ask students to think about how they would feel if someone "stole" their drawing or poem or music composition or computer program. Then I relate that feeling of ownership to plagiarism, to try to help students understand why citation is important. I use the Gananda (NY) Central School library site, Plagiarism Is No Big Deal – Is It? (http://www.gananda.org/library/mshslibrary/plagexamples.htm) to show examples of real world consequences of plagiarism.

When we use World Wide Web sites for research, it's important to note the date that we accessed the information, because web sites change so often. I use an electronic note-taking template that includes links to the simplified online Citation Maker (http://www.oslis.k12.or.us/elementary/howto/cited/) from the Oregon School Library Information System as well as the more sophisticated Citation Machine (http://www.landmark-project.com/citation_machine/index.php) which includes APA as well as MLA formats. Students copy and paste the citation as well as a portion of the document. Then they highlight the important words and phrases, summarize the information in their own words (or select a quotation to use), and reflect about how they will use this information in their product. Identifying relevant information and extracting it in an organized fashion helps students proceed to the Synthesis stage with confidence.

Attaining standards

In addition to the national information literacy and educational technology standards listed above, Big6 Stage 4, Use of Information, helps students achieve content standards like these (from ISTE's compilation of content area standards) (http://cnets.iste.org/currstands/):

English/Language Arts
"Students apply a wide range of strategies to comprehend, interpret, evaluate, and appreciate texts." "Students conduct research on issues and interests by generating ideas and questions, and by posing problems. They gather, evaluate, and synthesize data from a variety of sources."

Mathematics:
"All students … pose questions and collect, organize, and represent data."

Social Studies
Students "use appropriate resources, data sources, and geographic tools such as atlases, data bases, grid systems, charts, graphs, and maps to generate, manipulate, and interpret information."

The introduction to the English Language Arts Standards provides a rationale for using them: "The vision guiding these standards is that all students must have the opportunities and resources to develop the language skills they need to pursue life's goals and to participate fully as informed, productive members of society." And this, finally, is the underlying reason for all our instruction in information problem solving using the Big6 Skills: asking questions, finding answers, selecting, analyzing and interpreting information, extracting relevant information, and synthesizing that information to make a decision are all critical skills in today's world. When students protest that research is "just a school thing," I offer them examples of information problems they are likely to encounter outside of school:

- For whom should I vote? How can I decide?
- Which car/video camera/TV should I buy?
- What kind of job do I want?
- Should I go to college? Which college should I attend?

The ability to extract relevant information from accurate and reliable, unbiased sources will help them answer these questions, as well as other questions we can't even begin to anticipate.

Synthesis

A Good Way to Get Started: Synthesis

By Barbara Jansen / *From the Big6 website: www.big6.com*

Big6™ 5: Synthesis

5.1 Organize information from multiple sources

Decide how you will put together the notes you took and ideas that you will add. You may:

- Write a rough draft
- Create an outline
- Create a storyboard
- Make a sketch
- _____

5.2 Present the information

If your teacher assigns the product:

- Make sure that you follow your teacher's guidelines.
- Add value to the product by including your ideas along with the information you found in books, web sites, and other sources. Make sure that your final product or paper is more than just a summary of what you found in the other sources.
- Make a product or write a paper that you would be proud for anyone to read.
- Include a bibliography. This is an alphabetized list of your sources. See the citation page for help.

If you get to choose your final product:

- Make sure that you follow your teacher's guidelines.

- Decide which product will best suit your subject. You may give an oral presentation using *PowerPoint* or write a paper. You may make a video or audio tape. Use technology if it is the best way to show the results of your information finding.

- Add value to the product by including your ideas along with the information you found in books, web sites, and other sources. Make sure that your final product or paper is more than just a summary of what you found in the other sources.

- Make a product or write a paper that you would be proud to have anyone read.

- Include a bibliography. This is an alphabetized list of your sources.

Helping Students Use PowerPoint Effectively: Part I Focus on Presentation of Information

By Mike Eisenberg / vE2, no1

It's not called *PowerPoint* for nothing! This software is *powerful*—it's a powerful tool for presentation of information. From a Big6 perspective, we're talking about Big6 #5—Synthesis. *PowerPoint* has quickly become a staple of business and educational presentations and can be used to combine text, images, and media in a professional, organized manner. At the same time, *PowerPoint* is often misused, and students make some of the same mistakes that are found in business.

The problem is that students as well as business presenters sometimes get caught up with all the "cool" features, the bells and whistles of flying text that builds, sound, and graphics. They often overdo it, packing in too much content and using too much glitz. One way to help students recognize this is to have them critique a set of *PowerPoint* presentations on the same topic. Teachers can develop these sample presentations around a common theme. The more exaggerated and outrageous you can make them, the better. As students view the sample *PowerPoint* presentations have them analyze the following:

- Use of text: clear and large enough, minimal use of different fonts, consistent use of fonts.

- Layout on slide: consistent, plenty of open space around text and graphics, not too busy.

- Animation and sounds: limited use of animated "builds" as text appears on a slide or transitions between slides, appropriate use of sounds.

- Logical presentation of content on each slide.

The goal is to have students focus on the substance of the presentation in terms of content, organization, and flow. If the presentation format itself becomes the object of attention rather than the content, something is wrong.

PowerPoint Part II

By Mike Eisenberg / vE2, no2

This is the second installment of our series of TIPS about using PowerPoint. In this TIP we use PowerPoint for note-taking (Big6 #4.2). Part I focused on using PowerPoint for presenting information and Part III, scheduled for a future issue, will include great ideas for teaching organizational skills using PowerPoint's slide sorter function.

*P*owerPoint for note-taking? You bet. Librarians and classroom teachers have taught classic note-taking skills for many years. Note-taking usually involves some form of the "note-card" method—that is, recording a note by writing a single concept or idea from a source on a 3x5 card along with a notation that links the card to the full citation for the source. Information about the source is usually stored on a separate bibliography card.

The paper note-card method really isn't a very efficient way to take notes from a source: (1) it is laborious, (2) takes a lot of time, and (3) uses a lot of cards. And, most kids hate it! In fact, most teachers probably wouldn't use the paper note-card method themselves if they were asked to write a research paper on some topic. That's because the paper note-card method is actually not designed for efficient note-taking (Big6 #4.2); it's designed for efficient organization of information after all the notes are available (Big6 #5.1). Once you've got note-cards, it's very easy to organize and sort the cards—just like using the slide sorter function in *PowerPoint*!

PowerPoint offers an electronic alternative to the laborious and time-consuming problems of the traditional 3x5 note-card method. *PowerPoint* provides an efficient way to create and sort note-cards—electronically.

PowerPoint presentation 3x5 cards are very different from the paper 3x5 cards we used for note-taking from sources. With paper note cards, note-taking was done well before a presentation, and we were simply interested in capturing potential relevant information that we could use later. We can do the same here—create a set of *PowerPoint* note-taking slides that allow us to capture potential relevant information that we may or may not use later. These electronic note-taking slides are relatively easy and fast to create.

To create a baseline note-taking slide, use one of the "Autolayout" new slide templates provided in *PowerPoint*. I prefer the Autolayout option that includes a Title and a Body in the form of a bulleted list. Once a formatted slide is created, students can use the "Click to add title" space to enter their source information, and the "Click to add text" space for the related note. When ready to create another note-card, simply choose "Insert" from the Menu Bar, then either "New Slide" to enter entirely new information or "Duplicate Slide" to copy the previous slide. Copying the previous slide will allow students to keep the same source information in the Title and allow them to type over the Body section to enter new notes.

When entering notes, students can type them in from scratch or copy-and-paste from an electronic source. This latter approach is filled with danger because students can easily plagiarize. However, citing sources is part of what we need to teach. We need to continually reinforce the following:

1. Make sure that students always note their sources in the Title field provided on the PowerPoint slide.

2. Teach students to use quotation marks for any direct quotes.

3. Help students learn how to combine information from a range of sources in their final product and how to credit (i.e., cite) their sources.

I've also created a more elaborate note-taking *PowerPoint* template. This template has designated places on the slide for information about the source (on the bottom of the slide) and also provides a space on top for indicating a possible topic, subtopic, or section. If students are able to enter this information while taking notes, it will help them later to sort and organize. But, it is not necessary to fill in every field on the *PowerPoint* slide.

Once the slides are created, it is easy to try different sequences for the note-card slides. This is organizing information (Big6 #5.1) at its finest as students select, move, add, and delete individual note-card slides. I do recommend saving a backup of the **full set** of the note-card slides (using the "Save As" function) **before** sorting and organizing. Then, students can be as creative as they like—and save alternate versions along the way.

Finally, once the note-card slides are sorted and organized as desired, the slide text may be copied and pasted into a word processing file. Try the following:

- View the slides in "outline" mode
- Select all
- Click on copy
- Open a new document in a word processing program
- Paste what was copied.

The result may require some reformatting, but the basic text (and the citation information) will now be available to use.

Using PowerPoint to Teach Organizational Skills —Part III

By Mike Eisenberg / vE2, no3

*I*n this final installment of our series of TIPS focusing on *PowerPoint*, we look at using *PowerPoint* to organize a presentation through the slide sorter function (Big6 #5.1). Part one focused on using *PowerPoint* to present information and part two included great ideas for teaching note-taking using *PowerPoint*.

Sort Information by Using PowerPoint

The slide sorter function in *PowerPoint* makes it easy to move slides around so that a presentation is well organized. *PowerPoint's* slide sorter allows a user to view thumbnail sketches of all the slides on a screen. The order of the slides may be rearranged by using the drag-and-drop feature using the mouse. Since some novice users are not aware of the slide sorter function, it is a good idea to point this feature out to students.

The focus of Big6 #5 Synthesis is to organize information from multiple sources and present the result in a logical manner. To avoid confusion for the audience who will view the PowerPoint, encourage students to establish an outline or agenda of no more that six parts and to do so on the second slide of the presentation (after the title slide). Then, students can create slides that divide each section to help keep the audience on track.

Learn How to Organize Information

How can students learn to become better organizers? Again, we can also use the slide sorter function. A teacher can create a *PowerPoint* presentation with key information about a topic that the class has been studying. The teacher can then mix up all the slides, including the title and divider slides, and has the students use the slide sorter function to organize the slides in a manner that makes sense. Students could write a narrative summary of the information from the slide show and submit it to the teacher for comments. What a great way to review a topic and teach organization at the same time!

Here are some variations on the above technique:

- Create a presentation that includes divider slides but gives the students a number of new slides to include where appropriate.

- Give students a number of unorganized slides but with two different sets of outline and divider slides.

- Make a presentation that does not have an outline or divider slides and ask the students to create these.

CHAPTER 6

Evaluation

A Good Way to Get Started: Evaluation

By Barbara Jansen / *From the Big6 website: www.big6.com*

6.1 Judge your product (how effective were you)

Before turning in your assignment, compare it to the requirements that your teacher gave you.

- Did you do everything and include all that was required for the assignment?
- Did you give credit to all of your sources, written in the way your teacher requested?
- Is your work neat?
- Is your work complete and does it include heading information (name, date, etc.)
- Would you be proud for anyone to view this work?

6.2 Judge your information problem-solving process (how efficient were you)

Think about the actions that you perform as you are working on this assignment. Did you learn some things that you can use again?

- What did you learn that you can use again?
- How will you use the skill(s) again?
- What did you do well this time?
- What would you do differently next time?
- What information sources did you find useful? You may be able to use them again.
- What information sources did you need but did not have? Be sure to talk to your librarian about getting them.

Assessment Made Easy the Big6™ Way

By Gayle Schmuhl / vE3, no1

*B*eing able to effectively assess student-learning research activities has always been a difficult process for most teachers. Evaluating the end product of a student's research is limiting and often fails to provide insight into the extent of students' abilities. Were students able to effectively analyze, evaluate and make use of information? That's the challenge.

Teachers do evaluate students' final products to see if students have developed a neat presentation that fits their criteria. However, this often overlooks the whole process of research even though most curriculum areas (e.g., science, language arts, and social studies) use a process approach. Information problem solving—the Big6™ —is a process that students can use throughout their lifetime. This is why it is important for all classroom teachers as well as library, media, or technology teachers to be able to assess whether students are good information problem solvers.

The Big6 Assessment tool evaluates student competence at the various stages of the Big6 process. Each row in the tool examines one area of the process. Not every area of information problem solving is important all the time. There are times when one or more areas are of prime importance while others may have a lesser importance. Using the Big6 Assessment tool, teachers have a practical way of weighting the steps of the Big6 that need the most emphasis.

So, how is the Big6 Assessment tool used to evaluate students' research? Read on!

Creating the Big6™ Assessment Tool: Weigh Your Priorities

First, the classroom teacher and media specialist determine the priorities of the research:

- Which areas of the Big6 are going to be most heavily emphasized and which will have a lesser focus?

Write down the Big6 steps and then look over the research project from a Big6 perspective:

- Does locating resources using call numbers have great importance?
- Is being able to define the research task and carry it through to completion the predominant task?
- Will this research project cover all of the Big6 areas equally?

After considering these questions, it is time to create a table with the Big6 steps on the left and a scoring guide on the top. For example, the guide along the top could have a score of 1-4 labels such as Highly Competent, Competent, Acceptable and Not Yet Acceptable. Teachers can save time by creating a sample template that can be adapted for use in future situations.

Next, decide what evidence from the project will demonstrate the student's achievement level in each Big6 step. Place this information in the column next to the scoring guide. The final column will be the focus or emphasis placed on a particular Big6 skill area. Again, not all Big6 areas have to be emphasized equally. Classroom teachers traditionally emphasize the synthesis portion or end product and less emphasis is placed on the entire research process. Now, you may want to expand this to place a high focus on all areas in order to assess whether students are effective information problem solvers.

Figures 1 and 2 are two Big6 Assessment Tools that have been used with sixth and seventh grade students. Each one related to a specific research project designed collaboratively by media specialists and classroom teachers. In Figure 1, the tool developed for an introductory unit on the Big6 for sixth graders, the evidence column refers to worksheets that accompanied the unit for students to complete. The written work verified and gave evidence of the student's mastery of that particular Big6 skill area. This assessment tool was designed to evaluate all Big6 Skills equally. Therefore, the scoring of points is equal for all skill areas.

Figure 1

Big6™ Skills	Highly Competent	Competent	Acceptable	Adequate	Not Yet Acceptable	Evidence	Focus
	6	5	4	3	2		
Task Definition						R. Sht #1-2	High
Information Seeking Strategies						R. Sht #2	High
Location & Access						R. Sht #2 Collection Form	High
Use of Information						R. Sht #2-3	High
Synthesis						R. Sht #3 Collection Form & Oral	High
Evaluation						Evaluation Form R. Sht #4	High
Points Possible	36						
Total Points							
Percentage							
Grade							

Figure 2, developed for use by seventh graders, places the emphasis in only a few key areas such as Synthesis and Use of Information. Evidence of student mastery came from worksheets such as the Data & Synthesis Sheets.

Figure 2. Big6™ Assessment by Gayle Schmuhi

Attribute							
Big6™ Skills	Highly Competent	Competent	Adequate	Not Yet	Evidence Competent	Focus	Point Award
#1 Task Definition				2	Big6 Org.	2	
# 2 Information Seeking Strategies					Big6 Org.	6	
#3 Location & Access					Big6 Org.	4	
#4 Use of Information					Notes & Bibliography Log	6	
#5 Synthesis					Time Line & Notes	2	
#6 Evaluation					None	n/a	
					Total Points=	20	
					Your Points=		
					% Grade=		

Instead of placing the words low, high, or medium in the Focus column, point values are substituted. This allows the classroom teacher and media specialist to place a weighted value on a particular Big6 skill area. For example, Task definition was assigned 2 points while Use of Information received 6 points. For this project the emphasis was on evaluating the student's ability to write notes and to cite the sources of their information.

Does This Method of Assessment Work?

Using the Big6 Assessment Tool, each student receives a thorough evaluation of not just the product but the entire process. There are students who create an ineffective product (written report, PowerPoint presentation, etc.) but demonstrate the ability to take good notes, locate, use, and document a variety of sources. With the Big6 Assessment Tool, the focus is on the entire information problem solving process not just the product. In addition, teachers can use the Big6 Assessment Tool to diagnose any areas of concern they may have for students, and provide remediation as necessary.

Evaluation

By Barbara A. Jansen / From the Big6 website: www.big6.com

*H*ow do you know if the assignments you turn in will be just what your teacher wants? Most students just finish an assignment and turn it in without checking their work to see if they have done everything needed to get the best grade. Therefore, they may leave off an important part of the assignment or be content to turn in average work.

Get ahead of the class by using these simple checklists to make your best grades yet!

For the best results, look at the checklist before you start the assignment and before you turn it in.

All checklists follow article.

1a. Checklist for Evaluating a Writing Assignment. Grades 7-12

1b. Checklist for Evaluating a Writing Assignment. Grades 3-6

If you want to do your best writing ever, use the Writing Assignment Organizer to help you plan and write a great paper! It also includes a checklist.

2.   Checklist for Evaluating a Science Fair Project

Need help to get started on your science fair project? Use the handy Science Fair Project Organizer to help you find ideas and plan your project all the way through presenting your results, including the evaluation of your work.

3.   Checklist for Completing Any Assignment

Use this checklist before you turn in your work, to help you get your best grades on any assignment.

4.   Checklist for Evaluating the Big6 Process

How do you know if you defined the task or if you have selected the right materials? Use this checklist to make sure that you are successful with every step of the information search process.

Check List for a Writing Assignment Grades 7-12

Before you show your paper to others, make sure it is as perfect as possible. You should be proud to put your name on your paper.

You should be able to answer "yes" to these questions before you turn in your paper.

✔ Is your paper a thoughtful response to the assignment? _____ yes _____ no

✔ Does your final paper represent your ideas and conclusions? _____ yes _____ no

✔ Is your paper more than a summary of other people's ideas? _____ yes _____ no

✔ If you paraphrased or summarized information found in books or magazines, on the Internet, or from other people, did you cite the source at point of use in your paper (using a footnote or parenthetical reference)? _____ yes _____ no

✔ Did you give credit to all of your sources in a bibliography? _____ yes _____ no

✔ Did you do everything in the assignment? _____ yes _____ no

✔ Does your bibliography follow the MLA format? Find out if your teacher requires a format other than MLA. _____ yes _____ no

✔ Is your paper word processed (or very neatly typed or hand-written if you do not have access to a computer)? _____ yes _____ no

✔ Is your paper complete and does it include a title page with heading information (title, your name, your teacher's name, date, etc.) _____ yes _____ no

✔ If your teacher requests these, did you include your notes, copies of each draft, and an annotated bibliography? _____ yes _____ no

✔ Would you be proud for anyone to read this paper? _____ yes _____ no

From Big6™ Writing Process Organizer for Grades 7-12 by Barbara A. Jansen, available http://www.big6.com/kids.

Check List for a Writing Assignment
Grades 3-6

Before you you show your paper to others, make sure it is as perfect as possible. You should be proud to put your name on your paper.

You should be able to answer "yes" to these questions before you turn in your paper.

✔ Did you do everything in the assignment and include all that was required for the paper? _____ yes _____ no

✔ Does your final paper show your original ideas as well as other information you found? _____ yes _____ no

✔ Did you give credit to all of your sources in a list (bibliography) at the end of you paper? _____ yes _____ no

✔ Is your paper word processed (or very neatly typed or hand-written if you do not have access to a computer)? _____ yes _____ no

✔ Is your paper complete and does it include a title page with heading information (title, your name, your teacher's name, date, etc.)? _____ yes _____ no

✔ If your teacher asks for these, did you include your notes, copies of each version, and your list of books, people, and web sites? _____ yes _____ no

✔ Would you be proud for anyone to read this paper? _____ yes _____ no

From Big6™ Writing Process Organizer for Grades 3-6 by Barbara A. Jansen, available http://www.big6.com/kids.

Check List for Completing a Science Assignment

How will you know you have done your best on a school assignment?

Before you turn in an assignment to your teacher, make sure it is as perfect as possible. You should be proud to put your name on the assignment.

You should be able to answer "yes" to all these questions before you turn in your assignment.

✔ Is what I created to finish the assignment what my teacher wants me to do?
_____ yes _____ no

✔ Did I include all the information required for the assignment? _____ yes _____ no

✔ Do the results of my efforts reflect my original ideas or my own work?
_____ yes _____ no

✔ Did I give credit to all my sources, even if my teacher did not require me to do so?
_____ yes _____ no

✔ Is my work neat? _____ yes _____ no

✔ Is my work complete and includes heading information such as my name and the date? _____ yes _____ no

✔ Would I be proud for anyone to look at my work? _____ yes _____ no

Check List for Completing an Assignment

How will you know you have done your best on a school assignment?

Before you turn in an assignment to your teacher, make sure it is as perfect as possible. You should be proud to put your name on the assignment.

You should be able to answer "yes" to these questions before you turn in your assignment.

✓ Is what I created to finish the assignment what my teacher wants me to do?
_____ yes _____ no

✓ Did I include all the information required for the assignment? _____ yes _____ no

✓ Do the results of my efforts reflect my original ideas or my own work?
_____ yes _____ no

✓ Did I give credit to all my sources, even if my teacher did not require me to do so?
_____ yes _____ no

✓ Is my work neat? _____ yes _____ no

✓ Is my work complete and includes heading information such as my name and the date? _____ yes _____ no

✓ Would you be proud for anyone to look at my work? _____ yes _____ no

Evaluate Your Research Skills Using the Big6™
By Barbara A. Jansen and Robert E. Berkowitz

Before you turn in your assignment or project, think about and respond to the items below.

Big6 #1: Task Definition	☐ Does the information in your final product meet (or exceed) the requirements of the assignment? ☐ Does your final product meet your teacher's expectations?
Big6 #2: Information Seeking Strategies	☐ Did the books, web sites, and other resources you used meet the needs of the assignment? ☐ Did you select the best sources available to you? How do you know?
Big6 #3: Location & Access	☐ Did you locate the sources you needed? ☐ Did you find the information you need in each source?
Big6 #4: Use of Information	☐ Were you able to effectively identify the information you needed? ☐ Were you able to effectively take notes or gather information?
Big6 #5: Synthesis	☐ Did you effectively organize information? ☐ Does your product present the information clearly?
Big6 #6: Evaluation	☐ Does your product meet (or exceed) the assignment requirements? ☐ Did you use your time well?

The BIG6

CHAPTER 7

Big6 for All

Problem Solving Models: Another Connection for the Big6

By Janet Murray / vE4, no2

*I*n my high school, we have identified "problem solving skills" as one of the goals of our school improvement process. The North Central Association (NCA) Commission on Accreditation and School Improvement (CASI) accredits my school, so our school improvement process conforms to the "Performance Accreditation Framework" detailed on the NCA web site (http://www.ncacasi.org/standard/perf_accred_frame.adp). We have been examining problem solving models to select one we can adopt school-wide. This has been a difficult problem-solving process in and of itself for the team. However, what follows is my personal reflection on the process.

At first, we chose problem solving models and interventions by department. This chart compares the Big6 to two of those choices and the math model highlighted in the January, 2003 NCA CASI e-News.

Math *NCA CASI e-News January 2003*	Science	Social Studies *CCPL Study of Teaching 4 Categories of Thinking*	Information: Big6 Skills http://www.big6.com/
1. Clarify the problem or task	1. Explore the problem	xx	1. Define the task
2. Brainstorm possible solutions	xx	xx	2. Determine possible sources of information
xx	xx	1. Accessing information	3. Locate sources
3. Select a possible solution; try it.	2. Plan the solution	2. Organizing information	4. Extract relevant information
xx	3. Solve the problem	3. Transforming information	5. Synthesize the information
4. Debrief / Reflect	4. Examine the solution	xx	6.1 Judge the product
xx	xx	4. Thinking about thinking	6.2 Judge the process

Educator Perspectives

As a library media teacher whose job title is "Information Specialist," I have been using the Big6 as an information problem solving strategy for several years. I always emphasize the fact that the Big6 is a recursive process; I tell students that "research" literally means to "search and search again." For example, when we are conducting research, we need to continually re-evaluate our Task Definition (Big6 #1) and Information Seeking Strategies (Big6 #2) in light of the information we locate and extract from relevant sources.

Members of the Science department argue that the Social Studies department approach (as presented) addresses teaching strategies rather than learning strategies. Personally, I think it leaves out task definition and brainstorming. I also think the Math and Science models are too simplistic and omit some important steps in the "solution" process, although I know teachers elaborate the steps when they explain them.

The Robert D. Edgren High School (Misawa, Japan) in my district chose a model with six steps, as follows:

1. Identify the problem;

2. Brainstorm and list different choices;

3. Evaluate each choice in terms of its consequences;

4. Determine the best alternative;

5. Put the decision into action;

6. Evaluate the outcome of your solution.

This list of steps has the advantage of being broadly applicable to personal decision-making, a fact I always emphasize with students when I discuss the Big6 Skills. I want students to know that using the Big6 is not just a "school" thing, that it is pertinent to personal decisions like choosing a college or choosing a career.

Benefits of the Big6

As the Internet has become widely available, I have been focusing library instruction on using the World Wide Web for research (http://www.surfline.ne.jp/janetm/big6info.htm). Evaluating sources of information is critically important when students use the World Wide Web to select information, just as evaluating choices is important in the personal decision-making process. Although I'm sure our math and science teachers emphasize the importance of evaluating possible solutions, it is not obvious in the models outlined on page 63.

The Big6 focuses on information problem solving and information problem solving permeates all stages of more general problem solving processes. So, from one point of view, you can apply the entire Big6 process at each stage of problem solving. That is, for the model above, you can use task definition, information seeking strategies, location & access, use of information, synthesis and evaluation to "identify the problem" and each of the subsequent steps. Think of the "nested dolls" popular in Russia: the large one holds smaller and smaller versions within it. We have them in Japan, too, and I use them when I want to visually demonstrate processes within processes.

The Big6 bridges the gap between purely scientific, mathematical models and information research models because it expands the "solving" part of the process to emphasize that it involves more than a single step. The Big6 could become the "horizontal curriculum:" the unifying problem solving and research process common across the "vertical curriculum" of departmental subject matter.

As Art Wolinsky, author of books for kids about the Internet and Big6 trainer, says,

> "We all have a research process we teach kids, one that we are very comfortable using year after year after year. Yet each year we have to re-teach our process to a new group of students. The problem is that we are looking at the process from OUR point of view. From the students' perspective, they have to learn a slightly different process from every teacher they have. If we look at it from the student point of view, doesn't it make sense to adopt a single process that works? With the Big6 in place, all teachers have a common vocabulary and they can elaborate and refine the process each year."

Meeting Standards and Gaining Skills

In addition to the "specialized curricular requirements for each level of schooling" defined in the "Process of Schooling," the NCA cites (http://www.ncacasi.org/standard/emsu/ps.adp) "the application of technology as a tool for learning" at every level and expects schools "to enable students to become self-directed learners." Emphasis on technology as a "tool" corresponds to the language of the ISTE NETS-S (National Educational Technology Standards for Students) (http://cnets.iste.org/students/s_stands.html) and the goal of self-directed learning reflects the National Information Literacy Standards. (http://www.ala.org/aaslTemplate.cfm?Section=Information_Power&Template=/ContentManagement/ContentDisplay.cfm&ContentID=19937)

"Learning and Teaching Information Technology: Computer Skills in Context" by Mike Eisenberg and Doug Johnson (updated September 2002) incorporates both of these national standards in "Technology Skills for Information Problem Solving: A Curriculum Based on the Big6 Skills Approach." The authors note that "Educational technologists … are advocating integrating computer skills into the content areas, proclaiming that computer skills should not be taught in isolation and that separate 'computer classes' do not really help students learn to apply computer skills in meaningful ways." Similarly, "library skills" taught in isolation rarely produce independent, self-directed learners.

If we are truly dedicated to improving student performance, and our data indicates that students need to improve their problem-solving skills, we should consider a broad, school-wide implementation incorporating a problem solving model with cross curricular applications that involve computer literacy and information literacy skills.

The Big6 Sells Itself

By Karen MacDonald / vE1, no2

*B*e careful what you wish for—you just might get it! Look at me, a library-media specialist not even done with my Masters of Library Science (MLS) program at Syracuse…I wished to convince my public school system to use the Big6 instead of a grab-bag of assorted research processes, none of which are as simple and universally applicable. I wished teachers and students could apply the Big6 process consistently throughout their lives.

My wish was granted! I was invited to present the Big6 to the district's "What Is Taught and What Is Learned" curriculum subcommittee. "Well, gosh," I thought to myself, suddenly humble. "I'm no Mike Eisenberg, with nerves of steel and a wealth of Calvin and Hobbes' metaphors on the Information Age! Nor am I a Bob Berkowitz, with his sublime vision of the Big Picture—though occasionally I can answer the question, "Why are we doing this?" However, it was too late to bolt. Besides, I had eaten, slept, and breathed Big6 for the past two summers!

In '97 I took courses with Eisenberg and Berkowitz. And, I spent the lazy, hazy days of summer '98 glued to my computer, adapting my school system's outdated Information Skills Scope and Sequence (S&S) chart. Massachusetts' new Curriculum Frameworks (an offshoot of the Massachusetts Education Reform Act of 1993 (http://www.doe.mass.edu/frameworks) requires students "to frame questions and solve problems in real-life situations." I used the Big6 to update our S&S to incorporate this expanded mission, and added in media and technology skills, which didn't exist when Falmouth's Library Skills Scope and Sequence was created.

My Invitation to Speak

I was so proud of my new chart that I forwarded a copy to Ann Bradshaw, Falmouth's Director of Curriculum. When she neglected to respond immediately, I assumed she'd tossed my treasure . . . **until** she invited me to do the above-mentioned presentation. She said it was important to include classroom teachers, get their input and suggestions, to make them part of the process. "I'd love to do it," I said. "But only if you don't mind it being **very casual**." "Fine," she said.

"She has no idea what casual means," I thought, as I rummaged through my messy stockpile of real-life fourth grade graphics the morning of the presentation. I'd tossed them in the back seat of my car along with the orange Bible and the Big6 gravestones I'd used in October for a bulletin board detailing the steps in short phrases with humorous Mexican "Day-of-the-Dead" skeletons acting out each. The bulletin board was adapted from an idea conceived by Gretchen Baldauf, librarian at Alexander Hamilton Elementary School in New York, which I read about in the Sept.-Oct. '98 issue of *The Big6 Newsletter* (Lowe, 1998, p.3).

I'd hoped to open with the videotaped "I Love Lucy" episode that Mike Eisenberg used in IST 700 at Syracuse University. Unfortunately the tape was hung up in Location & Access when my interlibrary loan failed to arrive in time. So there I was, using the old "dump-the-whole-toolbox-on-the-table" strategy—you know the one where you've collected such a load of material and experiences that you can hardly decide where to start to explain. Nevertheless, my presentation was awesome!

As it turned out, everyone on the committee had seen reruns of the 1952 classic in which Lucy and Ethel try to earn money by wrapping candy on an assembly line. Remember "SPEED IT UP A LITTLE?" Mike says this is what the information explosion has done to classroom teachers. I can hear him now, "Though modern technology can deliver over ten-thousand characters per second, the average human can still comprehend only 300 words per minute." As a former classroom teacher, I know how busy teachers are and I like to reassure them, "You probably already **do** it!" I mean, I believe every teacher eventually improvises some form of the six steps, whether applying them to lesson planning or through helping students think for themselves but do their research first.

But it's one thing to do it and another to articulate it. So there I was, "scared stiff," as I set out my Big6 gravestones and posted the "Super Three" (PLAN, DO and REVIEW) under steps 1, 4 and 6. I gave a brief overview of my workshop. "First I'll introduce the six easy steps," I said, writing the mnemonic TILUSE on chart paper and explaining that T stands for Task Definition, I for Information Seeking Strategies, etc. "We'll do a little exercise together, proving how simple this process is. And then, for the rest of your life, Big6 will always be waiting there in the back of your mind, 'TIL you need to USE it.'"

At this point the process itself seemed to take over. I danced around the room gesturing at gravestones, pausing to share actual applications of each step. For example, at the "Information Seeking Strategy" stone (where a skeleton-lady fluttered her fan quizzically), I showed how children learn to brainstorm an assortment of keywords using a chart from *Information Problem-Solving: The Big Six Skills Approach to Library & Information Skills Instruction* (Eisenberg & Berkowitz, 1990, p.119).

How Children Used the Big6™

To demonstrate how children extract a task-appropriate topic from a multitude of options, I shared my worksheet featuring November motif cartoon drawings of Wampanoag clothing, pilgrim hats and shoes, canoes, muskets, etc. This worksheet required cooperative teams of students to graphically organize Major Topic [ships,] Subtopics [sails—wood—decks,] and Synonyms [cloth, planks, floors . . .]. Later, after the students completed the Location step on the school's OPAC, we would compare how many "hits" resulted from each brainstormed keyword.

Then I offered three examples of how they'd probably already used the process in solving fictional, school, and "real life" information problems. As an example from the school setting, I showed how I had used the Big6 with a fairy tale problem. I held up the laminated, reusable 11"x17" sheets with six sections. A class of fourth graders had used these sheets to record their notes as we deconstructed the plot of "Rumplestiltskin," Big6-style. I recalled the lesson for the committee, and showed them that when the fourth graders first analyzed "Rumplestiltskin," they had identified Task Definition as "The elf wants to get the baby."

"Notice how tricky the Evaluation step was," I pointed out to the teachers. "Though it **appeared** that Rumplestiltskin had succeeded in his task, the kids and I decided he'd "won the battle but lost the war." After looping back to Task Definition we added, "get and *keep* the baby" to our criteria.

In my second example, a fourth grade class prepared to set up a classroom aquarium. It was clear that students had learned to foresee the "assessment" step. For Task Definition number two, the kids now wrote, "build a salt-water aquarium **that works.**" Their Information Seeking Strategies were also more skillful. ("Ask people. Go on Internet. Find books by typing FISH on the computer catalog. Look in the Dewey Decimal 639 section.")

In response to questions from the audience, I taught a few web-browser tricks, then went on to my final example, the "Real-Life Problem." A biologist (who the fourth graders referred to as "the Fish Guy,") had recently visited the school, offering an exciting hands-on lesson about marine creatures. The class and I analyzed the steps the Fish Guy had probably gone through in order to present such a fine lecture and demo. We concluded that, although the Fish Guy may never had heard of the Big6, he'd obviously covered them all.

One Example of Using the Big6™ in Real Life

After about an hour, the whole committee was gaping in wonderment. Time to hook 'em with Bob Berkowitz's restaurant-choosing exercise. Here's a sketchy outline of our results.

Task Definition	Find a restaurant with food we want. Consider taste, cost, location, atmosphere, reputation, service, time.
Information Seeking around, **Strategies**	Consider friends, coupons, advertisements, the phone book, drive look at menus on walls, use the Internet.
Location & Access	Ask friend, phone a restaurant, check a bus or transportation map.
Use of Information	Go to the restaurant, decide on the section desired (smoking or non-smoking), wait.
Synthesis on the	Order, sit, relax, drink, spy on other diners, chat, have fun drawing placemat, eat.
Evaluation Would	Consider the cost, taste, and ambiance. Would you go back there? you recommend the restaurant to a friend?

As I closed the presentation, I shared some of the best resources in my toolbox—websites, book references, the Big6 mailing list address, and The Big6 Newsletter, as well as reminders about AskERIC (http://www.askeric.org) and KidsConnect (http://www.ala.org/ICONN/kidsconn.html). I was no longer a scared stiff speaker. In fact, I was looking forward to doing it again!

One thing I'd do differently next time would be to bring handouts. (When one of the teachers admired my colorful 15"x36" laminated Big6 data collection sheet, and I said, "Here, it's yours," you'd think I'd given her gold.) I'd bring a supply of Big6 bookmarks. Medfield's Dale Street School librarian, Allison Bernstein, jokes that she learned everything she needed to know from the bookmark—and I don't doubt it—the bookmarks offer a good explanation!

In the final analysis, it went well enough for my first presentation. As the full committee dismissed into subcommittees for "other business," I could hear that they were already using the vocabulary. And they asked me to join their committee—and maybe do a district-wide workshop. I can't wait to convince the entire educational system to reform the outdated "factory model" into a system that trains the students to solve problems methodically, using both intelligence and intuition.

But that's another story. The moral of this one is: if you're excited about the Big6 and want to share it with your school system, don't be scared! It practically teaches itself!

References

Eisenberg, M. B., & Berkowitz, R. E. (1990). *Information problem-solving: The Big Six Skills approach to library & information skills instruction,* (p.119). Stamford, CT: Ablex Publishing.

Lowe, C. A. (1998). Research reports: Bulletin boards. *The Big6 Newsletter,* 2(1), 3.

Why Do We Use the Big6?...
It All Points to FOCUS!

By Blythe Bennett / vE2, no1

*I*n November 2000, a request was posted on the LM_NET and Big6 listservs asking respondents who use the Big6 at their schools or higher education institutions to participate in a survey regarding the Big6. These surveys asked respondents to identify where and why they use the Big6 with their students as well as the impact of the Big6. The purpose of this article is to report on one question—the impact of the Big6—from the first 100 responses. Results from other questions and additional responses will be reported in upcoming issues of the eNewsletter.

The Big6 team wants to thank everyone who took the time to complete and return the survey. If you didn't get a chance to respond to the original survey, it is not too late!! It will only take 10-15 minutes and will help us a great deal. Please visit http://big6.com/enewsletter/e_survey.html to submit your responses.

What is the Impact of the Big6?

This was a central concern and key question in the survey (question 7 in the Big6 listserv survey, question 9 in the LM_NET version). The responses were varied and highly positive. Overall, they appeared to affirm the usefulness of the Big6 information problem-solving process. Most of the comments related that the Big6 helped students, teachers, and librarians to "focus." There were also a number of comments that students using the Big6 reported "less anxiety" and "more confidence" when approaching assignments and projects.

Focus

Respondents indicated that they use the Big6 because it provides a "logical," well designed process to work with and it provides the students with a "common vocabulary." Here is a sample of the statements made about having an impact on the students' ability to focus:

> "I know that this process gets our students organized, thinking about their needs and the work that they do." – Melinda Miller-Widrick, Colton, NY.

> "I think the most important impact of the Big6 has been that students are THINKING more before they start off on a task, being aware of the different options or sources for information (instead of just choosing the obvious) and evaluating information better." – Debbie Crumb, Bates Technical College, WA.

> "Students report that it has helped them prepare for the project or paper by providing them with structure that they would not have had otherwise." – Barbara Jansen, Austin, TX.

> "Students tell me it is much easier to do research when you go step by step. They find the Deciding aspect particularly helpful. Prior to using this model they used to wander around not really knowing where to start." – Clare Tuohy, Australia.

> "I see the difference it's made from the research angle. By grade 10 and up students know how to attack research problems with little direction and they are using a wider variety of resources available." – Verna LaBounty, Kindred Public School, Kindred, ND.

Librarians also noted that the Big6 process helps with focus in a slightly different way—to provide a focus for their library program:

> "It completely changed our library program because it gave us a focus. We have built around this and continue to use it as a backbone." – Joan Leach, TX.

Less Anxiety and More Confidence

Carol Kuhlthau (1989, 1993) has conducted extensive research on students' feelings and attitudes during the information search process. Kuhlthau found that students' emotions do change—usually from uncertainty and anxiety to security and confidence as they successfully proceed through the process.

Therefore, it was particularly revealing that when asked about the impact of the Big6, many of the respondents indicated that the Big6 model helps students by creating more confidence and less anxiety. Here is a sampling of responses:

> "From a personal view, on-the-ground, working with kids daily, I see them as being better organized and more confident with the Big6 as their framework." Marty Swist, The American School In Japan (ASIJ).

> "Students like the structure—they know that when they first come in the library to begin the project, I go through the steps with them in order to help them do their work faster and better. Step 1 gets rid of a lot of anxiety—they know exactly what the teacher wants handed in and what type of information is needed. Step 2 is extremely important—this is where I give them tips of the best resources our library has for that project after they brainstorm all possible sources. After a few projects, they even believe me when I tell them certain books would be a better first choice than the Internet!! —Sharon Talmadge, Oak Crest Middle School, San Dieguito Union High School District, Encinitas, CA.

> "I only introduced this half-way through last year, but already I see some of the anxiety (both students' and parents') about research diminishing. The teachers are happy with the process, because the students are doing more of their own work (as opposed to parents or tutors doing it for them). I have had a lot of positive feedback, particularly from the parents in primary grades, about how pleased they are that their children are learning good research skills at an early age and that they will be reinforced from kindergarten through 6th grade." – Yapha Mason, Brentwood School, West Campus (K-6), Los Angeles, CA.

> "…students approach assignments with less angst. Our activities for the first three steps have helped ease panic at the beginning." – Cecily R. Pilzer, librarian, Georgetown Day School, Washington, DC.

With heightened focus and less anxiety, students, teachers, and librarians are seeing grand results in their information problem-solving skills. Joyce Needham reports that the Big6 may have some relationship with test scores as assessments shift from content to process. "We are just beginning to discover how Big6 can improve our student's test scores by providing them with a 'process' for accessing, using, and communicating information." (Joyce Needham, MO).

It must be emphasized that these scores have not been tied directly to the use of Big6. Many respondents commented that it would be valuable to determine whether there is a correlation between the Big6 and student performance. It is clearly an area for further study.

From the preliminary 100 survey results on the question about the impact of the Big6, it does seem that some responding teachers and librarians see improvement in students' information problem-solving skills—particularly in terms of focus and confidence. The enthusiasm of the following statement is indicative of the overall responses of many:

> "There has never been a more exciting time to be involved with research. Now, kids can spend their time thinking, evaluating, and synthesizing, instead of just locating information." (Jo Chinn, WA).

Bibliography

Kuhlthau, Carol C.; And Others. (1989). *Facilitating information seeking through cognitive modeling of the search process.* A Library Studies Research Project.

Kuhlthau, C.C. (1993). *Seeking meaning: A process approach to library and information services.* Greenwich, CT: Ablex.

Lowe, C. A. (Sep-Oct 1997). The work of Carol A. Kuhlthau. *Big6 Newsletter*, 1(1) p11, 14.

Big6 in Action: The Big6 All Over the World

By Carrie Lowe / *vE1, no1*

*O*ne of the great benefits of the Internet is the ability to work with even our most distant colleagues. The following articles give us a glimpse of the way that two members of the Big6 mailing list—one in Israel, one in Germany—have used the Big6 with great success.

Reuven Werber, who lives in **Etzion Bloc, Israel**, is a long-time contributor to the Big6 mailing list and an active member of the Big6 community. His contribution to discussions and his perspective is invaluable! Last month, Reuven contributed a lesson about Chanukah (http://www.big6.com/showarticle.php?id=37). The lesson shares a great way to teach students about this meaningful holiday and reinforces their information problem-solving skills.

In his article, (see Article 1) Reuven describes his success in introducing the Big6 to the faculty and students of his school, **Neveh Channah High School for Girls**. He also introduces a lesson about neighborhoods, which can be applied to any community.

Deborah Stafford, Information Specialist at **Gen. H.H. Arnold High School in Wiesbaden, Germany**, is another Big6 enthusiast and an important contributor to the Big6 mailing list. Deborah's article (see Article 2) details a lesson that she created with the Junior Reserve Officer Training Corps (JROTC) instructor at her school. Her story is one of successful collaboration—so successful, in fact, that the instructor plans to repeat the lesson with future classes.

Thanks to Reuven and Deborah for contributing their articles. If you have a Big6 experience that you would like to publish in The Big6 in Action column, please e-mail me at carrie_a_lowe@yahoo.com.

~ Carrie Lowe

Article 1

The Big6™ in Israel
Reuven Werber

My name is **Reuven Werber**. I work at **Neveh Channah High School for Girls** in the **Etzion Bloc, Israel**. Our school is a 9–12th grade high school for Jewish modern Orthodox girls in the Etzion Bloc-Jerusalem area. We have two classes in every grade level with a total of about 250 students. I am a Judaic studies teacher and ed-tech coordinator at the school. I work with a staff (English teacher, math teacher, and school librarian) to develop and teach an educational technology information literacy course for 9th and 10th graders. I provide ed-tech support and professional development for our staff (about 50 teachers). I also teach a number of courses in ed-tech information literacy skills at the **Herzog Teachers College of Yeshivat Har Etzion** at the Etzion Bloc.

When I discovered the Big6 on the WWW, I joined and participated in the Big6 mailing list. Later, I bought and read a few Big6 books. Building on this knowledge base, I began translating Big6 materials and applying them at Neveh Channah. Two summers ago, it was my privilege to meet Bob Berkowitz who was in Israel for an International School Librarians conference. Bob visited our school and saw some of our projects. He gave us some very helpful tips and ideas for future program development. He invited me to present some of our projects at the school librarian conference, which I gladly did.

Our program teaches the students to use the Big6 model to complete various curricular projects (in cooperation with the curricular instructors). The projects emphasize different aspects of the model. Each year, we try to apply the Big6 model in a year-end team project. Last year, students in our 9th grade classes did a large project on Jerusalem neighborhoods. The students split into teams of four—chose a Jerusalem neighborhood, gathered information about it from books, periodicals, CD databases, the Web, visits to the neighborhood, and interviews with its residents. The teams utilized the information to prepare *PowerPoint* multimedia presentations. The students loved the project, and devoted many hours beyond the allotted class time for working on it.

The site is documented at http://www.nevnet.etzion.k12.il/jerusalem.htm (in Hebrew).

Title: Neighborhoods in Jerusalem

Authors: (from Neveh Channah Torah High School for Girls, Etzion Bloc, Israel)
- Tzila Yarhi
- Miriam Weitman
- Ita Munitz
- Phylis Goldman
- Reuven Werber

Subject Areas: Geography, history, holiday celebration (Jerusalem Day)

Grade: 9

Big6 Skills covered:
- Big6 #1 - Task Definition
- Big6 #2 - Information Seeking Strategies
- Big6 #3 - Location & Access
- Big6 #5 - Synthesis

Internet Uses:

- **Communication**—Students send e-mail to teachers for advice, and to submit assignments.

- **Information Resource**—Students search for Web sites and view information pertaining to the neighborhood.

- **Presentation**—Students upload *PowerPoint* presentation to the school Web site. Final student work will be viewed with Microsoft *Internet Explorer.*
  - **Goal:** Study the geographical, historical, and demographic development of Jerusalem.
  - **Content Area Objective:** Understand the history, geography, and life of Jerusalem and its residents.

Big6 Objectives:

1. Understand the assignment. (Task Definition)
2. Formulate relevant research questions. (Information Seeking Strategies)
3. Determine best sources for information gathering. (Information Seeking Strategies)
4. Search for specific information about neighborhoods. (Location & Access)
5. Construct a presentation on the neighborhood using Microsoft *PowerPoint.* (Synthesis)
6. Write a two page report on one of the problems facing the neighborhood and outline possible solutions. (Synthesis)

Overview:

Two 9th grade classes of 31-32 students each, are divided into teams of four. Each team chooses a neighborhood in Jerusalem and gathers, sorts, and organizes information about that neighborhood. Each team prepares a presentation about its neighborhood using Microsoft PowerPoint, and each team project will be exhibited to the school on Jerusalem Day (a day commemorating Jerusalem's liberation in 1967). Each team divides into two subteams of two students each. All subteams write a report on a problem facing its neighborhood today and propose some possible solutions. This lesson can be adapted to the study of neighborhoods, towns, or cities in any geographical location.

Materials (in Hebrew):

- Assignment online: http://www.nevnet.etzion.k12.il/jerusalem.htm (English translation is planned)

- List of online sources for Jerusalem information, linked to the Search Strategies step: http://www.nevnet.etzion.k12.il/jerusites.htm

- Document with rules for writing bibliography of text, digital, and Internet sources: http://www.nevnet.etzion.k12.il/mekorot.rtf

Activities:

1. Each team chooses a Jerusalem neighborhood.
2. Each team gathers information on the following:
   - Neighborhood name
   - Historical timeline of neighborhood from founding until present day
   - Demographic characteristics
   - Important buildings and institutions

- Important personalities
- Architecture and building styles
- The neighborhood in art (drawing, photo, poetry, music, etc.)

Additional points of importance and interest using the following recommended sources:

- Textual: encyclopedias, books, periodicals
- Digital: periodical guide, Jerusalem CD's, online catalogue
- Internet sources (see online list for ideas)

Additional: tours, museums, interviews, correspondence: e-mail and postal mail

3. Each team synthesizes this information into a 10-20 minute presentation using Microsoft *PowerPoint*. The presentation is shown to the entire school on Jerusalem Day. The presentation should contain a cover slide, text, pictures, maps, audio and video clips, and a rich and diverse bibliography.

4. Following the presentation, groups of two (from each team of four) write a report on their chosen neighborhood.

5. Students upload their *PowerPoint* presentations to the school Web site.

Logistics

- **Equipment:**
  During the course of the assignment, the teams have access to two computer labs outfitted with frame relay connections (20 computers). In addition to scheduled class time, the labs are open and accessible throughout the school day as long as no other class is using them. In addition, four computer stations are available in the school library.

- **Staff:**
  Two information technology teachers work with the teams in classes for two hours a week. One library media specialist works with the classes one hour a week, and two homeroom teachers are also involved in overseeing the project.

- **Evaluation:**
  The evaluation process will consist of three aspects:

1. Reflective evaluation
2. Peer evaluation
3. Instructor evaluation

Evaluation instruments are based upon project requirements as outlined above.

Article 2

Big6™ in Action

The Department of Defense Dependents Schools (DoDDS) Experience in Germany
by Deborah Stafford

My name is **Deborah Stafford** and I am the Information Specialist (this is our official title, though I prefer to be called a librarian) at **Gen. H.H. Arnold High School** (http://www.wies-hs.odedodea.edu/MediaCenter/media.html) in **Wiesbaden**, **Germany**.

Our school has approximately 550 students in grades 9–12. I am originally from Wyoming (USA) where I graduated from the University of Wyoming with a B.A. and a masters degree. My first job was as a high school librarian, and I wasn't much older than the students. After a stint as a teacher and librarian in Montana, I moved to Seoul, Korea to teach with the Department of Defense Dependents schools. From Seoul, I went to Nurnberg Germany and after a reduction of the U.S. military presence closed that community, I came to Wiesbaden, Germany.

I first heard about the Big6 by reading postings about it on the LM_NET mailing list. I became interested and looked into the process. Our local librarians association planned to do a conference and wanted a speaker to address the information process. Bob Berkowitz came and presented the Big6 Skills to our group and I began using the model in my school and encouraging others to do so. Later our school system had a conference for all librarians and again Bob Berkowitz presented to us. Now, the Big6 is used by many of us to teach information literacy.

An example of how we've used the Big6:

A couple of years ago, our Junior Reserve Officer Training Corps (JROTC) instructor wanted to do a research project with his cadets. He wanted to create a project that would require his students to look for information and produce a written report. The students would need to work in groups and there would be a group grade. Knowing that I was interested because I had talked with him several times, he asked me for some ideas. Our task was to develop a good project for his students.

Here's how we used the Big6 to help plan the project.

- **Task Definition -** Design a research project for JROTC cadets. The project should involve research, collaboration, and a final written report.

- **Information Seeking Strategies -** The instructor and I talked and looked at some previous projects. We also looked at the Big6 method.

- **Location & Access -** A message was posted to the Big6 mailing list asking for ideas.

- **Use of Information -** The posted ideas were printed and given to the instructor to read and analyze.

- **Synthesis -** After looking over the ideas, a project was created that incorporated several of the best ideas. The students were to plan an exercise program to counteract the effects of zero gravity in space. We established a time frame and scheduled library time.

- **Evaluation -** The JROTC instructor liked the process and the outcome. He will repeat the assignment in the future. From my perspective, the project was successful because student teams used a variety of resources and even stayed after school to use the library.

In evaluating the project, we decided to spend more time teaching students the Big6 method the next time the project is repeated. In addition we will involve the students in evaluating their own projects.

Here's how the students used the Big6 in this project:

- **Task Definition** - Students analyzed the project and formed teams. Each team completed a planning sheet before beginning the search for information.

- **Information Seeking Strategies** - Students determined that they needed two types of information:
  - What are the effects of zero gravity on the human body?
  - What exercises would be most useful in counteracting these effects?

- **Location & Access** - I presented a brief lesson on *subject* versus *keyword* searching. Students used CD-ROM databases such as SIRS Researcher, NewsBank Popular Periodicals, Science Source, Wilson Disk, encyclopedias, and the Internet. One site that was particularly useful was the NASA Spacelink search page (http://search.spacelink.nasa.gov/index.html). Students also established an e-mail contact at NASA.

- **Use of Information** - Teams analyzed their research and determined which parts would be useful in designing their exercise program.

- **Synthesis** - Teams used a variety of methods to present their research. Some teams wrote a fitness plan with illustrations. Other teams designed an exercise apparatus that would work in space. Some teams presented the problem then several solutions.

- **Evaluation** - Each member of the team had to sign the final document. In the final document, the role and contribution of each team member was stated. By signing the final document, the team members had to agree on both the final product and their role in completing it.

This year, the JROTC instructor will use the activity as a lead-in to NASA's Mars Millennium project (http://quest.arc.nasa.gov/ltc/mars/), a White House Millennium Council Youth Initiative that asks students to participate in the cooperative design of a community on Mars.

Big6 advice:

Over the past few years, the Big6 mailing list has been an invaluable resource for sharing ideas with other library media specialists and teachers. Some of the ideas that have been gathered and shared have included diverse topics such as mythology, health, Renaissance literature, math, and biology.

Since introducing the Big6 process, I believe that I have seen an increase in student projects at my school that involves information problem solving. I believe that using the Big6 process has enabled students to prepare better projects.

Collaborative Teaching Using the Big6

By Holly Barton / vE1, no4

When hardware and software are introduced into our schools, students need to learn new skills to gain intellectual access to the vast amount of online information. Mrs. Barton, library media specialist at Hope Valley Elementary School, the Chariho Regional School District in Rhode Island, noticed that some students who came to the media center lacked a research focus. She was concerned about the amount of time the students used as they searched the Web, and their limited flexibility and creativity in searching strategies surprised her. She was also concerned with the frequency with which the word *research* was equated with *Internet* these days. In short, the students needed to learn how to evaluate and use a variety of resources, and to realize that the Internet may not be the only source or the best source for research. In other words, students needed information literacy skills to access, evaluate and use information so that they could create their own discrete insights and new knowledge of a particular subject.

Planning a Science Project with the Big6

Hope Valley Elementary School third grade teachers came to Mrs. Barton to collaborate on a science research project. The project was linked to a unit on insects, and Mrs. Barton thought this was a good opportunity to introduce the Big6 research model to enhance the students' information literacy skills.

The teachers and Mrs. Barton collaborated to develop a schematic to use to plan the assignment. Mrs. Barton, Jane Carlson-Pickering, the district's multiple intelligences expert, and Prudy Patnoad and Ann Gardiner, third grade teachers, used Inspiration® software to prepare the schematic. The teachers included the district's third grade curriculum standards, information literacy standards, and the new National Standards and Benchmarks. They organized the process around the steps in the Big6 (see Figure 1 on page 80) (http://fp3e.adhost.com/big6/enewsletter/archives/winter01/barton_fig1.gif).

The Big6 and Life-Long Learning: Task Definition

It is important for a student to realize that he or she is doing important work. The information literacy skills the students gain will contribute to the student becoming a life-long learner. In the case of this insect unit, the student can imagine him or herself in the role of a real-life scientist. For this reason, the third grade teachers introduced the unit by having students imagine they were entomologists setting out to research a variety of insects. Using *Inspiration* software, the teachers and the "junior scientists" brainstormed what important facts needed to be discovered about insects. During this class brainstorming session, one of the teachers added students' thoughts about the project to the *Inspiration* schematic (see schematic at http://www.chariho.k12.ri.us/hv/overview.html). Each child received a copy of the brainstorming session to consult during the project. Teachers and students also brainstormed what sources of information would be available to the students, and teachers made sure that students realized the variety of both print and digital resources. The teachers used brainstorming to help students decide what the final product should be. The students and teachers selected a Web page as the final product (**Task Definition**).

Use Graphic Organizers for Information Seeking

Prior to this project, students had practice using "Trash and Treasure" techniques for finding information (see Barbara Jansen's Trash and Treasure Method, http://big6.com/lessons/reading_for_information.htm). Mrs. Barton had done several projects with these students as second graders in simple research using these skills. To extend their knowledge, the students used a graphic organizer called the "Fact Finder" to organize their efforts (**Information Seeking Strategies**, see Figure 2 on page 81) (http://fp3e.adhost.com/big6/enewsletter/archives/winter01/barton_fig2.gif). Fact Finder can be used for any research project conducted in or outside of the Library Media Center. Mrs. Barton developed this organizer to help students focus on the particular information they needed and to realize that the Internet was not the only source of information. For this reason, students were directed to find initial facts in print sources. Before doing so, the class brainstormed "treasure words" and each student entered these words in the left column of the Fact Finder (**Information Seeking Strategies, Location & Access of Information**). The students were asked to jot down short facts in the right column of the Fact Finder. The space provided for jotting down facts is intentionally limited to discourage copying the text word for word. After a sufficient amount of information was gathered, students were instructed to circle key words in these fact statements, and spelling was checked carefully. Only after these key words were determined, students were directed to look in digital sources for further information. The students were directed to use a child-appropriate search engine for their information. Mrs. Barton provided an extensive, annotated list of such search engines on the school Web page at http://www.chariho.k12.ri.us/hv/childinternet.htm.

The students entered any new information on a second page of the Fact Finder. Once information was gathered, students compiled their information into narrative form, using AlphaSmart® word processors (**Use of Information**). (AlphaSmart is a portable, battery powered word processor that will store work in eight different files. For more information, see http://www.alphasmart.com/). After composing their work, the students were ready to move on to the **Synthesis** stage of the project—developing a class Web page as their final product. The authors downloaded their work from the AlphaSmart word processors into word processing documents, and the material was cut and pasted into the Web editor. Students refined their work with the teacher's guidance. The students created their own graphic interpretation of their assigned insects by designing them with paper and crayon. These images were scanned and added to the Web page.

Figure 1: Insects Unit

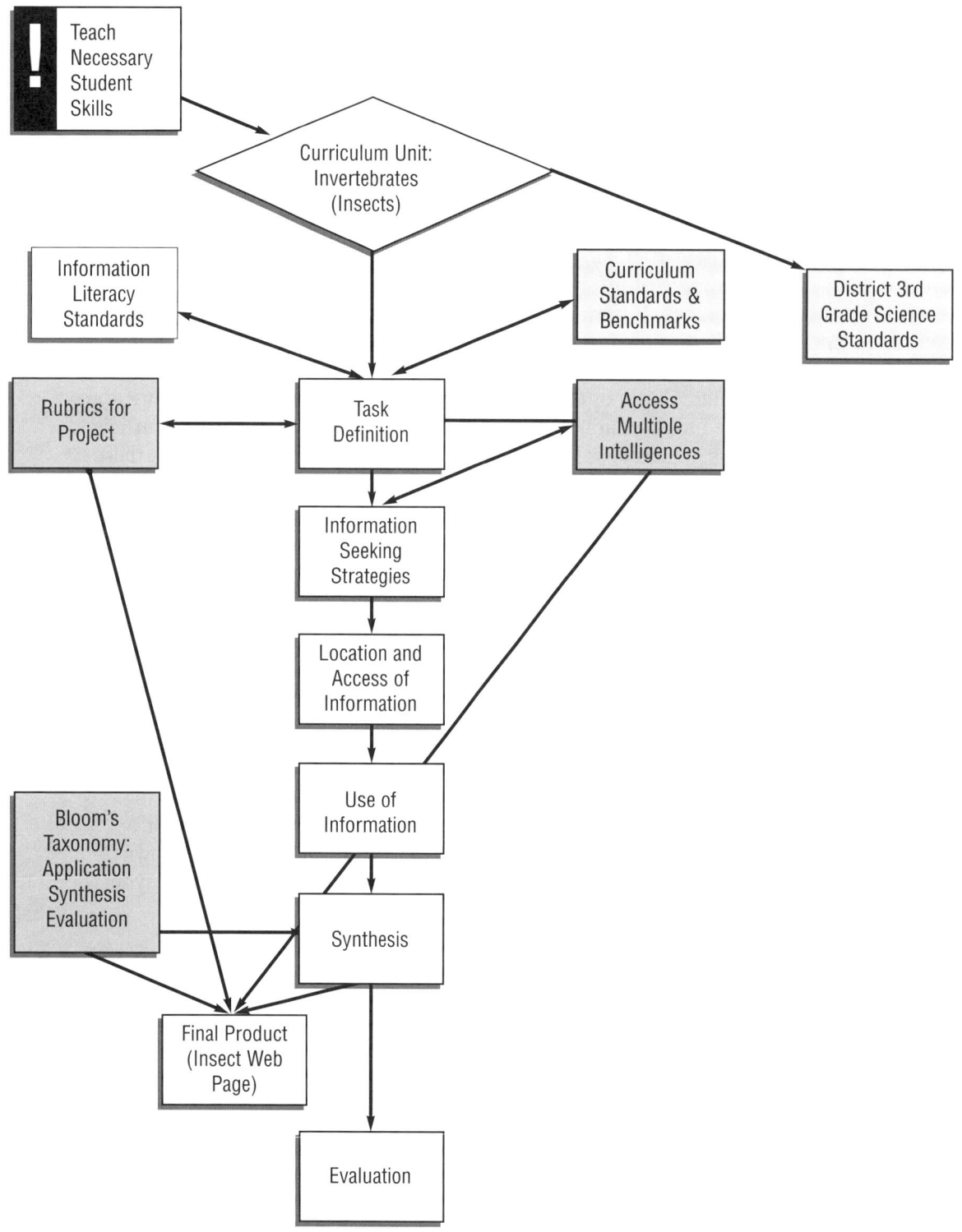

Figure 2

Figure 2: Fact Finder

Name: _____

This is my question: _____

Treasure Words

1. _____ 4. _____

2. _____ 5. _____

3. _____ 6. _____

Facts I have found in print form...

1. _____

2. _____

3. _____

4. _____

5. _____

6. _____

Keywords I will use in searching the Internet for information:

_____ _____

_____ _____

_____ _____

Reflections on Big6 Training:
Notes from an Experienced Big6er

By Joyce Needham / vE4, no4

I recently had the opportunity to attend a Big6 training session with a group of librarians and other educators who wanted to learn more about preparing their students to be information problem solvers. The session, presented by Big6 co-founder Mike Eisenberg, was held in the days leading up to the 2003 AASL Conference. The majority of participants were fairly new to Big6, however two of those in attendance have been on a quest to learn and teach Big6 for eleven years.

My Background with Big6™

I am one of those "experienced" Big6ers. Eleven years ago, my district's new superintendent made it clear that he was not satisfied with just having beautiful library facilities. He insisted our students should use the library to solve information problems and increase learning. In sharing his vision, he mentioned the widely-recognized Blue Valley Schools (http://www.bluevalleyk12.org/) in Kansas City, Kansas.

I had the opportunity to visit the Blue Valley System and observe the integrated, flexible library program they had developed in action. When I witnessed elementary school students independently using the library and learned how Big6 was a part of that program, I began my personal journey to learn Big6. That journey began with a one-day Big6 workshop taught by Barbara Jansen. I continued learning about Big6 by reading all the books and articles I could find on Big6, joining the Big6 e-mail list, attending Big6 workshops at our state conference, traveling to San Jose for a training session with Mike Eisenberg and Bob Berkowitz and attending the Big6 Conference there.

My Big6 journey has benefited my students. I have implemented flexible, collaborative, integrated library programs based on Big6 in both of my elementary schools in Springfield, Missouri and serve as one of two Big6 staff development trainers for our district. As I work with my own students and train teachers, I continue to learn about Big6 and its power in helping our students become information literate.

Discovering that the majority of the participants were beginners, I wondered very briefly, "Will this workshop be beneficial to me?" A few years ago, I might have thought "Since I know so much about Big6, I will learn nothing new in this session!" and probably would have proceeded to fulfill that prediction.

My in-depth experience in working with and implementing the Big6 has made it clear that there is still much to learn about this approach. I have made several realizations regarding the Big6 and implementation:

- My *knowing* Big6 does not increase student achievement.

- Teachers *using* Big6 in their teaching does not increase student achievement.

- Student achievement will only increase when students have *ownership* of the Big6 problem solving process and *apply* it as they solve both school-related and personal information problems.

- For students to learn to apply Big6, teachers must provide direct instruction (including vocabulary) and modeling. For the modeling to be effective, students must be *aware or cognizant* that Big6 is being modeled.

- There are levels of learning regarding Big6:
  - Level 1: Teachers learn the Big6 process.
  - Level 2: Teachers integrate Big6 into personal and professional information problem solving.
  - Level 3: Teachers, through direct instruction including vocabulary instruction and modeling help students learn the Big6 process.
  - Level 4: Teachers, through coaching, help students integrate Big6 into their personal and educational information problem solving.

The goal of my participation in the Big6 workshop was to reach level 4 with my students. While we as participants might be at various levels, I realized that the workshop could indeed be beneficial to me. I was not disappointed.

10 Things I learned or re-learned

A peek inside my notebook from the Big6 workshop shows that I am still learning about Big6, and I can't wait to implement my most recent discoveries. I had three primary takeaways from the session. First, affirmation of what I thought I knew about the Big6. The second thing I developed was the enrichment or development of deeper understanding of some concepts. Third, I benefited from new and forgotten learning. Some of the new and forgotten learning includes:

1. The Big6 process is not linear.

2. Give students choices when possible. Examples include choice of which source to use and type of product to create.

3. Apply Big6 to personal problems to help students make connections and increase learning: What should I buy Suzie for her birthday? Where should I go to college? How can I get into the college of my choice?

4. Repetition (practice) is important in learning.

5. Technology should be logically integrated into our problem solving. For example, what is the baseline tool we have used and what technological tool could be used instead?
    a. Instead of face-to-face conversation: e-mail, chat room
    b. Instead of magazines and books: Web sites, databases
    c. Instead of pen or pencil: word processor

6. Focus not only on what information is needed, but what types of information are needed: graphic or text; a lot or a little, et cetera. This relates to Big6 #1, Task Definition.

7. Keywords are essential in locating information, not only in text sources but especially in electronic sources.
    a. Use graphic organizers to help develop list of keywords
    b. Keywords equal synonyms. Thus a thesaurus can be helpful.

8. Transition students from using print indexes to electronic indexes. This is an Information Seeking Strategies skill, Big6 #2.

9. Have students brainstorm a list of criteria for what makes a good source (fun, reliable, fast, easy, etc). Post this list of criteria where everyone can see it. Have students evaluate sources throughout the year using their criteria. This approach reinforces Information Seeking Strategies and Evaluation.

10. Note taking is an excellent Use of Information skill to develop.
    a. PowerPoint can be useful as a note-taking device, not just for Synthesis.
    b. To help students "organize" information, give them a group of PowerPoint slides in no particular order and have them arrange the slides.
    c. Teach note taking in steps:
        i. First have students simply quote the needed information.
        ii. Once students have mastered locating the needed information, have them practice putting it into their own words.

Have students cite their source in every assignment. Their understanding of sources will greatly increase and they will develop the habit of giving credit. Start with little ones (Kindergarten and first grade) simply using stamps to identify if source was a book, person, computer, or themselves (Use of Information).

Despite my extensive experience with Big6, I found the workshop to be worthwhile. Now the challenge facing me as I continue my Big6 journey is to continue to implement this learning as I teach students and staff to be Big6 problem solvers.

Five Actions to Big6: Problem-Based Lessons Using Graphic Organizers

By Miguel Guhlin / vE1, no2

The communities of Santa Teresa, New Mexico and El Paso, Texas have something in common—the U. S. Border Patrol monitors both communities, but not in the way that many illegal aliens have come to expect their attention. The U. S. Border Patrol has set up outreach centers to bring about goodwill and provide teenagers with the opportunity to explore career possibilities. For the legal citizens of these communities, this is a wonderful initiative. For the undocumented aliens, parents of teenagers coming face to face with the U. S. Border Patrol in school, it's a nightmare.

Illegal immigrants fear that the U. S. Border Patrol may try to identify children of illegals, and then use this information to locate and prosecute the parents. Despite the U. S. Border Patrol's protests that this will not happen, the relationship between parents and school officials is tenuous. How will parents who are illegal immigrants attend school meetings if they fear encountering deportation officials? While the stakeholders of these border communities probably have not heard of ill-structured problems, they are certainly in the middle of one.

Ill-structured problems like this one are messy by nature. They are like the real-life situations students can expect to encounter when they leave school, and they can be great learning opportunities as a form of problem-based learning. Problem-based learning (PBL) uses real-life problems modeled after a contemporary or historical case to engage students as they pursue specified learning outcomes that are in line with academic standards or course objectives (Stepien & Pyke, 1997). Students work through the problem as a stakeholder. The teacher acts as a guide or advisor as students explore the issues involved, formulate questions, conduct research, and consider possible solutions to the problems.

Since most problems spring from a lack of information, problem-based learning makes an ideal tool to use and reinforce the Big6 Skills. The Big6 approach to information-problem solving provides a framework for students to find, organize, and present the information that they need to solve-real life problems. This accomplishes two goals—to help them complete their assignment efficiently and successfully, and to remind them that they must be information processors in their life beyond school. Combined with graphic organizers, the Big6 becomes a powerful tool to help students work through the U. S. Border Patrol scenario.

Using graphic organizers with the Big6 process can help students build their own knowledge and reflect on how new information links to their mental framework, or schema, of the world. This is important because, according to Buzan (1996), the human brain works primarily with key concepts in an interlinked and integrated manner. For each step in the Big6, there is at least one graphic organizer that helps students integrate new information with information that they already know (see Table 1).

Table 1. Matching Each Big6™Skill with a Graphic Organizer Tool

All Graphic Organizers follow article starting on page 93.

Big6 Skill	Graphic Organizer
Task Definition 1.1 Define the problem 1.2 Identify information needed	■ Chain of events: Use to plan out problem-solving process. ■ Fishbone Mapping: Use to identify problem causes and interrelationships between them as they relate to the problem. ■ Cycle: Use to show interactions between events. ■ Spider Map: Use to explore a topic and identify main ideas and details. ■ Problem/Solution: Use to identify a problem and consider multiple solutions and possible results.
Information Seeking Strategies 2.1 Determine all possible sources 2.2 Select the best source	■ Clustering: Use to generate ideas about possible sources of information. ■ Compare/Contrast: Use to compare/contrast information sources.
Location & Access 3.1 Locate sources 3.2 Find information within sources	■ Spider Map: Use to determine key words for searching. ■ Clustering: Use to generate ideas and key words.
Use of Information 4.1 Engage information in sources 4.2 Extract relevant information	■ Continuum: Use to develop timelines, rating scales or show historical progression. ■ Compare/Contrast: Use to compare/contrast information sources. ■ Venn Diagram: Use to identify similarities/differences.
Synthesis 5.1 Organize information from multiple sources 5.2 Present the result	■ Clustering: Use to pull together ideas organizing a product (project, presentation, or paper). ■ Compare/Contrast: Use to organize compare/contrast information. ■ Problem/Solution: Use to articulate problem and consider multiple solutions and possible results. ■ Storyboard: Use to map out presentation or Web page.
Evaluation 6.1 Judge the result 6.2 Judge the process	■ Interaction Outline: Use to judge the problem-solving process, and the interactions between team members.

Problem-based learning is a valuable tool for students of many levels. However, the task of designing a problem-based learning lesson can be daunting—the problems are large and messy, and it can be a challenge to know where to start. The following Big6-related five actions can help you keep your problem-based learning lesson under control and moving along.

Action 1—Select a Problem and Brainstorm an Idea to Explore Its Potential (Task Definition)

According to Stepien and Pyke (1997), a problem-based learning situation must meet several criteria. The situation must provide an effective way of engaging students with experiences that scaffold higher order thinking. The situation should also accomplish curriculum objectives and include age-appropriate topics. Further, the learning situation should take the form of an ill-structured problem to foster inquiry at a level that is cognitively engaging but not frustrating. Lastly, the situation should make efficient use of instructional time allotted to the unit.

When selecting a problem, the teacher can either look through academic standards and objectives for a dilemma, or search news stories for a problem that will allow the introduction of academic standards. In examining the problem, the teacher can use a brainstorming map to explore the content that students may encounter as they go about examining the issue and suggesting possible resolutions.

Brainstorming with some form of visual aid (e.g., spider map, clustering, fishbone mapping) can be an important tool for teachers to consider the breadth of the issue and to include cross-curricular connections. For example, in the past, the author worked with a sixth grade social studies teacher who was asking the class to examine the core dilemma involved in dropping the atom bomb on Hiroshima, Japan. By focusing only on activities to teach history, the sixth grade teacher missed the big question, "Should we have dropped the bomb?" and possible explorations through the stakeholders' points of view (for example, President Truman, U. S. Air Force Pilot, residents of Hiroshima, etc.).

Action 2—Engage Students in a Real-Life Problem (Task Definition)

This action builds a blueprint for inquiry and the investigation process to follow. As the teacher, you identify key curriculum goals and work forward from those to pose an engaging introduction that reflects a real world, ill-structured problem.

As in real-life, students must use the inquiry process and reasoning to solve the problem. The narrative that introduces students to the real-life problem is the key to a successful problem-based learning lesson. You can find sample narratives at: http://www.esc20.k12.tx.us/cut/ The Curriculum Using Technology (CUT) Institute Materials web page.

Action 3—Focus Inquiry and Investigation (Task Definition to Information Seeking Strategy, Location & Access and Use of Information)

Once students are engaged in the problem, they begin to write down their hunches about it and identify with a stakeholder. Following this, they can begin the process of locating, gathering and using sources of information using the Big6. Inquiry and investigation builds a basis for students to design a solution product.

Action 4—Support Problem Resolution (Synthesis)

As students work their way through the different points of view according to the stakeholder position they have taken, it is important that they share information with each other. One way to do this is to encourage students to suggest a solution to the problem that considers the various points of view of all stakeholders. The teacher will want to facilitate a discussion to determine how students will share information to arrive at such a solution.

Action 5—Facilitate Problem Debriefing (Evaluation)

After solving the problem, a key piece of problem-based learning is to debrief students. The debriefing step asks students to consider what steps they took to solve the problem and to determine the effectiveness of their reasoning. In addition, students reflect on whether or not they believe their solution will address the causes that were identified in Task Definition. For example, students can look at the criteria identified in Task Definition and ask themselves, "Did I find research from multiple sources?" and "Did I spend my time well in gathering and using information from various sources?" The role of the teacher is to help students focus on metacognition and to review issues inherent in the problem (Gallagher, 2000).

An Example: On the Border

This article began with a presentation of a problem that exists on the border of the United States and Mexico. Here's how the author used this situation to develop a problem-based learning (PBL) lesson called "On the Border," which reinforces essential Big6 information problem-solving skills.

Don't forget that preparing curriculum is an information exercise for the teacher, just as the lesson itself presents an information problem for the student. Since lessons based on real-life problems are broad and information-rich, Task Definition is a particularly important step for the teacher.

A particularly useful Task Definition exercise for lesson planning is the articulation of curriculum objectives and learning outcomes. When developing the On the Border lesson, the author identified four curriculum objectives:
Students will:

- Examine how history, culture, and geography influence a person's perception toward a particular issue.

- Construct an understanding of the various stakeholder points of view by immersing themselves in the role of individuals who live there.

- Research, analyze, and synthesize how the historical, geographical and cultural implications have influenced the views of various groups of people found on the border between the U. S. and Mexico.

- Apply what they have learned concerning differing points of view, and technology, to create a multimedia presentation to the class.

Once the teacher has defined the desired learning outcomes for the lesson, the next step is to consider possible issues associated with the central problem. This will help the teacher to identify and anticipate ways that students may potentially approach the problem. In developing the On the Border lesson, the teacher used a brainstorming map (http://www.edsupport.cc/mguhlin/ portfolio/writings/99_2000/ontheborder.jpg) to examine the issues connected with this particular ill-structured problem. The brainstorming map identifies possible stakeholders, issues arising from the influx of undocumented workers, the deaths of border patrol agents, the culture clash between Mexico and the United States, the impact of free trade policies the federal government has enacted and much more. Of course, as any experienced teacher knows, there is no way to anticipate everything the class will come up with–expect to be dazzled by your students' insight and creativity!

While Task Definition deals with the problem at hand, it also asks you to define the type of information needed. For the teacher, this means considering what he or she expects for the final product of the lesson. The author determined that as students progress through the lesson, they would build a portfolio for assessment. Each assessment task pinpoints specific learning objectives. An overview of the assessments for this lesson include:

Student Product Objectives (I=Individual Product; G=Group Product):

- Fishbone map of the causes and effects. (I)
- Cluster map of stakeholder questions. (I)
- Comparison/Contrast chart on information sources. (I)
- Spider Map that identifies stakeholder question responses. (I)
- Problem/solution map that reflects all stakeholders' information. (G)
- Venn Diagram with different points of view. (G)
- Multimedia Presentation (G) assessed using the Multimedia Presentation rubric.
- Peer Evaluation (G) assessed using the Peer Evaluation rubric.

Engage Students in a Real-life Problem (Task Definition)

Once the teacher has gone through his or her own Big6 process to plan the PBL lesson, it is time to present the lesson to the students and prepare them to engage in their own information problem-solving process to complete the lesson successfully. First, it is important to help the class understand the importance of the problem. Role playing is one way for the students to become actively involved in the problem. The student must say, "My mother is an illegal alien. How do I feel about the U. S. Border Patrol in school?" or perhaps, "As the U.S. Border Patrol Agent in charge of setting up the outreach centers, how can I reassure these children that I am not here on official business in order to hunt their parents?"

The teacher can use the Big6 and graphic organizers to help students identify with a particular group. Following is an excerpt from the lesson, where students use graphic organizers to help them begin to define the task of their particular stakeholder group.

Big6 #1: Task Definition

1.1 Define the information problem: The U.S. Border Patrol has created several outreach programs to provide teenagers the opportunity to explore career possibilities. With these programs, the Border Patrol hopes to improve its relationship with residents in El Paso and Southern New Mexico. One particular initiative in Santa Teresa, New Mexico seems to be doing just the opposite. As you listen to the National Public Radio (NPR) broadcast, do the following:

- Create a fishbone map of the situation.
- Identify the stakeholders involved with each cause and identify who is impacted in the result.
- Select a stakeholder that you would like to know more about.

1.2 Define the information needed to solve the problem: After selecting the stakeholder you would like to know more about, ask yourself as many questions as you can about the point of view you will represent. Use Inspiration software to create a cluster map of these questions. Develop specific questions about your point of view to which you do not yet know the answer.

Focus Inquiry and Investigation (Task Definition to Information Seeking Strategy, Location & Access and Use of Information)

2.1 Brainstorm possible sources of information: After you have done a Web search on your topic, organize the possible sources in a chart, like the one below. Use the chart to compare and contrast sources of information and to gather information for the questions you've written. Be sure to use citation guidelines for any information you find.

Sample Chart:

Stakeholder:	U.S. Border Patrol		
	Questions and Title/URL of possible information found at resources		
Sources/Inputs	Why are people afraid of the U.S. Border Patrol?	What can the U.S. Border Patrol do to make its outreach program more effective?	Are there other outreach programs run by federal programs?
News report, Internet search tools	1. CNN—U.S. Border Patrol-March 20, 1996 2. Border Shooting 3. NPR Report	1. Model Outreach Programs	1. NASA 2. FBI's Junior Special Agent Program
Books, magazines			
Interviews			
Other:			

2.2 Selecting the best sources: Look at your chart and decide which sources you will use to respond to your questions.

Support Problem Resolution (Synthesis)

5.1 Organize information from multiple sources: Once again, a graphic organizer can help with this task. Create a spider map that deals with your stakeholder questions and summarizes the information you have found to answer your questions. This will ensure that you include all of the important information that you have collected, and will help to illustrate the relationships between ideas. Next, develop a problem/solution map to show solutions from your point of view, what you think the results will be, and how these results will affect the overall situation. This is where the point of view of the stakeholder is particularly important—keep in mind what your group will think is a good idea, and what solutions the members of the group would be opposed to. Finally, share your information with your team (the other stakeholders) and then create a Venn diagram to show how the different points of view are similar and different. This will give you the information that you need to develop a problem/solution map that includes the ideas of all members of your group.

5.2 Present the information: Now that you have analyzed the results of your research, develop a multimedia presentation. Using eight slides, address the major points of your group's problem/solution map, such as:

- Title of your presentation and list of Group Members

- What's the problem?

- Why is this a problem?

- Who are the stakeholders?

- What are some of the attempted solutions and their results? (use a different slide for each solution and result).

- What do you see as the end result of these problems/solutions?

- List your references.

- Reflect on your success as a group.

Facilitate Problem Debriefing (Evaluation)

Since students worked both individually and as a group for this project, it is important that they evaluate their individual work as well as their team work.

6.2 Judge the process (Individual): Use the following checklist to judge your information gathering process.

- What I created to finish the assignment is appropriate for what I was supposed do in Big6 #1.

- The information I found in Big6 #4 matches the information needed in Big6 #1.

- I have given credit to my sources and have used a standard citation format.

- My work complies with copyright laws and fair use guidelines.

- My work is neat.

- My work is complete and includes heading information (name, date, etc.).

- I would be proud for anyone to view this work.

Judge the Process (Group): Use the following checklist to judge your group's information gathering process.

- The group received a high score on the multimedia presentation rubric.

- We have given credit to our sources and have used a standard citation format.

- The group's work complies with copyright laws and fair use guidelines.

- The group received a high score on the peer evaluation rubric.

- Our work includes the components outlined in Big6 #5.

- We would be proud for anyone to view this work.

Conclusion

Using graphic organizers with the Big6 information problem-solving model provides students with essential tools to participate in problem-based learning. Graphic organizers give students maps they can use to locate, gather, organize, and synthesize information from a variety of resources. Then, students can put that knowledge to use in developing possible solutions for real-life, messy problems. The process of growing up isn't easy . . . it requires us to work through problems, running into barriers as we gather information and trying to reconcile new information to what we already know. That's why information problem-solving processes, such as the Big6, are important; they allow us to externalize the process we go through. By making the process external, we can begin to approach the situation, not only as stakeholders willing to fight for our beliefs, but also as people who can recognize and reconcile different points of view.

On the Border Lesson Materials:

- RealAudio Player
- Internet Access and browser
- Inspiration Software (http://www.inspiration.com/)
- PowerPoint or other multimedia presentation tool
- Kid Safe search tools

References

Guhlin, M. (1999). Five steps to Big6™ problem-based learning lessons using graphic organizers. [Online]. Available: http://www.geocities.com/mguhlin

Freeman, G. (1999). *The graphic organizer.* [Online]. Available: http://www.graphic.org/ (current September 8, 1999)

Gallagher, S. A., & Stepien, W. (January, 2000). *Problem-based learning: Blueprint for bringing curriculum reform to the classroom.* Workshop presented at the ASCD Professional Development Conference, San Antonio, Texas.

Stepien, W., & Pyke, S. L. (Summer, 1997). Designing problem-based learning units. *Journal for the Education of the Gifted*, 20(4), 380-400.

On the Border Lesson

Brower, D. (no date). Border patrol outreach programs. [Online]. Available: http://search.npr.org/cf/cmn/cmnps05fm.cfm?SegID=68757 (Current 01/05/2000).

Buzan, T., & Buzan, B. (1996). *The mind map book: How to use radiant thinking to maximize your brain's untapped potential.* London, UK: BBC Books: NAL/ Dutton.

Creating web-based lessons: Webquests and other Internet projects. Rubric collection [Online]. Available: http://www.esc20.net/etprojects/rubrics/Default.htm (Current 1/15/2000).

Eisenberg, M. B., & Berkowitz, R. E. (1999). *Teaching information & technology skills: The Big6™ in elementary schools.* Worthington, OH: Linworth Publishing, Inc.

Fishbone map. [Online]. Available http://www.sdcoe.k12.ca.us/score/actbank/tfish.htm (Current at 1/15/2000).

Freeman, G. (1999). *The graphic organizer.* [Online]. Available: http://www.graphic.org (Current September 8, 1999).

Guhlin, M. (no date). *Graphically organizing the Big6.* [Online]. Available: http://www.edsupport.cc/mguhlin/workshops/wtic/ips.html (Current 1/15/2000).

Jansen, B. (no date). *Big6 assignment organizer.* [Online]. Available: http://www.standrews.austin.tx.us/library/Assignment%20organizer.htm (Current 01/15/2000).

*Author's Note: The Curriculum Using Technology (CUT) Institute guides teachers to develop problem-based learning units that integrate technology. In its second year, the CUT Model is simple enough to understand and encourages teachers to answer three questions: 1) What is the curriculum connection? 2) How is technology connected and used? 3) How are students assessed? Teachers developing a unit and planning lesson activities remember these questions as they answer the following three questions: 1) What is the real-life connection to academic or curriculum standards? 2) What information problem-solving approach will be used for research? 3) What products are students expected to produce?

Chain of Events

Chain of Events is used to describe the stages of an event, the actions of character or the steps in a procedure.

Key questions: What is the first step in the procedure or initiating event? What are the next stages or steps? How does one event lead to one another? What is the final outcome?

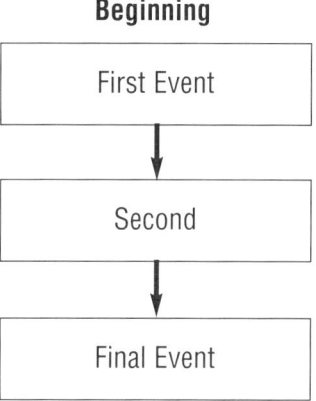

Fishbone Mapping

A Fishbone Map is used to show the causal interaction of a complex event (an election, a nuclear explosion) or complex phenomenon (juvenile delinquency, learning disabilities).

Key frame questions: What are the factors that cause X? How do they interrelate? Are the factors that cause X the same as those that cause X to persist?

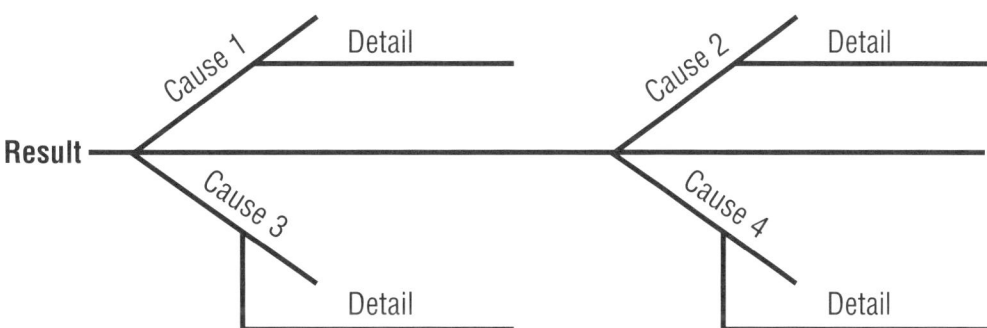

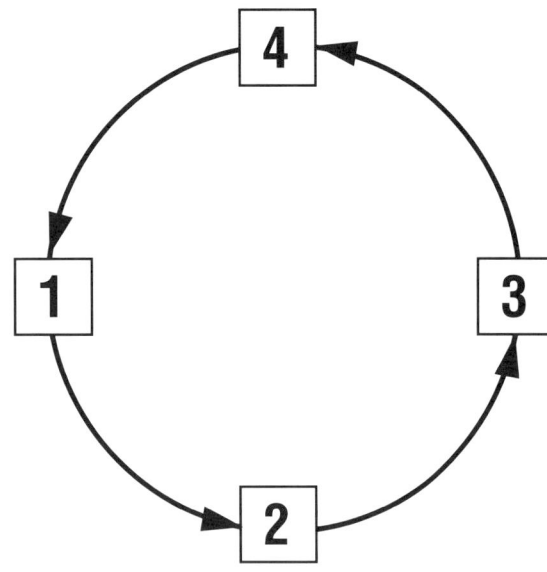

Cycle

A depiction of a Cycle attempts to show how a series of events interacts to produce a set of results again and again, such as the life cycle or a cycle of poor decisions.

Key frame questions: What are the main events in the cycle? How do they interact and return to the beginning again?

Spider Map

The Spider Map is used to describe a central idea: a thing, a process, a concept, a proposition. The map may be used to organize ideas or brainstorm ideas for a writing project.

Key frame questions: What is the central idea? What are its attributes? What are its functions?

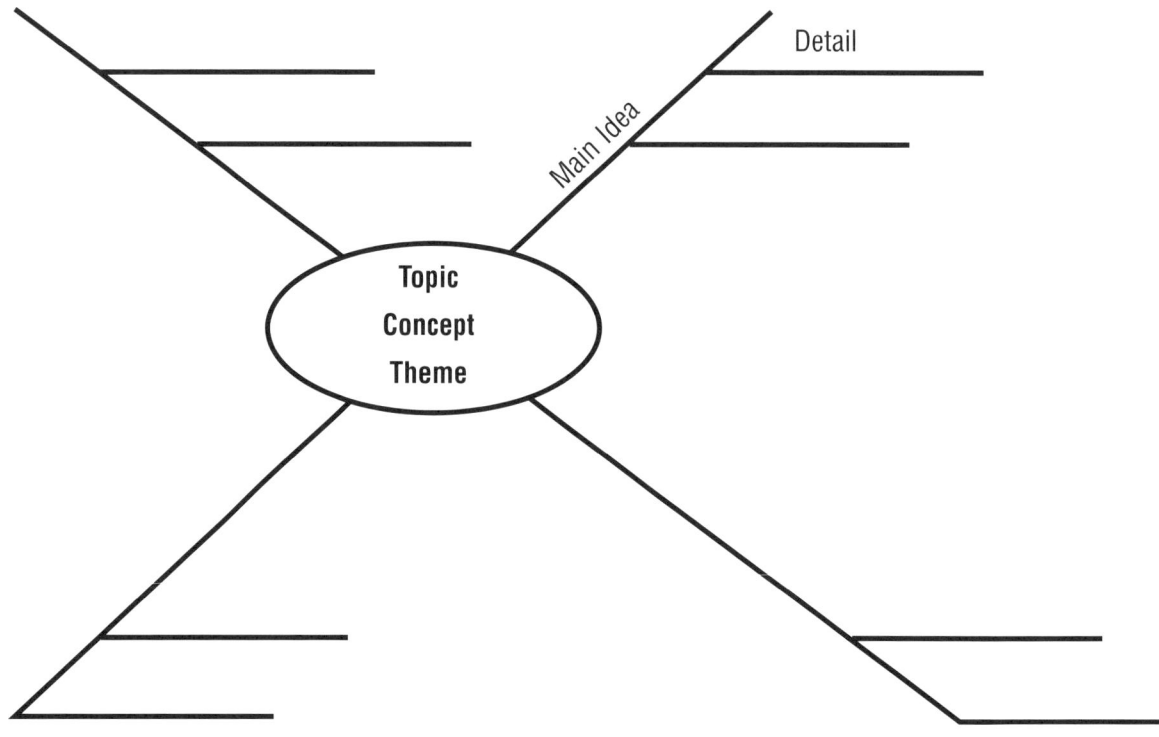

Problem/Solution

Problem/Solution requires students to identify a problem and consider multiple solutions and possible results.

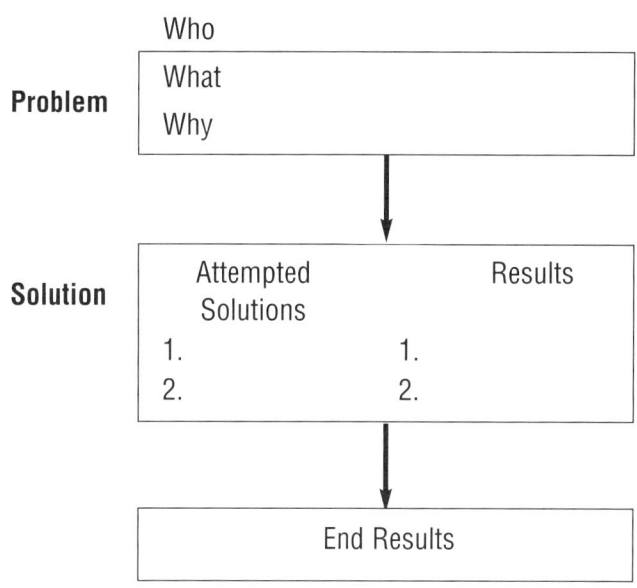

Clustering

Clustering is a nonlinear activity that generates ideas, images and feelings around a stimulus word. As students cluster, their thoughts tumble out, enlarging their word bank for writing and often enabling them to see patterns in their ideas. Clustering may be a class or an individual activity.

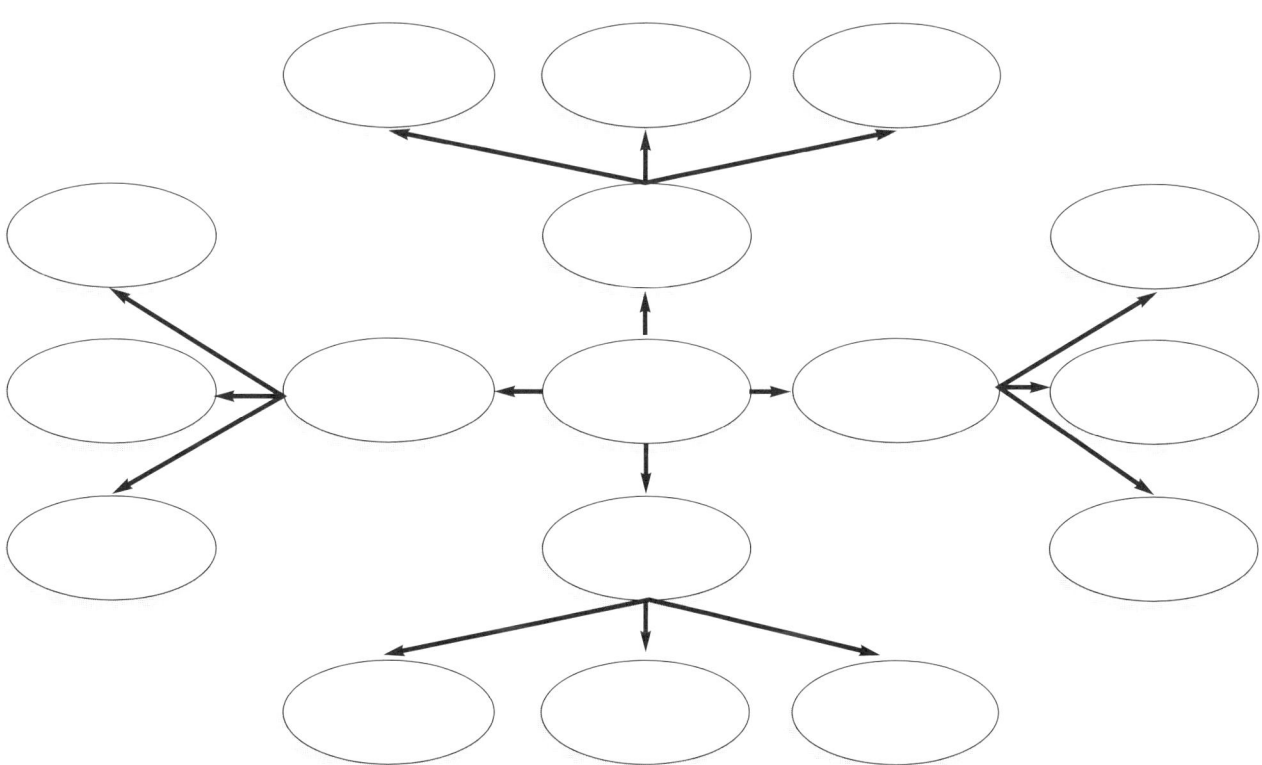

	Name 1	Name 2
Attribute 1		
Attribute 2		
Attribute 3		

Compare/Contrast

Comparison/Contrast is used to show similarities and differences.
Key frame questions: What are being compared? How are they similar? How are they different?

Continuum

Continuum is used for time lines showing historical events, ages (grade levels in school), degrees of something (weight), shades of meaning, or rating scales (achievement in school).
Key frame questions: What is being scaled? What are the end points or extremes?

Low   **High**

Venn Diagram

The Venn Diagram is made up of two or more overlapping circles. It is often used in mathematics to show relationships between sets. In language arts instruction, Venn Diagrams are useful for examining similarities and differences in characters, stories, poems, etc.

It is frequently used as a prewriting activity to enable students to organize thoughts or textual quotations prior to writing a compare/ contrast essay. This activity enables students to organize similarities and differences visually.

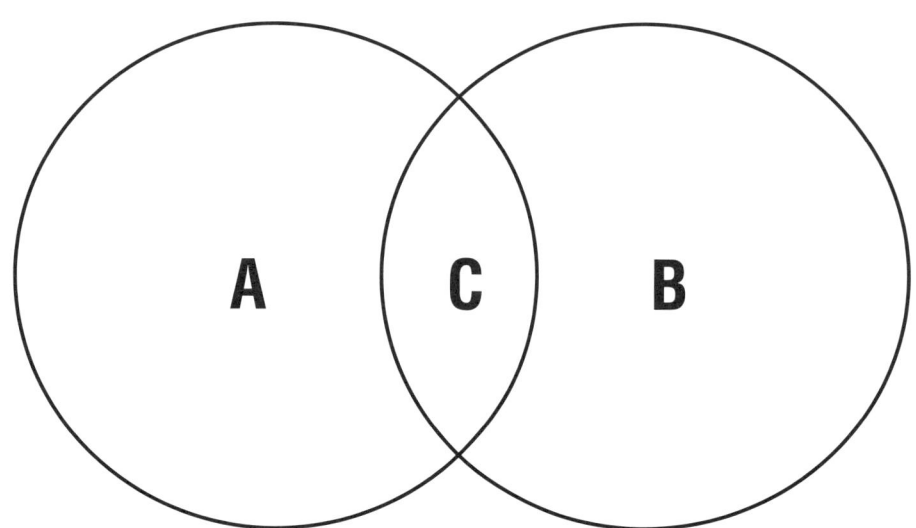

Storyboard

A storyboard is a graphic, sequential depiction of a narrative. Students recall major events of the story, then illustrate the events in the squares provided.

Interaction Outline

Interaction Outline is used to show the nature of an interaction between persons or groups, such as the interaction between European settlers and American Indians.

Key frame questions: Who are the persons or groups? What were their goals? Did they conflict or cooperate? What was the outcome for each person or group?

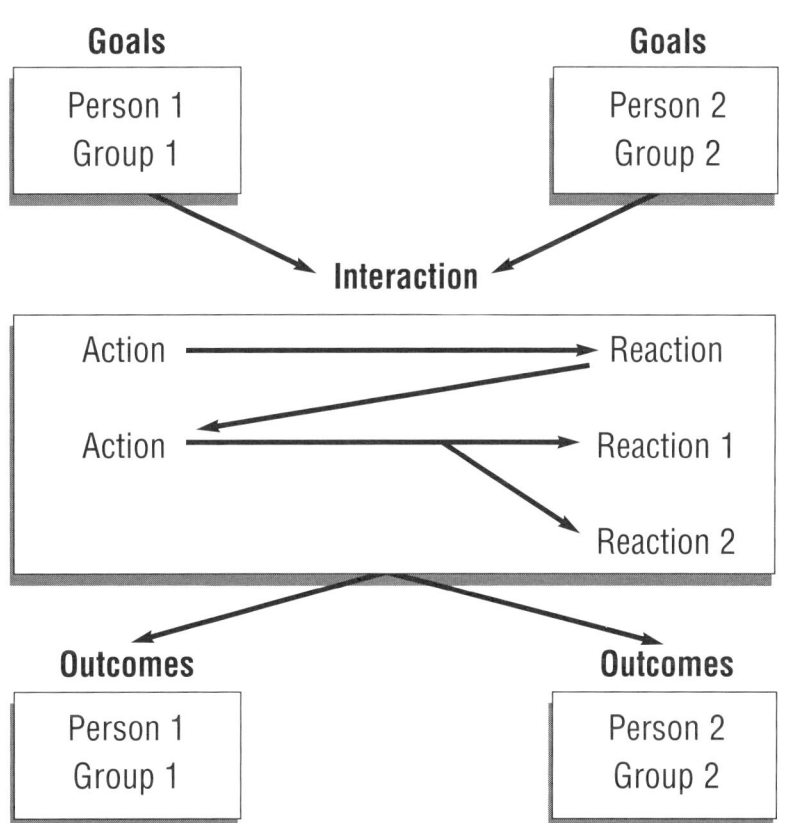

Part II:

Big6™ in Action: K-Higher Education

CHAPTER 8

Little Kids

Super3 - The Early Childhood Version of the Big6 Skills

By Tami J. Little / From the Big6 website: www.big6.com

The Super3 is the early childhood version of The Big6 Skills. The Big6 Skills was written by Mike Eisenberg and Bob Berkowitz.

What is the Super3?

The table below shows the comparison of the Big6™ and the Super3.

The Super3	The Big6™ Research Program Map (http://www.squires.fayette.k12.ky.us/ library/research/research.htm)
Beginning	Task Definition
	Information Seeking Strategies
Middle	Location and Access
	Use of Information
End	Synthesis
	Evaluation

Why the Super3?

Some teachers and librarians were concerned that the Big6 was too much for children. With the Super3, teachers are able to use vocabulary that children understand.

Beginning

When students get an assignment or a task, BEFORE they start doing anything, they should think:

- What am I supposed to do?
- What will it look like if I do a really good job?
- What do I need to find out to do the job?

Middle

In the Middle the students DO the activity. This is where they read, view, tell, make a picture, something about the activity.

End

Before finishing the product and turning it in, students should stop and think:

- Is this done?
- Did I do what I was supposed to do?
- Do I feel ok about this?
- Should I do something else before I turn it in?

Authentic Applications of the Big6 in the Primary Grades

By Rosemarie Granger / vE2, no3

Rosemarie Granger's second grade class at Fisher-Mitchell School in Bath, Maine is involved in an Internet based project, Owney the Traveling Dog.

The project, based on a book by Lynn Hall, involves sending a stuffed dog, a postcard, and e-mail from school to school in the group. During the project, a class in Idaho e-mailed:

"We are interested in Maine because it is easier to find on the map than some states. Are there still lighthouses there?"

Good question! This e-mail request presented Mrs. Granger's class with a genuine purpose to conduct authentic research.

Education Projects and Maine Learning Standards

When the class did its first research project, Mrs. Granger was a member of the Maine Assessment Portfolio Project (http://www.state.me.us/education/g2000/map.htm). This 3-year state sponsored project encourages teachers to develop tasks that can measure student achievement toward meeting the Maine Learning Results standards (http://www.state.me.us/education/lres/homepage.htm). Writing a research paper was one of the anchor tasks.

SEED (Spreading Educator to Educator Developments) recognized Mrs. Granger's project as a Developer's Packet (project) because it integrates technology in an innovative way to achieve state standards. SEED shares these packets with educators on the main SEED website (http://seed.mainecenter.org/index.cfm?section=1).

Teachers are encouraged to view and adapt the packets. In fact, teachers from Maine can adapt a packet and receive an award that will help provide needed materials or extensive consultation, if needed. To see a list of fifty packets and descriptions of each, visit the website.

SEED is a collaborative initiative of Maine's major educational institutions. The SEED project was introduced by the Maine Center for Educational Services. SEED is one of the twenty-two affiliates of national IMPACT II -The Teacher Network, and is funded by the United States Department of Education Technology Innovation Challenge Grant #R303A990295. For more information about these grants, visit the website.

The Big6™ Assignment Organizer

This SEED project launched the second grade class into an interesting research project and allowed Mrs. Granger to introduce the Big6™ Skills. To answer the question from the class in Idaho, "We are interested in Maine because it is easier to find on the map than some states. Are there still lighthouses there?" students used the Big6™ Assignment organizer. Using the Big6™ for units of study prepares children to plan for and think about conducting research. The Big6™ supports students in writing their response through several drafts and shows students how to write a bibliography. The initial Big6™ Assignment Organizer, which Mrs. Granger's class used, was adapted by our librarian, Charlotte Brown. This organizer has become a resource in our Language Arts curriculum notebook.

As a first step in the research project, students completed the first five sections of the Big6™ Assignment Organizer. It takes about one 30-minute period for second grade students to fill out the organizer. The time is well spent because the organizer serves as a plan that will help students to access information.

- **Task Definition:** Part 1 of the Big6™ Assignment Organizer is Task Definition and includes the questions "What am I supposed to do?" and "What information do I need in order to do this?" The latter question has places for four statements to help students clarify what they want to find out.

- **Information Seeking Strategies:** The Information Seeking Strategies section includes a list of possible sources for "information needs" that students have identified in Task Definition. The students analyze these sources and write down the strategies they think would work best to locate the information they need. Mrs. Granger's students selected the Internet, reference books, and people as the best sources of information about lighthouses. They decided that information in encyclopedias and dictionaries would not be specific enough. To finalize this section, students also need to write some keywords that would help with their search.

- **Location & Access:** Part 3, Location & Access, asks the students to write where they will find these resources and what or who can help them. The students determined that the library was a good resource and that the computer in the classroom connected to the Internet would also be helpful. The students found quite a number of links from the Maine Secretary of State's Kid's Page. The Kid's Page was one of the links that our class included on our Owney page because they wanted students in other states to know about the State of Maine. Students also executed searches using Yahooligans. One advantage of using the Big6™ Assignment Organizer is that the teacher can check the keywords and phrases that the students have brainstormed and suggest modifications prior to searching. As students continued their searches, they evaluated the Internet sites for interesting information and pictures that would help explain the text.

- **Use of Information:** The Use of Information section of the Big6™ Assignment Organizer asks students how they will record their information and how they will credit their sources. Students recorded the title, author, and some notes about the book on 4 x 5 file cards. They also recorded the Web page URLs, which were later used as links on a Web page for the project.

- **Synthesis:** Part 5, the Synthesis section, focuses on how to organize information, what the final product will be, and how students will give credit to the information sources of their final product. Students wrote rough drafts on paper but the final product was created on Claris Home Page. The students copied and pasted their response into an e-mail message to send directly to the Idaho class that had originally posed the question.

- **Evaluation:** Students must check the Evaluation section of the Big6™ Assignment Organizer before they turn in their final product. In this case, the product was the creation of the e-mail to answer the question and a Web page for other students around the country to see. The rest of the class evaluated the e-mail and decided that it should also become part of a Web page.

Not all of the students in the class researched the question about lighthouses but other classmates were excited by the prospect of doing their own research project using a variety of research resources. They looked up topics like apples, watermelons, chocolate, pies, and "Where did pizza came from?" and so forth. When the projects were taken to a Maine Assessment Portfolio (MAP) meeting, Internet research and online publishing were evaluated as a new way to research and present material. This online presentation format is now part of the 1999/2000 Maine Assessment Portfolio English Language Arts Entry Slip.

Conclusion

The Big6 is an organized, logical way to assist young children in conducting research. It is adaptable to fit the individual needs of students and teachers. In fact, other teachers at the Fisher Mitchell School have successfully adapted the assignment organizer form for their students. Donna Smith, a first grade teacher, has adapted the form and used it with her students as they created reports on animals. See how Donna's students used the Big6 process. The Big6™ Assignment Organizer is an indispensable tool for conducting research and for helping students become critical consumers of information. It encourages student independence with effective teacher support. I strongly recommend its adaptation to meet learners' research needs.

New Game: Match the Super3 (Grades K-2)

By Barbara A. Jansen / vE4, no1

Directions

Plan

Gather: 2 pieces of construction paper, blunt scissors, glue.
Print: 2 game sheets on pages 107 and 108.

Do

Prepare the game pieces:

1. Cut the game sheets apart on the dotted lines.

2. Cut each piece of construction paper into 4 parts the same size (fold it first, open the page, and cut on the folded lines)

3. Glue each of the game pieces onto the pieces of cut construction paper to make cards. Let them dry.

Play the game:

1. Mix up the cards.

2. Put them face down on a table or the floor. Mix them up again.

3. Turn one over. Turn another over. Does the Super3 match its description? If not, turn them face down again and try again. If you get a match, put the pair—2 cards—to the side. Keep trying until you get three matching pairs.

Review

Do you know which Super3 (Plan, Do, Review) goes with each description? Do you know what Plan, Do, and Review mean? If you did not make matches, who can you ask for help?

Super3 Matching Game

Plan

Gather: 2 pieces of construction paper, blunt scissors, glue.

Print: these 2 game sheets

Do

Prepare the game pieces

1. Cut the game sheets apart on the dotted lines
2. Cut each piece of construction paper into 4 parts the same size (fold it first, open the page, and cut on the folded lines)
3. Glue each of the game pieces onto the pieces of cut paper to make cards. Let them dry.

Play the game:

1. Mix up the cards.
2. Put them face down on a table or the floor. Mix them up again.
3. Turn one over. Turn another over. Does the Super3 match its description? If not, turn them face down again and try again. If you get a match, put the pair—2 cards—to the side. Keep trying until you get three matching pairs.

Review

Do you know which Super3 (Plan, do, Review) goes with each description? Do you know what Plan, Do, and Review mean? If you did not make any matches, who can you ask for help?

Plan

Do

Review

What am I supposed to do?

What will the result look like if I do a really good job?

What do I need to make to show what I learned?

What do I need to find out about in order to do the job?

How can I do the job?

What can I use to find what I need?

Now I need to make something to show what I learned!

Is my job done?

Did I do what I was supposed to do?

Do I feel ok about this?

Should I do something before I turn it in?

CHAPTER 9

Middle Kids

On an Information Treasure Hunt: Using Props to Illustrate the Research Process

By Jeanita Lovelace / vE4, no3

How many times have you taught a lesson that seemed to go right over the heads of your students? It is at times like this that you can become frustrated, perhaps even lose some of your confidence in your own teaching abilities. One thing I've learned from my combined years of teaching high school and as an elementary librarian—to borrow a football term—times like this require that you drop back and punt. I have had to go back to the drawing board many times in my twenty-two years of educating our future leaders because they have become increasingly less capable of grasping concepts that do not come wrapped up as an action packed adventure or required skilled thumbs on a video game controller. Especially at the introductory level, younger students may struggle with many of the abstract concepts involved in doing research.

Creating a Visual Representation

Because my students were struggling with the concept of digging for information, I decided that I must come up with a concrete example to bring the concept into focus. Many of the students could not grasp the abstract concepts involved with so much of the research process. Though I had encountered the idea of digging for treasure, like Barbara Jansen's "Trash and Treasure" (http://www.big6.com/showenewsarticle.php?id=45) method related to the Big6, many of my students still couldn't apply the graphic illustrations to their own information searches. I began to brainstorm how I could convert locating answers to specific questions from printed material into real objects to assist my students in the application of the steps of the Big6, particularly the fourth step, Use of Information. I successfully developed and used the following concrete example of "Trash and Treasure."

I developed a concrete "Trash and Treasure" to go with a biography research project used by our third graders. I needed to show my students how to find information from a book about Hank Aaron. I purchased a large cardboard trunk that I painted to look like a treasure chest. Inside the chest, I placed a baby bottle, a toy school bus, a foam football, a foam baseball, a foam basketball, and a small foam surfboard painted to look like a tombstone. These objects would represent his birth, education, sports played, what made him famous, and death respectively. I placed the trunk on the bottom shelf of a rolling AV cart then covered the entire cart with a brown cloth to represent dirt. I placed a large black "x" on the cloth at the front of the cart to represent the digging spot.

Presenting the Lesson

I was then ready to present the research treasure chest to my students. We had already done lessons on selecting keywords, using the parts of a book to narrow searches (such as the index, table of contents, headings and subheadings), and the basics of the "Trash and Treasure" method. I had also shown them transparencies that explain the information search as a search for hidden treasure. Next, I showed the Hank Aaron book to my students and discussed how to start a search by choosing keywords that represent the main areas of research. I then told them that we would be going on a treasure hunt for key information about Hank Aaron.

I previously placed dashed line cutouts on the floor that would remind them of the path marked off on treasure maps. I walked around, following the trail until I got to the cart where the treasure chest was hidden. I pulled the cart into the view of the students. I explained that this would be like using the first steps of the research process to actually get the source of information (book) in front of you (Big6 #2—Information Seeking Strategies). I then used a small shovel that I had hidden on a bottom shelf of the cart to begin digging for the actual answers needed to answer our information search (Big6 #4—Use of Information). I pretended to dig out shovelfuls of dirt—the "trash" that is eliminated because these sentences do not contain the answers needed. I reminded them that this would be done in a real search once the paragraphs containing needed answers were narrowed down using the book's index and table of contents. I then brought the chest up on top of the cart, signifying that we had actually located one of the answers for which we'd been searching.

Now I brought the discussion back to the types of information we would probably want to know about Hank Aaron. This took some guidance. As the students began to relate the needed information, I would bring up the object that matched that answer. The students became quite excited as they waited to see what item I would pull up next. One at a time, I brought up each item—the toy school bus, the baby bottle, the nerf balls, and foam tombstone, and one at a time, I pointed out to students what each item represented in the life of Hank Aaron.

Results of the Lesson

I concluded the lesson by actually going to pages from the book that I had transferred to transparencies so that we could actually mark through sentences that were "trash" (sentences that did not supply the required information) until we located the "treasure" (sentences that did supply the required information). Suddenly, lights were going off in student's heads. All they had needed was a way to transfer the abstract searching concepts into a concrete concept that they could actually feel. We spent more time at the next class meeting practicing their newfound skills.

Even though my fourth and fifth grade students were not researching for a biography unit, I used this same demonstration with them. Next year, I will build on my success by creating representations of other types of research. Everywhere I go now, I keep an eye out for objects that can be used to demonstrate key words for researching animals, or places, or inventions. I hope to develop chest objects that can apply to the precise type of research the students are assigned so that the concepts can go from the abstract to the concrete no matter what type of research is assigned. In addition, next year I will attach paper labels to each item that will include the actual answer from the research source. For example, the baby bottle label will list the birthday of Hank Aaron, the school bus label will list the name of one of his schools, and so on. In the end, I consider the demonstration to be a great success and will definitely repeat it with future lessons.

The Big6—Dig It!: Bringing Research Process to Life

By Shayne Russell / vE4, no3

"*M*ake it real. Make it relevant." As educators, we know that this is a key factor in helping students to make the connections needed to learn. A few years ago, I had an experience that helped me understand just how important those connections to something real and relevant are—and from that experience, the Web site "Big6—Dig It!" (http://home.earthlink.net/~s.russell/bigsixdigit.html) was born.

I had already been teaching the Big6 Information Process to my students. Although the six steps are logical and made perfect sense to me, I found I still had trouble remembering what order they came in and what occurred during each step. I suspected my students had the same difficulty.

Digging the Research Project

Six years ago, I had the opportunity to work as a field scientist—an archaeologist to be specific! I was a recipient of a grant from Bell Atlantic that funded my participation in an Earthwatch (http://www.earthwatch.org/) archaeological expedition in Springerville, Arizona.

For two weeks in July 1997, I was part of a research team comprised largely of educators from the United States and Australia working under the supervision of three archaeologists. Each morning at the dig site we unearthed artifacts that would help identify ties between the Mogollon people who once lived there and the present day Hopi and Zuni cultures. During the hot Arizona afternoons, we cleaned and cataloged our finds in the lab, attended lectures, and participated in field trips to other archaeological sites in the area. Long hours in the field gave me lots of time to think, and I made some important connections.

When I reflected on the work we had done in the field, I realized I had a new way to teach the Big6—one that was interesting and unusual and exciting. Now the steps really made sense to me and were easy to understand and remember because I had seen (and been part of) the process in action in a real-life research project. I knew I could use my experience to help my students understand them, too.

Bringing the Big6™ to Life for Students

I begin by telling my students to look around at all the books, magazines, videos and other materials we have in the Media Center. We talk about all the information that is available to us through these resources. Much of this information exists because of the "original research" conducted by scientists in the field. Through their observations, experiments and studies, scientists make new discoveries and learn things we never knew before. Then they make this information available to us through newspaper and magazine articles, books, videos, etc. "And you know what?" I ask them, "The process they use to do that research and learn all those new things is exactly the same as the process that you use when you do research here in the Media Center." It's time to introduce the Big6! "And I need you to know," I tell them confidentially, "this isn't just 'library stuff' we're talking about here. This is a process used by scientists who are doing real research, and I learned it by working side by side with archaeologists." By this point, I have their interest.

The Big6 process is presented to students as a puzzle. Working in groups of five or six, students are given a set of six "archaeology cards." Each card represents a step of the Big6 as seen through the eyes of an archaeologist. Their challenge is to use all the clues available to them (the picture on the card, the text on the card, the definitions of Big6 terms such as "Task Definition," "Location & Access," "Synthesis," and so on) to put the steps in the proper order. Once the group has agreed on the order, they are to move on to discussing what each step would look like in the library. I tell students that the kinds of things I expect to hear when they are having this discussion would be things like, "Oh, that step is kind of like when we use the online catalog to find a book in the library," or "That's like when we take notes," or "We'd be doing that when we write our bibliography."

Once each group has their cards in the order they've agreed upon (I have them lay them out on the table so I can see when they're done), we work as a group to make sure everyone ends up with the correct sequence. I added some interactivity to this finale by using our new SmartBoard, an interactive, digital whiteboard (http://www.smarttech.com/products/whiteboards.asp) for more information.

Using a Web page with pictures of each step (http://home.earthlink.net/~s.russell/bigsixdigit.html), I have a student come up to move each step into place as we discuss them one at a time. Sometimes I use a worksheet for students to take notes. Of course, you don't need a SmartBoard to do this—you can do it with a computer and projection or even just large post-it notes.

Following a discussion of all the steps of the Big6 process, I ask students how many of them enjoy doing research. There are always a few who do, but not many. Going quickly back over the six steps, I suggest they look at it this way:

- Task Definition: thinking step
- Information Seeking Strategies: thinking step
- Location & Access: "doing" step
- Use of Information: "doing" step
- Synthesis: "doing" step
- Evaluation: thinking step

There are six steps in this process. Three of them are "thinking" steps. So you are only working half the time— the rest of the time you're just sitting around thinking. How hard can it be?!

Conclusion

Sharing our personal experiences helps to bring life and relevance to our lessons. In this case, I've found that photographs attached to each step have been powerful visual clues that help students remember key aspects of the research process. Students sometimes describe the research process to me with an archaeological "spin" based on what they remember from the photos they've seen. Ah, but they do remember!

Just Imagine—Stew, Do, Review Technique for the Big6

By Earl J. / vE1, no4

Editor's Note: Here's an interesting twist on the Super3 – Plan, Do, Review (Beginning, Middle, End) approach. Earl encourages us to "stew" and to use our imaginations by beginning at the end—or is it end at the beginning?

Stew, Do, Review can be used by students who have the ability to think through a project from start to finish and imagine that the project is completed before they even begin. It is an exercise of the imagination in learning. It helps emphasize the contemplative nature of collecting information or completing a project. It might also be used by sports coaches to prepare their teams for an upcoming game—sort of a visualization exercise before the main event.

Stew: Begin at the End

The Stew step is the most involved and yet requires the least amount of physical activity. It only involves thinking of what needs to be accomplished. Stew involves thinking about what the final project will look like—What color is it? How many pages long is it? Where is it sitting for final display? Students begin at the end, and work their way to the beginning using their imagination. They ask and answer very specific questions in their minds along with the general notions from the Big6 steps 1-4—What am I supposed to do? What types of information will I need to complete the project? What sources might I use? What sources can I obtain? Where would I obtain the most relevant sources? Who can help me find the sources I need? How will I record the information I find? How do I identify the sources I have used?

This process begins with a very vivid picture in the individual's mind as to what the outcome will look like before anything else is started. In the project sense, the individual must be able to visualize the project sitting on a table in the corner of the library or classroom for all to view. The individual must be able to explain in detail the light coming in a certain window and shining on the items on display. The individual must be able to describe the documents included in the project. If the final product is an event, the individual must be able to describe the event in very close detail…including how happy students are; or how many other students showed up; or perhaps how parents and teachers were so surprised at the success of the event prepared by only students.

In the area of sports, the individual must be able to describe the winning score, the teams' elation at beating an opponent of such skill, or the joy of the coach upon beating an old rival "just one more time." In all cases, focus on the positive feelings and the joy of the final event or project. Steer clear of any negative emotions or images—don't focus on the dejection of the losing team; don't focus on having a better project than Jack or Jill; and don't focus on how much work it will be to complete—just savor the moment of completion and triumph.

This final image is not cast in concrete or stone. Ultimately, these imaginary solutions must be tempered with the facts of reality. In fact, the final project should take on a number of variations before it is actually complete. In general, younger students will tend to be more ambitious with their final project. They might anticipate videotapes of major motion picture quality captured with a home video camera … part of the challenge of the teacher/librarian here is to continue to encourage the enthusiasm of the students without setting them up for disappointments at the end. Have samples handy of previous projects or prepare a few simple projects to demonstrate the acceptable quality of work for display in the classroom or library. Let them build their castles in the air just as long as they can place their foundations solidly on the ground.

Let this *Stew* segment last a while … it might be a topic of discussion for a few days … in the event of weekly meetings, let it stew for at least two weeks. Discuss it openly in class with student input and encourage each student to continue to think through each step of the process. This backward-planning process (think of the end and work to the beginning before you start) should get the student enthused about starting. The longer and more detailed the student ponders the process (to a point—not to the point of distraction or loss of interest), the more smoothly the process will run once it is begun.

Individuals may begin to collect information for the completion of the project during the *Stew* process (some students will want to start immediately no matter how one attempts to restrain them). This situation is to be anticipated. Some students will think more often of the project and have it completed in their minds before others. A few students will only think of the project while in the presence of the person in charge of the project and not think of it at all outside the class or library. Students are students. If those students who want to begin have a firm grasp of what is to be done next, let them begin.

Do: The Building Process

The *Do* process is the actual building of the project, preparation of the event, or performance of the sporting endeavor. This point is the culmination of all the thinking that has been accomplished before; the accumulation of the information required to complete the project; and the actual completion of the project. The more detailed and vivid the image in the beginning, the more closely the final project will mimic that image. Consequently, the final project represents the finest product that the individual is capable of producing. This *Do* portion of the project should probably take about one-third to one-half of the time required for the entire project. Those time estimates are simply a general guide for most projects. If the project involves videotape and interviews with individuals and family members from surrounding communities, this *Do* process might very well take up three-fourths of the time required or more. *Stew, Do, Review* is a flexible method similar to the others mentioned above.

Review: What Could I Do Better?

The *Review* process is the Evaluation step from the Big6. Here the student, with guidance and coaching, reflects on the process of the project or event and determines what could have been accomplished in a more efficient or effective manner. The *Review* process is important to provide the student an opportunity to determine what has been learned from the project… not only the information learned in the searching and locating steps, but also what was learned from implementing the *Stew, Do, Review* process.

The Importance of Imagination

Students might also glean from this exercise that the mind has a difficult time differentiating between reality and fantasy. If one can imagine an event or object vividly enough, the mind can be fooled into believing that the event or object can exist for real. When the logical, rational mind is let go and the imagination is put in charge, it does its best to bring the fantasy notion to fruition. "Seeing is believing" might become "believing is seeing" – what you believe can happen could become reality. For those of you who would scoff at this imagination approach, here are a few quotes from some of our more notable forefathers:

- "Imagination is more important than knowledge." Albert Einstein

- "Anybody can do anything that he imagines." Henry Ford

- "The imagination imitates. It is the critical spirit that creates." Oscar Wilde

- "Every great advance in science has issued from a new audacity of imagination." John Dewey

- "Your imagination has much to do with your life. It pictures beauty, success, desired results. On the other hand, it brings into focus ugliness, distress, and failure. It is for you to decide how you want your imagination to serve you." John Erskine

- "Imagination lit every lamp in this country, produced every article we use, built every church, made every discovery, performed every act of kindness and progress, created more and better things for more people. It is the priceless ingredient for a better day." Henry J. Taylor

In the long run, let's not kill imagination in order to instill knowledge. Imagination and knowledge must necessarily co-exist if we are to progress successfully into the new millennium. Let's bring a sprinkling of imagination to everything we do; let's encourage imagination in every student to bring us a better tomorrow beginning today!

New Game: Match the Big6 (Grades 3-6)

By Barbara A. Jansen / *vE4, no1*

Match the Big6 and test your problem solving power! Directions for preparing and playing the Big6 matching game.

Gather: 3 pieces of construction paper, blunt scissors, glue.

Print: these 3 game sheets on pages 118-120.

Prepare the game pieces:

1. Cut the game sheets apart on the dotted lines.
2. Cut each piece of construction paper into 4 parts the same size (fold it first, open the page, and cut on the folded lines)
3. Glue each of the game pieces onto the pieces of cut construction paper to make cards. Let them dry.

Play the game:

1. Mix up the cards.
2. Put them face down on a table or the floor. Mix them up again.
3. Turn one over. Turn another over. Does the Big6 Skill match its description? If not, turn them face down again and try again. If you get a match, put the pair—2 cards—to the side. Keep trying until you get six matching pairs.

Have fun!

Big6 #1

Task
Definition

Big6© Eiisenberg, Berkowitz, 1990.

Big6 #2

Information
Seeking
Strategies

Big6© Eiisenberg, Berkowitz, 1990.

Big6 #3

Location
&
Access

Big6© Eiisenberg, Berkowitz, 1990.

Big6 #4

Use of
Information

Big6© Eiisenberg, Berkowitz, 1990.

Big6 #5

Synthesis

Big6 #6

Evaluation

What am I supposed to do?

What can I use to find what I need?

Where can I find what I need?

What information can I use?

What can I make to finish the job?

How will I know if I did my job well?

I Spy: Crafting Library Media Opportunities to Learn Big6

By Jeanita Lovelace / vE4, no4

*A*pplying the Big6 in the library media center can be a challenge, especially when the librarian has a fixed schedule that does not lend itself towards easy collaboration with teachers. Even though there were just three more class meetings before the end of our school year, I solved just such a situation at my elementary school.

This situation was essentially an information problem, so I used the Big6 process to solve it! Just as I taught my students, I followed the 6 steps to brainstorm a lesson that would require my students to use the Big6. Although collaboration with the classroom teacher would have been preferable, it was not possible with such a short timeline. For this reason, collaboration was limited to having teachers grade a small portion of the projects and allow students to store their projects in their classrooms during the three-week project period.

Big6 #1, Task Definition—Develop a lesson that would demonstrate the use of the Big6, involve minimal intervention by teachers, and be fun for the students.

Big6 #2, Information Seeking Strategies—I brainstormed a list of popular activities for my students. I chose Scholastic's popular *I Spy* (Marzollo) book series as my focus. I knew that these books were in constant circulation among students from second through fifth grades at my school—the books never seemed to spend any time on the shelves. To capitalize on the series' popularity, I challenged the students in grades 3-5 to make their own *I Spy* pages. I would use the digital camera to photograph their work, and then I would incorporate these photos into a PowerPoint presentation to create a book for each grade level (Big6 #5, Synthesis).

Children were put into small groups of two to five students. Each group would use the Big6 process in order to complete the I Spy project. The assignment: Use newspaper and magazine pictures and text to create a poster-sized page of hidden pictures. The completed project would be digitally photographed then added as one slide in that grade's PowerPoint show. Students would include a written description of each Big6 step they took. Teachers would grade the descriptions and count the assignment as one daily grade. Each student was evaluated on his/her active participation to ensure that all students, skilled and unskilled, could be successful with the project if they contributed.

Big6 #3, Location and Access—I furnished each group with old newspapers and magazines. Students were encouraged to bring in their own materials if they wished. I also furnished scissors, glue sticks, markers, and large chart pad sheets.

Big6 #4, Use of Information—The students were to select objects or words from the newspapers and magazines that would become the hidden things on their *I Spy* pages.

Each group had to choose a theme for their pages, although "no theme" was also an acceptable choice. The student who had the best handwriting and was the most reliable was designated as the recorder. The recorder's job was to keep track of all project pieces, record how his/her group applied each step of the Big6, and write the captions at the bottom of the project page. Other students were responsible for locating and cutting out pictures, words, or numbers from the newspapers and magazines. The remaining students were to plan, position, and paste these items onto the chart paper.

Big6 #5, Synthesis—Students were limited to three class meetings to complete the project, and then I photographed the projects and constructed the PowerPoint presentations.

Big6 #6, Evaluation—The students in each group worked enthusiastically during the time allowed for completion. I was quite impressed with their grasp of the process. This gave me an opportunity to Evaluate (Big6 #6) my own work in creating the lesson, and I was pleased with my results! The students were eager to see their presentations and liked the idea that others would be able to view their work since the presentations would be placed on the campus network.

The project was a great success. I look forward to repeating it with some minor adjustments. For example, the next time I will have the students be responsible for taking their own digital photos and preparing the PowerPoint presentations as well. Also, I will schedule the project earlier in the year so that their pages can be displayed in the school hallways.

In a perfect world, Big6 projects are done in collaboration with teachers. However, this is one example of working within the limitations of imperfect schedules yet creatively teaching skills that are useful to students inside the classroom and beyond the school setting.

Note: I Spy *books are available by searching Amazon.com online or at your local bookstores.*

Assignment Organizer for Grades 3-6

From the Big6 website: www.big6.com

Fill out Big6 #1-5 **before** you begin to work on your assignment.
Fill out Big6 #6 **before** you turn in your assignment.
You will need to print this form before exiting the page.

Name: _____

Today's date: _____ Class: _____

Big6 #1: Task Definition

What am I supposed to do?

_____
_____
_____
_____
_____

What information do I need in order to do this? (Consider listing in question form.)

1. _____
2. _____
3. _____
4. _____
5. _____
6. _____
7. _____
8. _____
9. _____
10. _____

Big6 #2: Information Seeking Strategies

What are the best sources I can use to find this information?

1. _____

2. _____

3. _____

4. _____

5. _____

6. _____

7. _____

8. _____

If using web sites, how will I know that they are good enough for my project?

☐ I will use only those evaluated by and provided by my teachers.

☐ I will ask my librarian, teacher, or parent for help in finding good web sites for my project.

Big6 #3: Location & Access

Where will I find these sources?

☐ school library

☐ public library

☐ personal library

☐ provided by my teachers

☐ Internet

☐ other:_____

Who can help me find what I need?

☐ I can find the resources myself.

☐ my librarian

☐ my teacher

☐ my parent(s)

Big6 #4: Use of Information

How will I record the information that I find?

☐ take notes using cards

☐ take notes on notebook paper

☐ take notes using a word processor on a computer

☐ take notes using a data chart or other graphic organizer

☐ illustrate concepts

☐ record into a tape recorder or use a video or digital camera

☐ other: _____

How will I give credit to my sources?

☐ use the guide given to me by my teacher

☐ use the Classroom Connect web site for citing Internet resources
http://www.classroom.com/community/connection/howto/citeresources.jhtml

☐ use the Quick Guide for citing other resources
http://www.standrews.austin.tx.us/library/WorksCited.htm

Big6 #5: Synthesis

How will I show my results?

☐ written paper

☐ oral presentation

☐ multimedia presentation _____

☐ performance or _____

☐ other: _____

How will I give credit to my sources in my final product or performance?

☐ include a written bibliography

☐ after the performance or presentation, announce which sources I used

☐ other: _____

Materials I will need for my presentation or performance (list, separating by commas)

_____

_____

How much time do I estimate it will take to find the information and create the product?

☐ 2-3 hours   ☐ 4-5 hours   ☐ 5-6 hours   ☐ 7-8 hours

☐ 9-10 hours   ☐ more than 10 hours

Timeline for assignment

Ideas for project (task definition) completed by: _____

Information searching (note taking) completed by: _____

First draft due: _____

Completed assignment due: _____

Include here any additional information needed to successfully complete the assignment:

_____

_____

_____

Big6 #6: Evaluation

How will I know if I have done my best?
Before turning in my assignment, I need to check off all of these items (on the printed Organizer):

☐ what I created to finish the assignment is appropriate for what I was supposed to do in Big6 #1

☐ the information I found in Big6 #4 matches the information needed in Big6 #1

☐ credit is given to all of my sources, written in the way my teacher requested

☐ my work is neat

☐ my work is complete and includes heading information (name, date, etc.)

☐ I would be proud for anyone to view this work.

Alphabetizing for a Reason

By Lyn Ballam / vE4, no1

Related Big6 Skills:

#1 Task Definition – We need to put words in alphabetical order.

#2 Information Seeking Strategies – Consider the entire word list.

#3 Location & Access – Look at our list and compare to the A – Z order.

#4 Use of Information – Arrange the list in A – Z order.

#5 Synthesis – Present the ordered list.

#6 Evaluation – Is the list in order? How could we do it differently?

Goals:

1. This lesson helps students learn how to alphabetize. Alphabet letters are sequential just like numbers.

2. Students will learn to alphabetize beyond the first letter of a word.

3. Students will learn to alphabetize through the entire word. This skill will help students use the guide words in the dictionary, the phone book and other alphabetized reference sources. This skill will also help students locate books in the library.

Learning Context: Elementary students 1st through 6th grade. For all skill levels.

Discussion: Students learn to say their ABC's and the corresponding sounds for the purpose of learning to read. However, once they have mastered reading, the use of the alphabet as a tool is often overlooked in the curriculum. This oversight makes the simple task of locating alphabetical information a setup for failure. As students progress through school they are required to use the dictionary and other alphabetical reference guides for various purposes, including research. It is extremely frustrating for students to try to locate information in an alphabetized information source without the necessary skills.

Alphabetizing for a Reason

1. Simple ABC's – Practice the alphabet. Start in the middle of the alphabet and ask "What letter comes after M?"

2. Simple ABC's Using Flash Cards – Make one card for each letter of the alphabet. Randomly distribute the cards to students and have students line up in alphabetical order by the letter on the card. This activity can be done with small or large groups of students.

3. Simple ABC's Using Names – Have students line up by first name or last name (students with the same or similar names lead into next step).

4. Names: Second Letter – Introduce how the second letter effects alpha ordering. Make cards with two letter combinations (usually two or three students will have the same first letter in his or her name). Randomly distribute cards to students and have them line up in alpha order.

5. Third Letter – Make cards with three letters (or have students do it), and repeat lesson from above (be sure to have 2 to 4 cards with the same first two letters).

6. Book Author Names – Show the spine label of a library book and discuss how books are shelved by the first three letters of the author's last name. Distribute one library book to every student and have each student line up according to the book spine label code.

7. Locate Titles – Using the library's catalog have students find titles in the fiction and picture book sections, and practice locating the exact book in the library.

8. Fourth Letter – This activity teaches alphabetizing beyond the third letter in a word or name. You may use the dictionary (or other sources) for this game. Distribute one dictionary per student or have students work in a group. Chose a word that is not a guide word and announce the word to the class. Student must locate the word in the dictionary. The first student to find the word can read the definition (if they want) and now have the privilege to choose the next word.

9. Phonebook – Using the phone book guide words look up your phone number and a friend's phone number. Use the yellow pages to look up business services.

10. Silent ABC Mixer (5th Grade and up) – Have students line up alphabetically by his or her name (either first or last), but they must do it silently. This is a good mixer and checks their skills.

Banana Splits

By Tami J. Little / *From the Big6 website: www.big6.com*

1. Task Definition:

1.1 Define the problem. The Information Problem — We are hungry for Banana Splits.

1.2 Identify the information requirements of the problem. Are we going to make the banana splits or buy them? How do we make them? We need to decide how much money we have to spend, what store we will go to? What grocery items we will need? How many banana splits we want to make?

2. Information Seeking Strategies:

2.1 Determine the range of possible sources. We can gather recipes from the Internet, call Dairy Queen, call other ice cream stores, check cookbooks, etc. We can go to the convenience store, the super market, etc. We will need to choose bananas, ice cream, toppings, dishes to put them in, spoons, whipped topping, etc. Find the aisles to get the food items.

2.2 Evaluate the different possible sources to determine priorities. From above list, prioritize the items that best fit our needs, make a grocery list of items.

3. Location and Access:

3.1 Locate sources (intellectually and physically).

3.2 Find information within sources. You are in the right aisle, in the store you chose, now choose the best items for the money and description you need from all of the possible brands.

4. Use of Information:

4.1 Engage (read, hear, view, touch) the information source.

4.2 Extract the information from a source. Begin making your banana split. First you put the ice cream dish on the table, then scoop the ice cream out of the container, peel the bananas. Take each item from its original container and put it on to the table or in bowls, etc.

5. Synthesis:

5.1 Organize the information from multiple sources. Place each of the items in the banana split dish in a neat order, following the recipe or directions chosen. Make sure that it looks "pretty."

5.2 Present the information. Share the banana split with friends. Everyone eat and enjoy!

6. Evaluation:

6.1 Judge the product (effectiveness). How did the banana split look? How did the banana split taste? Was it good? What was the quality of the ingredients? Would you choose a different banana, different dish or different spoons?

6.2 Judge the information problem-solving process (efficiency). When making the split next time, would you do anything different? How easy was it to find the recipes and did the directions work? What problems did you have when shopping? Would you go to the same store?

Comments:

Banana Split Presentation — Ideas/Modifications for consideration— Suggested by Dr. Nancy Thomas from Emporia State University, Emporia, Kansas. Thanks to Dr. Thomas for taking the time to do this!

Be sure to note that if you present other process models that Kuhlthau's model is not conceptually the same or equal to the Big6 Model. It is a process model. Kuhlthau's model was derived from what people actually do in seeking information. It also helps us to plan our professional intervention based upon what she learned about how people feel at various stages in their searches in school and public libraries.

The other models present ways to teach problem solving and project creation and evaluation. Although we can teach the Big6—we don't necessarily teach the Information Problem Solving (IPS) as articulated by Kuhlthau.

An idea about the actual banana split presentation—It might be useful to put all of the goodies that people will use to make the banana splits into several plain brown paper bags.

In this way, part of their job will be to decide how they will go about information seeking—i.e. the universe method (unpacking everything and then deciding what is relevant to their needs) or the berry picking method (go through the bags item by item, choosing what may be useful and leaving in the bag items which are not); or other method they might find useful based on their own preferences.

This also means that you may want to provide some items which may have little value to people, instead of providing only what is necessary for making the banana split (we get lots more information than we need when we are getting started in researching a project— and have to decide which information is relevant and which is not. We don't necessarily ever use everything that we find, right?) A monkey wrench, string, crayons, mustard, or scissors, for example, while useful tools for some purposes may be of very little value in this exercise.

You might want to provide some cookbooks that contain recipes for banana splits.

Provide some articles in the bags of goodies that force participants to make some more serious choices among alternatives—i.e., choices which call for evaluation at more than one step in the overall process. This is a way to ensure that evaluation occur at every step.

Maybe define a task as making the most healthful banana split, and thus provide options (sugar free toppings, vs. natural flavor—thus engaging with this activity on a higher cognitive level). Ask that participants consider food preferences of members, or allergies (to nuts).

Finally, provide each group with a large sheet of paper with the Big6 steps indicated — then have one person in each group write down the steps taken and the activities or decisions made at each step. This can serve as a record or journal that can be the basis for discussion about their experience after they have eaten.

Don't forget the moist towels or something to clean up—this activity gets sticky!

The Big6 at the American School of Japan

By Marty Swist / vE1, no1

Here's a detailed look of how to use the Big6 in a middle school situation. The location of the middle school is somewhat unique—in an American school in Japan! **Marty Swist** *has attended Big6 classes by Bob Berkowitz and me, and I was fortunate to visit and work with Marty and other teachers at his school in fall 1998. Needless to say, I was impressed! So, get ready for some good ideas and some fun!* —Mike Eisenberg

*I*t's clearly the information age at **The American School of Japan (ASIJ) middle school**! During a recent nine-day period, more than 40 classes were scheduled for formal Big6 Skills training at the middle school library. And, that certainly didn't account for all the action. You would need to add the:

- Classes that came for booktalks
- Teachers who wanted to discuss further projects or get replacement lamps for their overhead projectors
- Students who came to find a fact during class, or for an award-winning book to read, to borrow the digital cameras, or to check e-mail during an unassigned period.

As you can see, we live life in the fast lane at ASIJ—or The Fact Lane as neighboring teacher, Josh Reckord, and I call it. Your library is probably very much like ours. During these nine days, students in grades six through eight were engaged in a variety of research activities for a wide range of outcomes. As we know, these projects would require varied strategies, and carefully selected, appropriate resources. Conducting all of this instruction from a Big6 perspective empowers students to complete their assignments in a methodical and productive way—efficiently and effectively.

Seventh Grade Science and Big6 Training!

The highlight of seventh grade science is a week-long springtime study trip to the island of Miyake, Japan. The island of Miyake, or *Miyake-jima*, is located in the Sea of Japan 200 miles south of Tokyo. Twenty-eight students at a time, plus five teachers, experience the natural wonders of Miyake each week until all 110 seventh grade students have had a chance to see Miyake. Miyake is an active volcano and the home of a world renowned marine biology study center (and resident marine biologist-guru, **Jack Moyer**, listed in the *1999 Marquis' Who's Who in the World*).

Before our student scientists embark on this journey, they conduct several weeks of research throughout the year on the local land forms and sea life, as well as the many colorful birds of the island. This year will be the 31st consecutive year that ASIJ Middle School students have studied the delicate ecosystem on Miyake. The library has acquired most of the materials needed. In addition, we continue to discover many useful Web sites to assist students with this project.

The Miyake science unit begins with Step 1, Task Definition, an integral part of every Big6 exercise in the library. Obviously, all students need to know what is expected of them. In addition, working on Task Definition together gives me the opportunity to demonstrate to the students and to their teacher my co-ownership of this project from the ground up. We are on this journey together.

At the conclusion of Step 1, I go into my Carl Malden routine. No, I don't push The American Express Card (for any fellow "boomers" who might remember him and his commercials). I tell the students, *"Don't leave class without it."* We discuss how crucial it is to be sure of the assignment. Can they repeat the assignment in their own words? To further illustrate the significance of Task Definition, I simply ask: "If you don't know the assignment, how can you complete it successfully? How can your friends, parents, or librarian help you?" The teacher is usually with us at this stage and invariably wears a smile as the class accomplishes Step 1. The emphasis on Step 1 takes approximately five minutes.

To reinforce Task Definition this year I will place a message in the student section of our Daily Bulletin four times. I am also sending an e-mail message to all middle school teachers advising them of the upcoming short message. The message to the students is, you guessed it, *"Don't leave class without it."*

In the e-mail to faculty, I ask them to monitor any discussion after the message is read aloud and to reinforce the importance of Task Definition. My goal is to make teacher intervention unnecessary by the end of the school year. This step takes 15 to 20 seconds once each quarter, or approximately one minute of the year's morning announcement prime time. The return on this investment can be remarkable.

After discussing the project with the science teacher, and reviewing the seventh grade students' Big6 progress in the library, I decided to emphasize Big6 Steps 3 and 4, **Location & Access**, and **Use of Information**. I had ulterior motives—as we sometimes do. Last year, we switched to a different on-line catalog. We migrated from *Columbia* in DOS to *Spectrum* by Winnebago in Windows. Although many of this year's seventh graders had enjoyed an introduction to *Spectrum* during their sixth grade rivers unit, I knew they needed another guided opportunity to become competent and comfortable with *Spectrum*.

The second motive was to remind the students that they can locate and access selected web sites for this project on our middle school library web site. Our curriculum links pages contain tested sites that support major units. I like to emphasize this proactive, outreach aspect of our library services to students living one-and-one-half hours away from the school. Some students are ecstatic when I remind them that they can access these Web pages and complete their homework while on vacation as long as they have an Internet connection. In an international school environment, students may travel out of the country for major holidays. A major holiday in Tokyo ranges from a four-day weekend excursion to Guam, Beijing, or Seoul, to three weeks spent between Honolulu and Grandmother's house in Connecticut during the winter holiday.

Location & Access for this project began with "Easy and Expanded" searching in *Spectrum*. Students suggested search terms, or subjects, and reacquainted themselves with the physical location of the 500's in the library. They discovered which books had indexes, which books were easy to use, and which ones weren't easy. Students were directed to CD ROMS through *Spectrum*, as well as to links for selected Web sites also cataloged in, and accessible through, *Spectrum*.

Students took turns demonstrating how to search, sort, and select Web sites while the rest of us watched on the large screen monitor. The class used the rest of the period and the following few days to conduct their research, locate and access the appropriate materials, take notes; and in this case, write their papers, answer pointed questions, and create their illustrations.

We began the second day with a discussion about Step 4, Use of Information. I reminded them that I have seen many of their wonderful art projects throughout the year. They know this is true because my wife, **Jessica**, is their art teacher. I frequently admire student work in her classroom. Next the students and I discussed the futility of beautiful pieces of abstract "highlight art" in alternating fluorescent colors for research purposes.

Entire paragraphs usually need not be highlighted. It's hyperbole; they know it. But it is a segue for me to discuss effective note-taking strategies. I asked if their teacher has a specific method he wants students to use. He did not. We discussed a few options that were demonstrated by the students. These strategies included mind mapping, underlining, and making notes in the margins of photocopied text.

The science teacher, assistant librarian, and I continued to assist the students in the library for the duration of the assignment, as needed. Some students came to the library for additional research before school, during lunch, during an unassigned period, or after school. Step 5, **Synthesis**, was completed outside of the library. I am not formally included in Step 6, **Evaluation**, with this project.

This spring I will go to Miyake for one week with a group of seventh grade students. I will be with them as they apply the Big6 Skills they have learned in their other research projects. We will discover more about science together—by climbing the active volcano (about 11 kms up one side, across, and down the other) and snorkeling over the hard coral beds in a cove in the sea. I think of this as Step Seventh Heaven. :-)

A Little Background

My present position as middle school librarian is my third overseas school library position in twenty-two years of expat ex-libris. The ASIJ middle school library serves 330 students in grades six through eight. The student enrollment at ASIJ is about 1400, K–12. There are three libraries on our campus and three librarians. For the most part, our middle school curriculum is similar to a stateside middle school curriculum. Melinda Kehe, my assistant, is a recent graduate of the MLS program at the University of Wisconsin. I am fortunate to have her for an assistant.

During three summers in the mid-1990's **Kathy Tobiason**, our elementary school librarian; **Vicky Downs**, our former high school and head librarian; and I, attended Bob's and Mike's excellent classes at Syracuse University that featured the Big6 problem-solving skills. In November 1996, while working in different schools in different countries, Kathy and I had the good fortune to attend Mike's presentations at our regional teachers' conference, CERCOS, which was hosted by International School Manila. Also presenting a Big6 workshop at CERCOS was **Jennifer Merchant**, high school librarian at **Teipei American School**. In the fall of 1999, Jennifer joined ASIJ as our new high school and head librarian. Kathy and Jennifer are steadfast proponents and conscientious practitioners of the Big6. As the middle school librarian, I enjoy outstanding collegial support and inspiration.

Peter Cooper, ASIJ headmaster, and **Dan Bender**, elementary school principal, attended Mike's keynote address and presentations at CERCOS and at EARCOS, the administrators' conference that immediately followed. After learning about the Big6, all of our administrators were very receptive to, and supportive of, our request to invite Mike to work with us at ASIJ. In November of 1998, Mike worked in our classrooms modeling the Big6 for classroom teachers for three days—every period for three days! Mike used our teachers' actual lesson plans and student outcomes. This was *real*.

We three librarians had already implemented the Big6 strategies in our instruction. We were very comfortable with it; we knew it helped students. But Mike showed us all that the Big6 doesn't just happen in the libraries. Mike also presented a well attended workshop for parents highlighting the work he and Bob have done in *Helping with Homework* (Eisenberg & Berkowitz, 1996). Mike's visit greatly accelerated our efforts to become a K-12 Big6 school.

Real Life Connections: From Citations to Charting Their Futures

By Tina Hudak / vE4, no2

Library media specialists are often asked by classroom teachers to instruct students on the use of bibliographic citations. This is not a topic that generally inspires middle school students to shouts of joy. Yet, my story is about one serendipitous journey undertaken by a seventh grade class, beginning with this challenge, and taking them through a three-month process of self-discovery and adventure. Yes, creating bibliographic citations for different sources actually led to a much broader exploration and learning experience.

Understand the Task (Big6 #1)

The classroom curriculum objective states "students will be able to cite the correct bibliographic citation for their sources." How many times have we started on this path only to see eyes glaze over, notes being passed, and attention wandering to the windows?

I teach in a Title I, high-immigrant, low-income, Catholic school that has recently become connected to the Internet. This is an exciting and thought-provoking teaching position. My main challenge is to help students who have little or no experience with the Internet or software to become technologically skilled. At the same time, they needed to learn the research process. Doing these together makes a lot of sense—especially with the Big6.

First, I used the Big6 approach as my own tool for designing a lesson. For a moment, do as I did. Ask yourself, why is this skill important? What relevance does any citation have in student lives? What is my "task definition" for this class? This meant throwing out content explicitly directed to the curriculum and replacing it with one that "grabbed" student interest. As any middle school teacher knows, it's all about the students; as any media specialist knows, its process, not content.

Project Relevance and Information Seeking Strategies (Big6 #2)

Using this challenge as an opportunity provided a starting point for the lesson on "Discovering Careers" that emerged. Our circuitous route to bibliographic citations began by introducing students to why it is important for them to be in school in the first place. Statistics can be boring. Yet, show a group of students the chart with statistics from The Bureau of Labor Statistics comparing educational level and income in the area where they live and others, and they pay attention. Suddenly, this is their life, their education, their future and their research project.

During the next two-to-three months students completed a series of activities. They took an online career key test (http://www.careerkey.org/english/you/) to help them focus on choices and interests (Big6 #3 Location and Access). Students had to find specific information by following a rubric designed for a *PowerPoint* presentation. They researched in the Computer Lab using online sites at Occupational Outlook Handbook (http://www.bls.gov/oco/home.htm), Bureau of Labor Statistics for Kids (http://www.bls.gov/k12/html/edu_over.htm) along with hard copies of reference materials in the Media Center.

These activities allowed students to transform their "ideal career" into something more tangible (Big6 #4 Use of Information): define the career; describe the working conditions;

the educational requirements; the employment outlook and income; decide on appropriate high-school courses to help them along; professional organizations in this field; evaluate the project, and finally, write the bibliography! (Big6 #5 Synthesis)

Career Day—Face to Face

Halfway through this project, students' interest began to wane. This reminded me of Carol Kuhlthau's extensive research on students' attitudes during the search process. (Kuhlthau, 1993) Students were learning that research is hard work, and that re-evaluating (Big6 #6 Evaluation) their choices meant rewriting a lot of what they had completed.

Breathing life into our "real life" activities meant modifying the lesson plan, once again. So we scheduled a "Career Day" to reinforce the importance of the project and to let students talk one-on-one with professionals in their chosen fields. It was a way to bring the outside world of work and accomplishment directly into their lives. In the third month of our work, students finalized their projects. Twelve professionals including (doctors, teachers, and business people) participated, sharing their personal experiences and stories with our students, and then visited the Computer Lab to view the final student projects.

This unexpected journey began with a seemingly simple task for the student to write a bibliographic citation; students accomplished this and more. I accomplished my own task: "the teacher will initiate a lesson that shows students the importance of learning and supports her belief that everyone in her class will be successful."

Works Cited

Kuhlthau, Carol. *Seeking Meaning: A Process Approach to Library and Information Services*, Ablex Publishing Co. (Available through Greenwood Publishing), 1993

Big Kids

Big6 Research Paper Organizer

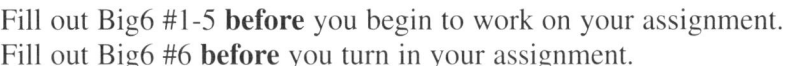

vE4, no3

Fill out Big6 #1-5 **before** you begin to work on your assignment.
Fill out Big6 #6 **before** you turn in your assignment.

Name: _____

Today's date: _____   Class: _____

Pre-Search Strategies

If you don't have an idea for a topic or if your teacher did not assign a specific topic for your paper, consider the following suggestions:

1. Think about what is interesting to you and see if you can connect that interest to the requirements of the paper. For example, if the teacher has assigned a broad topic such as "Change over time in U.S. History" and you are passionate about Corvettes, consider connecting the topics in this way: "How has the design of automobiles over time influenced the way Americans buy and use their cars?"
   Here is another example for a student who loves photography: "How has photography and its advances changed the definition of what it means to be an American?"

2. Use the online reference databases in which the school has subscriptions (see your librarian for help accessing these).

3. Talk to your parents, teachers and friends about good topics

Big6 #1 Task Definition

Determine a purpose and need for information
In order for your paper to be more than a rewrite of the facts you find about your topic in print and online sources, or a summary of someone else's ideas, you need to develop an essential question (http://www.standrews.austin.tx.us/library/ResearchPaper.htm) for inquiry. If written correctly and thoughtfully, the essential question will ensure that you critically and creatively process the information you find.

Write your essential question here. You should have already had a draft of it approved by your teacher.

_____

_____

_____

What questions should you ask to support your essential question?

You will find information on what types of supporting questions to ask to support your essential question in the document "Did you ask a good question today?"
http://www.standrews.austin.tx.us/library/Questioning.htm
    You should consider writing supporting questions from each of the four categories:

Memory (http://www.standrews.austin.tx.us/library/MemoryQuestions.htm),

Convergent (http://www.standrews.austin.tx.us/library/ConvergentThinkingQuestions.htm),

Divergent (http://www.standrews.austin.tx.us/library/DivergentThinkingQuestions.htm), and

Evaluative (http://www.standrews.austin.tx.us/library/EvaluativeThinkingQuestions.htm).

List below the questions that you feel you need to answer at this time. You will most likely find interesting additional information as you use print and online resources.

1. _____

2. _____

3. _____

4. _____

5. _____

6. _____

7. _____

8. _____

9. _____

10. _____

Big6 #2 Information Seeking Strategies

Examine alternative approaches to acquiring information. List the best sources to find this information. Don't forget traditional print and human sources as appropriate.

1. _____

2. _____

3. _____

4. _____

5. _____

Big6 Research Paper Organizer *continued*

If using web sites, who will evaluate them for relevancy, accuracy, and authority?

☐ I will use only those evaluated by and provided by my teachers or librarian, including the databases to which the school subscribes

☐ I will find free web sites and use a web site evaluation guide (http://www.standrews.austin.tx.us/ library/Web%20evaluation.htm) for each that I use in my project

If you need help with this (or any) step of the process, please see your librarian!

Big6 #3 Location & Access

Locate sources and access the information within them—Where will I locate these sources?

☐ school library   ☐ provided by my teachers

☐ public or university library   ☐ Internet

☐ personal library   ☐ other: _____

If using a search engine list likely key words.

_____   _____

_____   _____

_____   _____

Big6 #4 Use of Information

Use a source to gain information—How will I record the information that I find?

☐ take notes using cards

☐ take notes on notebook paper

☐ take notes using a word processor

☐ take notes using a data chart or other graphic organizer

☐ illustrate concepts

☐ use a tape recorder, video, or digital camera

☐ other: _____

How will I give credit to my sources?

☐ use the Slate Citation Machine (http://www.landmark-project.com/citation_machine/index.php) web site for citing Internet resources

☐ use the Quick Guide (http://www.standrews.austin.tx.us/library/WorksCited.htm) or Writer's Guide to MLA Documentation (http://webster.commnet.edu/mla/index.shtml) for citing other resources

☐ use footnotes (see Writer's Guide) http://webster.commnet.edu/mla/index.shtml) for help on using footnotes

Big6 #5 Synthesis

Integrate information from a variety of sources—How will I show my results?

☐ written paper

How will I give credit to my sources in my final paper?

☐ include a written bibliography

Timeline for assignment

Idea for topic (task definition) completed by: _____

Information searching (note taking) completed by: _____

First draft due: _____

Completed paper due: _____

Include here any additional information needed to successfully complete the paper:

_____

_____

_____

Big6 #6 Evaluation

Before turning in my assignment, I need to check off all of these items (on the printed Organizer, which needs to be turned in with my paper):

☐ my final paper is a thoughtful presentation of my essential question and represents my ideas and conclusions

☐ I have not represented others' ideas as my own

☐ credit is given to my sources, written in standard citation format (http://www.standrews.austin.tx.us/library/WorksCited.htm)

☐ my work is word processed

☐ my work is complete and includes a title page and bibliography

☐ I would be proud for anyone to read this paper

Big6 Assignment Organizer copyright 1999, Barbara A. Jansen.

Preventing Victimization: Strategies for Personal Safety

By Kim Baker / vE4, no2

Subject: Physical Education

Teacher: Kim Baker, Physical Education Department
Wayne Central High School, Ontario Center, NY

Grade Level: 9-12 high school

Learning Strategy: Round Table, Group Work

Objective: The objective of this lesson is to teach students to identify strategies to successfully prevent themselves from being a victim of a physical attack.

Big6 Objectives
Task Definition: Understanding verbal directions
Use of Information: Listening for information from a story
Synthesis: Sharing and organizing information on a response sheet
Evaluation: Judging the quality of the responses to the problem-solving situation

Materials
- 5 copies of "Jodie Robertson's Story"
- 5 large sheets of paper
- 5 marking pens / masking tape

Activities

1. **Introduce the activity and the lesson objective.**
   - Prompt for active listening.
   - Talk about key words in assignments related to Task Definition.

2. **Group students and hand out materials.**
   - 5 students per group / 1 piece of paper / 1 pen / 1 story

3. **Have one student from each group read the story out loud to their group.**
   - Discuss use of information strategies—listening and note-taking.

4. **All groups must answer the following question:**
   - "What are some things Jodie Robertson could have done to prevent this violent attack?"

5. **One student in the group writes a response and shares it out loud with the group.**

6. **The response paper is passed to the right, and the second student writes her response, etc.**

7. **If students don't have an answer, they may "pass."**

8. **Each group has 10 – 15 minutes to complete the exercise, writing as many responses as the group can generate.**

9. **Once time is called, all groups meet together to share their ideas.**

10. Students justify their responses and determine the best strategies.

11. Teacher compiles a master list of the best strategies for personal safety given this situation.

Closure

1. **Content Side: Review and discuss with students the importance of:**
   - being alert to their surroundings
   - trusting their "safety" instincts
   - using personal safety strategies

2. **Big6 Side: Review and discuss Synthesis with students**
   - generating as many ideas as possible
   - building on the ideas of others
   - combining ideas and summarizing

3. **Big6 Side: Review and discuss Evaluation with students**
   - listening skills
   - quality of responses
   - working in groups

Article

Jodie Robertson's Story
From: Home Journal, February 1997, p66.

I was thirty-four years old and on vacation at my brother's in California. I was driving back to his apartment at about 11 p.m. when I stopped at a light. A sports car pulled up and drove slowly past me. The same car then pulled into the parking lot at my brother's building. The driver got out, leaving the motor running, and walked past me, then grabbed me and put a knife to my throat, almost before I could blink. "You're going with me," he said.

He shoved me into his car and drove me to a house outside of town, where he tied my hands with a rope that was waiting, neatly coiled on the bed. Then he laid me down on the bed and raped me. Afterward, he drove to a deserted place and walked me into the bushes. He grabbed my hair, pulled my head back and slashed my throat from ear to ear. At this point I couldn't focus at all. Then he took a rock and slammed it into my skull. Two women out for their morning walk found me at about seven a.m.

The Big6: Helping Teens Build Resiliency

By Jami L. Jones, East Carolina University / vE4, no3

Author's Personal Note

Many teens experience difficulties they are unprepared to manage. The death of my son's girlfriend caused me to reconsider my role as media specialist in helping teens cope with the pressures of life in an increasingly complex and confusing world. Information seemed to me to be the key to help teens develop the practical life skills to overcome life's challenges. The results of resiliency research bore this out. The research showed that teens who were able to problem solve were more apt to be resilient – to bounce back from adversity. The Big6 teaches teens to use information to overcome life's challenges.

Why do students need information literacy?

Many students walking the halls of America's schools are experiencing complex challenges they are unprepared to manage. Many of these problems are rooted in economics, family dysfunction, and mental or physical health. Statistics indicate that in a typical middle school one in two students has experienced the upheaval and confusion of their parents' divorce (Divorce and its Impact on Teens, par. 1); one in four lives with a parent who abuses alcohol, and one in five lives in poverty (Indicators of Children's Well-Being, p. 17).

While many problems are rooted in the home, school and peer issues can cause a great deal of confusion as well. For example, many middle school students face the daily problem of bullying. In a study conducted by the National Institute of Child Health and Human Development of almost 16,000 students in grades six through ten, it was found that one in three had either been the victim of bullying, had bullied others, or had been both victim and perpetrator (Nansel et al. p. 2094). In a typical high school, one in three students report either they or a friend has experienced violence in a dating relationship (What You Need to Know About Dating Violence, p. 4-22) and one in five suffers from depression (Koplewicz, p. 5). America has the highest teen pregnancy rate of any other developed country in the world. Some teens—especially girls—suffer from eating disorders and use self-inflicted violence as a means to control their emotional pain.

It used to be that educators developed programs and interventions only after teens had been identified at risk of educational failure because of such things as drug abuse and pregnancy. Now the focus is on providing teens with supportive environments and teaching life skills to buffer them before they succumb to risky behaviors. The concept of resiliency— defined by Bonnie Benard as the ability to "bounce back despite exposure to severe risks"— is embraced as one way to strengthen children and adolescents (Benard, p. 44).

The Kauai Longitudinal Study and Resiliency

Much of what is known about resiliency was learned from the Kauai Longitudinal Study. In this study, which began in the 1950s, social scientists Emmy E. Werner and Ruth Smith followed all children born on the island of Kauai in Hawaii for more than 30 years to determine their response to such problems as family conflict, poverty, and poor health. As a result, Werner and Smith were able to identify many factors that helped these children and adolescents succeed despite adversity. Five of these factors are especially relevant to library media specialists. These five factors are:

- mentoring and making connections
- reading
- problem solving and information skills
- social skills, and
- hobbies and interests (Jones).

In the book *A Tribe Apart: A Journey into the Heart of American Adolescence,* Patricia Hersch monitored a group of adolescents to gain an understanding of the realities of their world. Hersch found that a significant problem facing adolescents is the lack of adult role models to help them develop problem solving and decision making skills. She writes, "The more we leave kids alone, don't engage, the more they circle around on the same adolescent logic that has caused the dangerous situation to escalate" (p. ix). The purpose of this lesson is to teach middle and high school students to apply the Big6 information problem solving process to the real-life issues, problems, and challenges facing them. The power of information literacy is not limited to academic pursuits, but extends to personal decision making and improved quality of life.

Helping Teens Cope Big6™ Lesson Plan (Grades 6-12)

By Jami Jones / From the Big6 website: www.big6.com

Objectives: To teach teens to apply critical thinking skills to everyday living and to develop an information product to enlighten students about the challenges faced by their peers.

Subjects: Psychology, sociology, health, critical thinking

Grade Level: This lesson can be modified to use with students in grades 6-12.

Big6 Stage One: Task Definition

As a class, students brainstorm and identify 10 to 15 "difficulties" their peers might be experiencing. Students select a difficulty to research. The following scenario is then read to students:

You are worried about your friend who is struggling with a particular issue, problem, or challenge – we'll call these "difficulties." You know other teens in your school who are struggling with this difficulty, too. Working with a partner, you are to research your friend's difficulty so you can help him or her become proactive in resolving the problem. You are to develop a report to give to your friend that contains a brief summary of your findings as well as a list of national and local resources such as hotlines, web sites, organizations, computer listservs, and support groups. The report must also contain bibliographic information of teen fiction and nonfiction books to recommend to your friend. The information you provide your friend must be detailed enough so he or she can begin to develop a personal plan to prevent, minimize, or eradicate the difficulty.

Big6 Stage Two: Information Seeking Strategies

In this Stage, students develop a search plan whereby they identify various resources most likely to contain the information needed to successfully fulfill the task as defined in Task Definition, Stage One. Note: Because of the sensitive nature of these topics, it is essential that students only use resources that have been peer reviewed or authored by learned and credentialed individuals and respected organizations.

Big6 Stage Three: Locate and Access Information

In this Stage, students use proper search techniques to implement the search plan identified in Stage Two, (Information Seeking Strategies). Students will locate the information to implement the next Stage – Use of Information.

Big6 Stage Four: Use of Information

Students read, take notes, skim and scan information in order to become knowledgeable about the difficulty they are researching. Next, students organize what was found to make sure that the information requirements of the task have been met. If additional information is needed, students will need to repeat Stages Two, Three, and Four.

Big6 Stage Five: Synthesis

As stated in Stage One, students are to develop a report to help their friend learn about his or her difficulty. In addition to the report, students may develop a product such as a pamphlet, web site, article for the school newspaper, book cover, or fast food tray liner to distribute to their friend and other teens. Either the report or optional product may be delivered in an oral presentation.

Big6 Stage Six: Evaluation

Students are evaluated on the following elements:

1. **Information resources.** Did the student utilize quality information that was written by credentialed professionals or reputable organizations that are knowledgeable about the difficulty? Students must be able to defend their information choices.

2. **Range and diversity of resources.** Did the student identify and use a variety of resources such as web sites, hotlines, support groups, organizations, and fiction and nonfiction books?

3. **Summarization.** Did the student distill the salient points of the information into a readable report and optional product?

4. **Mechanics.** Did the student use grammatically correct language with no spelling and punctuation errors? When citing resources, did the student adhere to a bibliographic format such as MLA or APA? The student must not plagiarize.

5. **Report.** Did the student organize and utilize resources effectively to write an informative report based on research, not opinion or personal experience?

6. **Optional product.** Did the student produce a product with the potential to impact teens?

Works Cited

Benard, Bonnie. "Fostering Resiliency in Kids." Educational Leadership, 44-48.

Divorce and its Impact on Teens. U. of New Hampshire Cooperative Extension. 27 Aug. 2003 http://ceinfo.unh.edu/common/documents/divorce.htm

Hersch, Patricia. (1998). *A Tribe Apart: A Journey into the Heart of American Adolescence.* New York: Ballantine.

Indicators of Children's Well Being. Federal Interagency Forum on Child and Family Statistics. 27 Aug. 2003 http://www.childstats.gov/ac2002/pdf.econ.pdf

Jones, Jami. "Library Ladder of Resiliency." AskDrJami.org. 27 Aug. 2003 http://www.askdrjami.org/pdf/LibraryLadderofResiliency.pdf

Koplewicz, Harold S. 92002). *More than Moody: Recognizing and Treating Adolescent Depression.* New York: G.P. Putnam's Sons.

Nansel, Tonja. "Bullying Behaviors among US Youth." *Journal of the American Medical Association* 285.16 (2001): 2094-2100.

What You Need to Know about Dating Violence. Liz Claiborne Inc. 27 Aug. 2003 http://www.lizclaiborne.com/lizinc/lizworks/women/pdf/teen_handbook.pdf

You're Not Alone. 27 Aug. 2003 http://www.girlpower.gov/girlarea/notalone/thefacts.htm

Big6 Assignment Organizer for Grades 7-12

From the Big6 website: www.big6.com

Fill out Big6 #1-5 **before** you begin to work on your assignment.
Fill out Big6 #6 **before** you turn in your assignment.

Name: _____

Today's date: _____ Class: _____

Big6 #1 Task Definition

Determine a purpose and need for information—What am I supposed to do?

_____

_____

_____

What information do I need in order to do this? (Consider listing in question form.)

You will most likely find interesting additional information as you use the resources. List below information that you feel you need to know at this time.

1. _____

2. _____

3. _____

4. _____

5. _____

6. _____

7. _____

8. _____

9. _____

10. _____

Big6 #2 Information Seeking Strategies

Examine alternative approaches to acquiring information. List the best sources to find this information. Don't forget traditional print and human sources as appropriate.

1. _____

2. _____

3. _____

4. _____

5. _____

If using web sites, who will evaluate them for relevancy, accuracy, and authority?

☐   I will use only those evaluated by and provided by my teachers or librarian, including the databases to which the school subscribes.

☐   I will find free web sites and use a web site evaluation guide for each that I use in my project.

Big6 #3 Location & Access

Locate sources and access the information within them—Where will I locate these sources?

☐   school library

☐   public or university library

☐   personal library

☐   provided by my teachers

☐   Internet

☐   other: _____

If using a search engine list likely key words.

_____   _____

_____   _____

_____   _____

Big6 #4 Use of Information

Use a source to gain information—How will I record the information that I find?

- [ ] take notes using cards
- [ ] take notes on notebook paper
- [ ] take notes using a word processor
- [ ] take notes using a data chart or other graphic organizer

How will I give credit to my sources?

- [ ] use the Quick Guide or Writer's Guide to MLA Documentation for citing other resources
- [ ] use footnotes

Big6 #5 Synthesis

Integrate information from a variety of sources—How will I show my results?

- [ ] written paper
- [ ] oral presentation.
- [ ] multimedia presentation _____
- [ ] performance _____
- [ ] other _____

How will I give credit to my sources in my final paper?

- [ ] include a written bibliography
- [ ] after the performance or presentation, announce which sources I used
- [ ] other _____

Materials I will need for my presentation or performance list (list, separated by commas)

_____

_____

_____

How much time do I estimate it will take to find the information and create the product?_____

Timeline for assignment

Idea for topic (task definition) completed by: _____

Information searching (note taking) completed by: _____

First draft due: _____

Completed paper due: _____

Include here any additional information needed to successfully complete the paper:

_____

_____

_____

Big6 #6 Evaluation

Before turning in my assignment, I need to check off all of these items (on the printed Organizer, which needs to be turned in with my paper):

☐ what I created to finish the assignment is appropriate for what I was supposed to do in Big6 #1

☐ the information I found in Big6 #4 matches the information needed in Big6 #1

☐ credit is given to my sources, written in standard citation format

☐ I am in compliance of copyright laws and fair use guidelines.

☐ my work is neat

☐ my work is complete and includes heading information (name, date, etc.)

☐ I would be proud for anyone to read this paper.

Powers of the President: A Study in Presidential Decision-Making

By Bob Berkowitz, John DonVito / vE4, no1

Overview

This instructional unit provides students with the opportunity to study the powers of the President, and the growth of Presidential power over the years. Through library research and the use of their textbook, students access information to be analyzed, evaluated and applied to a simulated situation. Students are required to prepare both written and oral products to demonstrate their knowledge.

Content Objectives Include:

Students will demonstrate the ability to:

1. list the Constitutional powers of the President in Article II

2. describe how the powers of the President have been extended and the impact on the country

3. describe how the American democracy functions through the executive branch

4. make rational and informed decisions about social, political and economic issues

Big6™ Objectives Include:

Students will demonstrate the ability to:

Task Definition - restate the requirements of the assignment in his or her own words

Information Use - read and analyze information; interpret and apply information

Synthesis - organize and create an information based response to a simulated historical situation

Basic Instructional Sequence:

Day 1.

1. Explain the purpose of the assignment.

2. Explain the requirements of the assignment.

3. Model Presidential decision-making. (Use an example of a Presidential decision that the students have studied previous to this unit.)

   a. define the problem

   b. list those groups affected by the problem and how they are affected

     • gather information

     • analyze information

     • determine criteria for a successful solution

   c. list potential solutions

d. analyze features, pros/cons of each solution

e. make recommendations

f. implement solution

g. evaluation solution based on criteria

4. Students are divided into groups of three. Each group will be assigned a president to research. Each student will be required to focus on either the (1) social, (2) political or (3) economic perspectives of the president.

Day 2.

5. Students use library and other resources to complete the data worksheet. (Library and Homework)

6. Students use their notes to prepare for class discussion.

Day 3 & 4.

7. The class discussion will take place in a round table interview format lead by teacher.

8. Students in the audience will take notes on data sheets during the presentations.

9. The process of decision-making will be reviewed. Students will be given the "Jerindon" scenario, and required to prepare a written response to the assigned questions.

Homework

10. Students will respond in writing to the "closure" question.

A model process that a President might use for decision-making

a. define the problem and its aspects

b. list all those who are affected by the problem and how they are affected - gather information

  • analyze information

  • determine criteria for a successful solution

c. list potential solutions

d. analyze features, pros/cons of each solution

e. make recommendations

f. implement solution

g. evaluate solution based on criteria

Situation

The country is concerned about the large unemployment rate among citizens ages 18-23 who do not attend college, other post-secondary training, or go into the military. During his campaign the President promised that he would lower the unemployment rate, and raise the rate of 18-23 year olds who go to work at job sites that pay above minimum wage and provide technology training. The President is committed to this promise. Using the decision-making process, outline a solution that the President might recommend to congress so he can turn his promise into action.

Some sample brainstormed ideas:

- define the problem and its aspects
- reduce unemployment among 18-23 yr. olds
- create an atmosphere where jobs and on-site training are available
- provide incentives for job providers to keep costs down

list all those who are affected by the problem and how they are affected
- 18-23 who do not attend college, other post-secondary training, or go into the military
- employers
- federal government agencies (dept. of labor, education, etc.)
- state government
- local government

gather information
- discuss the kind of information needed (costs, numbers, implications, etc.)
- analyze information
- discuss what you would be looking for in this information determine criteria for a successful solution

list potential solutions
- provide incentives for employers
- provide incentives for perspective employees (daycare)
- public relations... encourage employers to support the idea so that they see the benefits and run the program on a no-government-involvement basis...

analyze features, pros/cons of each solution
make recommendations (this may be a combination of the potential solutions)
implement solution
evaluate solution based on criteria

See Worksheet 1 on page 154

- Based on your research, what was this President's perspective on the powers of the president as expressed in the constitution?
- From the perspective assigned by your teacher (social, political, or economic) discuss historical evidence that illustrates this President's beliefs. Give the situation, the President's response and the effect on American history.
- Did this President extend the "powers of the presidency" in any way? If so, how? What has been the result?

Some sample questions/issues for the students to prepare, and the teacher to use to prompt interaction, during the roundtable discussions.

Economic:
- Explain the economic conditions of your times, and the major influences on the economy.
- What were your ideas on the economy?
- What actions did you take to improve the economic situation for the citizens and business and industry?

Powers of the President: A Study in Presidential Decision Making

By Bob Berkowitz, John DonVito

Individual Worksheet #1

Name: _____

President: _____

Directions: Answer the following questions about your assigned president.

1. List the Constitutional Powers of the President:	
2. Based on your research, what was this President's perspective on the powers of the president as expressed in the constitution?	
3. From the perspective assigned by your teacher (social, political, or economic) discuss historical evidence that illustrates this President's beliefs. Give the situation, the president's response and the effect on American history.	
4. Did this President extend the "powers of the presidency" in any way? If so, how? What has been the result?	

- What was the impact of your economic policies?

Political:

- Explain the political issues and concerns of the times.
- What was your point of view on these issues?
- For each of these issues, what actions did you take to and what was their impact?

Social:

- Explain the social conditions of the times.
- What were your priorities with regard to social issues and concerns?
- What policies and/or laws were implemented during your presidency that improved the social condition for Americans?
- In what ways were the peoples' social conditions improved and what was the effect?

Foreign Policy

- What were the major foreign affairs issues of the time?
- What was your philosophy toward foreign policy?
- How did you implement your philosophy?
- What was the impact of your foreign affairs policy?

Historical Background

Jerindon is a small democratic republic in the Western Hemisphere. Its basic resources include small amounts of oil, good farmland, large deposits of coal, iron and copper ore. Its geography includes warm water ports, and river that connects its major cities. However, much of Jerindon has remote and mountainous areas. Its population, which lives in both city and rural settings, is culturally diverse. The diversity includes both ethnic and religious groups.

Jerindon is a country in turmoil. It has a variety of social, political and economic problems. Throughout the country there is a growing population of dissatisfied citizens who feel that their human rights are restricted because of their lack of education, and unequal employment opportunities. For example, the remote Northeast Region is the richest natural resources area in the country. Despite that fact, the citizens have the lowest standard of living per capita. The people in this region are hard working people, however, they are poorly educated and lack the range of social resources to which the urban population has access. Such resources include hospitals, schools, newspapers, doctors, dentists, and other social service agencies. They are a proud, hardy people, who have little hope for advancement or change.

The country includes a growing faction of discontented citizens who are highly conservative, religiously minded and believe in the supremacy of individual rights. The most outspoken members of this group are located in the Southwest region. These people are often farmers, militant, and outspoken. Known as Revisionists, this group is fast becoming a powerful base for anti-government sentiment.

Donaragus is the country that borders Jerindon on the west. A violent civil war is being fought in Donaragus. A significant portion of Donaragus's citizens want to overthrow the military government because they feel it is not responsive to their social and economic needs. Donaragus's economy is based on manufacturing and textile production. Its main export is textiles. Donaragus sells about 90% of the clothes worn by the citizens of Jerindon. In the last 4 years they have increased their prices by 25%. Jerindon sells large amounts of steel to Donaragus and provides 90% of its heating oil. Jerindon's citizens are upset that the price of clothes continually increases while their wages remain steady. Additionally, Donaragus provides Jerindon with most of its farm equipment and spare parts. Because of the civil war, shipments of farm equipment to Jerindon have decreased 20% each month for the last 6 months. Much of Jerindon's equipment is breaking down and in need of spare parts or replacement.

This is an election year, and the President of Jerindon must make important policy decisions that will increase his popularity, and have a positive impact on the citizens of his country. He also wants to ensure reelection.

Assume that the US President you have been learning about is the president of Jerindon. Use the historical information presented, what you know about the powers of the president in a democratic republic, and the research you did regarding how the US President you were assigned interpreted and used those powers, to prepare a written reaction to each of the following

Social Issue

1. All of Jerindon's citizens expect a basic standard of life guaranteed by the government. What actions, if any, should the president take in response to this expectation?

Political Issue

2. Do citizens' rights take precedence over the rights and responsibilities of the government? How should the president of Jerindon respond to the political needs of the citizens, and how can he justify his actions.

Economic Issue

3. The citizens of Jerindon believe that it is the obligation of the government to ensure a free market economy and to provide economic security to all citizens. What should the president of Jerindon do to address this fundamental belief, given its economic relationship to Donaragus?

Foreign Affairs Issues

4. Under what conditions should Jerindon get involved in Donaragus's internal affairs. What foreign policies or actions would the president of Jerindon take, knowing that there will be costs in terms of men and machines and money?

Key Terms:

Social: Presidents perspective on the relationship between the federal government and people.

Political: Presidents perspective on the relationship between the federal government, the state government, and foreign governments.

Economic: Presidents perspective on how the federal government spends money in relation to Social, Political and Foreign Affairs issues.

Foreign Policy: Presidents perspective on the relationship between the federal government and Foreign Countries.

Worksheet #2

Student worksheet

Situation:

The country is concerned about the large unemployment rate among citizens ages 18-23 who do not attend college, other post-secondary training, or go into the military. During his campaign the President promised that he would lower the unemployment rate, and raise the rate of 18-23 year olds who go to work at job sites that pay above minimum wage and provide technology training. The President is committed to this promise. Using the decision-making process, outline a solution that the President might recommend to congress so he can turn his promise into action.

The 6 BIG™

CHAPTER 11

Higher Education

The Big6 at La Salle University

vE2, no2

Bernetta Robinson Doane, library instruction librarian, and Martha Lyle, faculty coordinator for La Salle University (Philadelphia, PA) developed an information literacy information session "Introduction to Computing" course. They collaborated to prepare this program as a result of a recommendation from the Middle States Commission on Higher Education. Their first goal was to conduct an information session at the beginning of August 2000 (Big6 #1) and already the beginning of July was fast approaching. Bernetta and Martha quickly reviewed articles and Web sites about information literacy (Big6 #2). They decided that elementary and secondary schools had the most logical presentations using the Big6 problem-solving model. Therefore, they started to develop six modules plus an introduction to information literacy for their August faculty presentation.

The Big6 modules are summarized in the faculty presentation and may be viewed at http://www.lasalle.edu/library/BigSix. To create the presentation, Doane and Lyle started with ideas and handouts they had already developed for library classes (Big6 #4). For example, Doane had already developed a short handout called CARDS Click Library Research Guides. The CARDS (http://alpha.lasalle.edu/library/) method is a mnemonic to help students identify and determine the appropriateness and validity of information resources. C-A-R-D-S uses 5 (five) basic criteria: 1. Credibility, 2. Accuracy, 3. Relevancy, 4. Dates, and 5. Sources. These criteria describe what to look for when evaluating reference and Web publications. The CARDS criteria fit perfectly into the final Evaluation section of the Big6. Doane and Lyles had also created illustrations of the differences between a proprietary database and popular Web search engines. These were incorporated in the Location & Access (Big6 #3) section of the presentation module.

Doane and Lyles only stumbling block was to learn Microsoft PowerPoint quickly to engage the attention of the computer science faculty (Big6 #5). The Instructional Media Coordinator came to their rescue by critiquing the slides (Big6 #6). After a few small changes, they overwhelmed the faculty with their PowerPoint and Information Literacy knowledge.

The original faculty presentation has been modified to use with library instruction classes, special groups on campus, and other faculty groups. The Big6 presentation is versatile and adapts to almost every type of lecture offered.

The components of the Big6 step-by-step approach helped the librarians to successfully incorporate the use of teaching strategies associated with problem-based learning and information problem-solving techniques.

The Big6 Graduates — on to College

By Ru Story-Huffman / vE2, no2

*I*nformation literacy is alive and well in higher education. Academic faculty—including librarians—are exhibiting an increased awareness of the information literacy movement and its importance. Numerous books, journal articles, conference programs and grassroots movements are in place to spread the information literacy concept through college and university campuses. Academic administrators, teaching faculty and librarians are working to extend the information literacy skills that are currently being taught in numerous elementary and secondary schools in our country. The Big6™, as one of the premier information literacy models, is a natural tool for use in higher education as well as in K-12 settings.

Information Literacy Organizations

Two key organizations are deeply involved with developing understandings and promoting information literacy in higher education: the Association of College and Research Libraries and the National Forum on Information Literacy.

- The Association of College and Research Libraries (ACRL)

  The Association of College and Research Libraries (ACRL), a division of the American Library Association, recently adopted "Information Literacy Competency Standards for Higher Education." (http://www.ala.org/ala/acrl/acrlstandards/informationliteracycompetency. htm) Information Literacy, as defined by the ACRL document, is based on the 1989 definition of the American Library Association Task for Information Literacy:

    > "a set of abilities requiring individuals to recognize when information is needed and have the ability to locate, evaluate, and use effectively the needed information." (ALA, 1998)

  These skills will help lead students to succeed in college and ultimately in their chosen careers. ACRL developed five well-articulated standards that are very close conceptually to the Big6.

- The National Forum for Information Literacy (NFIL)

  The National Forum for Information Literacy (NFIL) (http://www.infolit.org/) is an organization that actively promotes information literacy in higher education. An initiative of the American Library Association's Presidential Committee on Information Literacy, The National Forum on Information Literacy was established in 1990. The NFIL encourages other governing bodies to institute information literacy guidelines into college curriculum. It also works with teacher education programs in United States colleges and universities to ensure that pre-service teachers learn the concept of information literacy so that they are able to incorporate information literacy into their classrooms. Additionally, the NFIL works with various academic accrediting agencies to ensure the inclusion of information literacy in the accreditation process. For example, the Southern Association of Colleges and Schools and the Middle States Association of Colleges and Schools both have clauses in their accreditation procedures that address the topic of information literacy.

When preparing for an accreditation review, a college participates in numerous activities, including self-studies, committee work and the actual accreditation visit. The academic library and librarians are usually heavily involved in the accreditation process for the campus as a whole and most especially in the presentation and evaluation of information literacy criteria. Successful implementation of the criteria required for information literacy will aid in the overall accreditation process.

Information Literacy in Higher Education

Many models of teaching information literacy in higher education have been adopted and are used. "Bibliographic instruction" or "library instruction" are two terms that are used in the academic library world to indicate instruction of the location, use, and evaluation of information and library resources. Often each freshman student is required to attend some type of library instruction session. Sometimes this will be basic information about how to use library databases, location of materials in the library and library policy for use of books and journals. Some colleges and universities envision their libraries as "teaching libraries." That is, these institutions accept that one of the primary goals of the library is to instruct students in obtaining the necessary skills to accomplish information literacy goals. Colleges will often have a selected set of courses that are taken which may include such concepts as identifying information, defining research needs, formulating search strategies, selecting appropriate information tools, evaluating the quality of information, and organizing information. At many colleges and universities students must take a course and demonstrate a mastery of information literacy skills in order to meet graduation requirements.

A move is afoot to collaborate with the faculty to incorporate information literacy initiatives into existing curriculum and everyday instruction. This pedagogical activity may include team teaching of the course in which information literacy skills are a vital aspect of the research and learning process. With student-centered learning, problem-solving skills are utilized and fostered. Working with other faculty, academic librarians can be at the forefront of the movement to instill the skills to successfully find, evaluate, use, and synthesize information.

The Big6™ in Higher Education

One of the goals of the information literacy movement, and college in general, is to develop lifelong learners who will go into the world, establish themselves in their chosen careers, and prosper emotionally, personally, and professionally. The attributes of successful lifelong learners include critical thinking, reasoning, logic and independent learning. In developing these attributes, many college professors go beyond the "traditional" classroom to present their students with real-life situations. In addition, students are often required to complete a field experience in their major concentration of study as a requirement for graduation. Having the ability to investigate, evaluate, synthesize and use information adds to the potential success of college graduates.

Working with faculty to incorporate information literacy into everyday lectures, assignments and research activities is a natural extension of the Big6 in an academic setting. This also expands the scope of instruction beyond the traditional resource-based approach of bibliographic or library instruction to the full information problem-solving process. Librarians are becoming more pro-active, taking the responsibility to plan and conduct faculty workshops to instruct and facilitate information literacy on campus. A librarian can use the Big6 model as a method for instructing faculty, who can then incorporate the Big6 into their coursework. In addition, the Big6 is designed so that each separate stage can be broken into numerous components for instruction purposes. The Big6 serves as a model for leading faculty down the information literacy highway by providing the instructor with the steps necessary for successful implementation.

Selected Examples of the Big6™ in Action in Higher Education

- **La Salle University:** Bernetta Robinson Doane, Reference Librarian/Coordinator of Library Instruction at Connelly Library, La Salle University, states, "I'm a big fan of the Big6™ and have been using it in our library instruction program here at La Salle University for the past year…I like to use all the steps of the Big6™ model because it clearly outlines a problem-solving technique. I found this to be very important in promoting the concept of information literacy on my campus." Ms. Doane and her collaborator, Martha Lyle, have used the Big6 as a model for working with faculty to establish information literacy components within the curriculum. Presentations developed by Doane and Lyle may be viewed at http://www.lasalle.edu/library/BigSix.

- **University of Denver Library:** The University of Denver Library and Information Services Program uses the Big6 as a model for their online information literacy tutorial. Marcy Phelps, the designer of the tutorial offered by the Penrose Library details her choice of the Big6 in "Designing Web-Based Library Instruction for Adult Learners," an article published in Colorado Libraries. She states "because of its emphasis on process, the Big6 approach can be used with any information problem or decision-making situation and is applicable across grade levels and throughout life. For this reason, I based the tutorial on the Big6, using six modules, one for each of the Big6 skills." (Phelps, p. 19). Visit the Penrose Library Information Literacy (http://www.du.edu/~miclark/tutorial/) Web site to view the tutorial.

- **Kenyon College:** Janet Cottrell, Director of Information Access at Kenyon College (Gambier, Ohio) offers a unique approach to using the Big6 in higher education. Cottrell used the Big6 stages to assess the different type of reference questions that were presented at the reference desk in an academic environment. Rather than analyzing reference questions "using traditional categorization techniques," Ms. Cottrell decided to look at the questions and see if the reference questions in a "mid-sized University's reference desk fit gracefully into a specific Information Problem-Solving Model" (Cottrell). In addition to assessment information, Cottrell, notes that the use of the Big6 affected her approach to reference, and that the Big6 model helped with "nearly every question that presented itself, just because it provided a combination of checklist and guide" (Cottrell). Cottrell's use of the Big6 to categorize reference questions will be detailed in "Applying an Information Problem-Solving Model to Academic Reference Work: Findings and Implications" by Janet R. Cottrell and Michael B. Eisenberg in the July 2001 issue of College & Research Libraries.

- **Cumberland College:** Another initiative, a work in progress, is the one developed for use at Cumberland College, where the author is a faculty member serving as Public Services Librarian. Cumberland College is a small, private liberal arts college located in the foothills of the Kentucky Appalachian Mountains. The college serves a traditional student body, with a small percentage of non-traditional undergraduates and graduate students. As part of the Information Literacy initiative at Cumberland College, the author developed a tutorial that is based on the principles of the Big6 model of information literacy. At this time, the college does not have a "set" campus wide information literacy component, but due to the author's interest in the area, she developed a tutorial for use with students. The author tailored each of the Big6 stages to the academic setting at Cumberland College. The tutorial provides specific information such as databases to use to locate information, location of materials, organization of materials, etc. It is hoped that through exposure to the tutorial, students will hone their research skills and become more information literate. The tutorial will be used in all future library instruction sessions that are presented to classes. As a result, students will be exposed to information literacy and the way it aids in their research in addition to basic instruction on database use, the library homepage, Internet searching techniques, web page evaluation and subject specific Internet sites.

Conclusion

Though many are still not aware of it, information literacy is a vital component of our everyday lives. Without the ability to seek information, we may be at a loss in simple situations. Decision-making can become easier, problems and solutions may become more apparent and the ability to understand, use, and locate information will be more important each day. In our world, information is available 24 hours a day, 7 days a week, 365 days a year. As we educate our young students to enter the world of work, and the world in general, we need to provide them with the skills to successfully use information. As educators, we are charged with the development of critical thinking, information seeking skills and lifelong learning. College should be the time when students are exposed to the world beyond what they have already experienced, and this includes the information that is available at every turn we take. Understanding the necessary components to develop and deliver a successful information literacy experience is a vital aspect of the work being done by librarians and other faculty.

Designed as a model to teach information and technology skills in the K-12 environment, the Big6™ has proven to be adaptable, innovative and useful in a variety of educational situations. In higher education, the Big6™ can be a natural and vital component of a successful college experience. It allows all involved in the information seeking process; students, librarians and teaching faculty, to fully experience the wonders of information.

References

American Library Association Presidential Committee on Information Literacy. (1989). *Final report*. Chicago: Author.

Association of College and Research Libraries. Information literacy competency standards for higher education. ACRL, 2000. (http://www.ala.org/ala/acrl/acrlstandards/informationliteracycompetency.htm)

[On-line]. (Current May 8, 2001) Cottrell, J. (personal communication, April 12, 2001)

Doane, B. (undated). Big Six presentations. [On-line]. (http://alpha.lasalle.edu/library/BigSix/)

Penrose Library Information Literacy Tutorial, Penrose Library, University of Denver, Denver, Colorado. [On-line]. (http://www.du.edu/~miclark/tutorial/)

Phelps, M. (2000) Designing web-based library instruction for adult learners. *Colorado Libraries*, 26, 19-20.

Big6™ Presentations

Connelly Library, La Salle University, Philadelphia, Pennsylvania
http://www.lasalle.edu/library/BigSix

Information Literacy with the Big6™: Cumberland College

Hagan Memorial Library, Cumberland College, Williamsburg, Kentucky
http://www.cumber.edu/library/Li/infolit.htm

Information Literacy Organizations:
A Selected Webliography and Bibliography

Links:

- Information Literacy in Higher Education – A Selected Bibliography An ongoing process, this is the author's webliography of useful web pages, books and journal articles on information literacy. Many of the links in this webliography are included.

- Institute for Information Literacy. (http://www.ala.org/ACRLTemplate.cfm?Section=ACRLs_Institute_for_Information_Literacy) An initiative of the American Library Association and Association for College and Research Libraries, this site is dedicated to preparing librarians to be effective in the teaching of information literacy and as a support location for information.

- ACRL Information Literacy. Maintained by the Association of College and Research Libraries, the web page offers a listing of useful materials on the subject for academic librarians.

- Best Practices and Assessment of Information Literacy Programs. (http://www.earlham.edu/~libr/Plan.htm) From the Institute for Information Literacy, one of the goals of The Best Practices is to identify criteria for academic information literacy programs and current benchmark programs.

- Christine Bruce: Information Literacy. Christine Bruce's Ph.D. dissertation was one of the first to address the topic of information literacy. Her main interests on the subject are information literacy theory and practice.

- Directory of Online Resources for Information Literacy (DORIL). (http://www.lib.usf.edu/ref/doril/) Maintained by the University of South Florida School of Library and Information Science, DORIL is a useful gathering of definitions, bibliographies, conferences and information literacy programs.

- National Forum on Information Literacy. (www.inforlit.org) An initiative of the American Library Association, the National Forum works to increase awareness of information literacy and helps to establish information literacy competency guidelines.

- Assessment of Information Literacy: Lessons from the Higher Education Assessment Movement. (http://www.ala.org/ala/acrl/acrlevents/acrls8thnational.htm) All educators understand the concept of "assessment," and this paper addresses assessment of information literacy in higher education.

- Information Literacy as a Liberal Art. http://www.educause.edu/pub/er/review/reviewarticles/31231.html Considered by the author as a benchmark in the information literacy literature, this article was published in 1996. A good introduction to the practice, theory and need for information literacy in higher education.

- Integrating Information Literacy into the Curriculum. An excellent article that can be used to evaluate information literacy programs in an academic setting, that can be adapted to all levels of education. Includes an "Information Literacy IQ Test."

- Information Literacy Sites – College and Research Libraries News. http://www.ala.org/ala/acrl/acrlpubs/crlnews/internetresources.htm The electronic version of an article first published in "College and Research Libraries News," February 1990, Vol. 60, No. 2.

Publications:

Breivik, P. S. (1988). *Student learning in the information age.* Oryx Press.

Bruce, C. (1997). *The Seven faces of information literacy.* Auslib Press.

Iannuzzi, P. (1999). *Teaching information literacy skills.* Ally and Bacon.

Grassian, E., Kaplowitz, J. (2001). *Information literacy instruction, theory and practice.* Neal-Schuman.

Jacobson, T. and Gatti, T. H., (Eds.). (2001). *Teaching information literacy concepts: Activities and frameworks from the field.* Library Instruction Publications.

Ryan, J. L. (2001). *Information literacy toolkit.* American Library Association.

Snavely, L., and Cooper, N. (1997). "The Information literacy debate." *Journal of Academic Librarianship*, 23, 9-14.

Sonntag, G. (1996). "The Development of a lower-division, general education, course-integrated information literacy program." *College and Research Libraries*, 57, 331-338.

Spitzer, K., with Eisenberg, M.B. and Lowe, C. (1998). *Information literacy: Essential skills for the information age.* ERIC Clearinghouse on Information & Technology, Syracuse University.

Young, R. M. (1999). *Working with faculty to design undergraduate information literacy programs.* Neal-Schuman.

Using the Big6 in a University Writing Course: A Collaborative Teaching Experience

By Abby Kasowitz-Scheer / vE4, no1

Introduction

Academic libraries today play an important role in teaching students to use information resources effectively and responsibly. As is true in K-12 education, information literacy instruction is most effective when taught and learned in context with course and curriculum goals. Collaboration between libraries and academic departments is a key component to successful information literacy instruction.

This article discusses a collaborative project between the Syracuse University Library and the Writing Program, using a process based on the Big6 to teach information literacy skills in the context of an actual research assignment. The project illustrates that the Big6 can be successfully adapted to online instruction in a multiple-section course and stresses the importance of carefully aligning information literacy instruction with specific course goals and objectives.

Project Background

The Writing Program at Syracuse University offers a writing studio course (Writing 205) for sophomores enrolled in the College of Arts and Sciences. This course is taught in many sections by teaching assistants and faculty to more than 500 students each year. Writing 205 examines research as critical inquiry and exposes students to the wide range of information available in a variety of formats and presented from multiple perspectives.

The Syracuse University Library has played a role in this course in past semesters, mostly by teaching on-demand, faculty-requested instruction sessions during regularly scheduled class periods. Librarians who have taught these sessions focused on using Library resources, such as the online catalog and databases, often with little knowledge of the students' long-term course projects or research needs. Furthermore, the Library only reached a portion of the students enrolled in the many sections of the course.

In the fall of 2001, the faculty of the Writing Program contacted the Library to discuss a possible solution for teaching research skills to a greater number of students without necessarily requiring all sections to attend formal library instruction sessions. A project team was formed including representatives of the Writing Program faculty, the subject librarian specializing in Writing, and the Library's Head of Instructional Programs. The team decided to develop a Web-based "guide" to instruct students in steps of the research process as well as to point them to resources related to their assignment: an annotated bibliography of resources relating to September 11, 2001 and the war on terrorism.

Project Description

This Web guide, designed by librarians and Writing faculty, was a key component in the second unit of several Spring 2002 Writing 205 courses. (Experienced Writing instructors had the option of creating their own research units if desired.) The content and activities of the Web guide were intended to be used throughout the unit as students worked towards their final project; this differs from the "one-shot" instruction sessions that the Library has traditionally provided, which are sometimes viewed as separate from the "real" work of the course. The librarians on the team presented the Web guide to the Writing instructors at the beginning of the semester.

The Web guide, entitled "9/11 & the War on Terrorism: Questioning, Researching, & Re-questioning" (http://libwww.syr.edu/instruction/tutorials/wrt205/index.htm), was based on the Big6, although language was changed slightly to turn the steps into questions.

The steps of the Big6 provided the basis for the Web guide and the overall unit. The Web guide included introductory information about the site and the information problem-solving process, information and suggestions on each of the steps of the research process (see below), supplemental pages with additional tips and supporting information, downloadable worksheets to allow for hands-on practice opportunities, and a feedback form.

The research process was outlined and presented as follows:

1. What is my task?
(http://libwww.syr.edu/instruction/tutorials/wrt205/index.htm)
The task is defined using a description of the assignment supplied by Writing Program faculty. In order to help students understand the concept of an annotated bibliography, the project team asks students to imagine themselves as interns at the fictional Journal of Complicated Perspectives charged with conducting preliminary research on the topic. They would later present their findings to an editor (their course instructor) in the form of an annotated bibliography and oral presentation. Sample research questions, also provided by faculty, are linked from this page.

2. What do I need to get started?
(http://libwww.syr.edu/instruction/tutorials/wrt205/step2-start.htm)
The project team designed this page to assist students in brainstorming the types of information and resources needed to answer their research questions. The content describing types of information resources was adapted from TILT (Texas Information Literacy Tutorial) http://tilt.lib.utsystem.edu/. This page provides a worksheet to help students record their thoughts during this brainstorming process.

3. How do I find the information?
(http://libwww.syr.edu/instruction/tutorials/wrt205/step3-find.htm)
Subtitled "Ready, Set, Search," this page focuses on search tools (e.g., online catalog and databases) and search terms. A sample resource list (http://libwww.syr.edu/instruction/tutorials/wrt205/resources.htm) is provided to guide students to databases, Web sites, print resources, and multimedia resources to assist students in finding information on September 11 and the war on terrorism. This section of the Web guide also includes worksheets on navigating the online catalog and databases and brainstorming search terms.

4. What do I do with the information?
(http://libwww.syr.edu/instruction/tutorials/wrt205/step4-assess.htm)
This step encourages students to "interact" with the information found in step 3 by assessing their sources and recording key information. This page asks students to record two types of information required for the annotated bibliography assignment: rhetorical elements (i.e., publishing context, audience, point of view, claim, and evidence) and citation information. Worksheets are provided to help students evaluate print and electronic sources and record their notes.

5. How do I complete my task?

(http://libwww.syr.edu/instruction/tutorials/wrt205/step5-create.htm)
Step 5 focuses on incorporating the information found into the final project: the annotated bibliography and oral presentation. This page refers to information recorded in step 4 and provides additional suggestions and examples for composing bibliography entries and citations according to MLA style.

6. How did it go?

(http://libwww.syr.edu/instruction/tutorials/wrt205/step6-evaluate.htm)
This page offers a very short statement on evaluating the project and research process. Students are encouraged to share their reflections with their classmates during their oral presentation.

Evaluation

The library team evaluated the Web guide using a variety of methods: a student evaluation form located in the summary section of the Web guide, an evaluation form for instructors, and informal feedback from instructors collected during a panel discussion at the Writing Program Spring Conference in March 2002.

Overall, the Web guide was considered successful as a way of bringing "the library to the students" (a term offered by one instructor), or providing convenient, easy access to library and Web-based information resources on the students' research topics. It was also considered helpful in preparing students to conduct future research using an information problem-solving approach.

The feedback also indicated several challenges relating to the Web guide and the overall course unit. In general, the Web guide did not always match the individual instructor's goals or teaching styles. Based on the feedback received, the project team may consider the following revisions for future projects:

- **Offer faculty guide with instructions for using Web guide.** It was clear that some instructors did not fully incorporate the Web guide as the project team had intended. For instance, some instructors assigned the worksheets after the students had completed most of their research, making the exercises appear tedious and irrelevant. Although instructors received a brief training session on the Web guide at the beginning of the semester, they may have also benefited from a handbook outlining the goals and intended uses of the Web guide in the context of the unit.

- **Make purpose of Web guide clear to students.** It appeared that some students had expectations of the Web guide that went beyond the original goals. The project team should communicate more clearly that the Web guide is intended to help students understand the research process as well as guide them in searching databases, the library catalog, and the World Wide Web. The team should clarify that the Web guide is not intended to provide specific information on the students' research topics or to teach "computer" or "Internet" skills, as some students expected. Students should also be encouraged to visit the library and speak to librarians when they require help not available on the Web guide.

- **Examine different ways to present content.** Many students indicated that the language used in the Web guide was too immature for the sophomore level. In addition, some felt that the research process was too confining as presented. The project team should consider different levels of skill and experience in the research process and use of library resources.

- **Consider less sensitive research topic.** Some instructors indicated that students had trouble focusing on the research process, because they were too emotionally involved in the topic only months after the September 11 attacks.

A more general recommendation is to have the team explore possibilities for incorporating an information problem-solving model like the Big6 across the Writing curriculum. Students could learn the general research process in the freshman Writing class (Writing 105) and build upon their knowledge in Writing 205 as they explore more advanced skills in writing and rhetorical analysis. While this research unit combined concepts from the Writing curriculum with general research skills, there is much more potential for establishing a comprehensive program of information literacy instruction within the required Writing courses.

Conclusion

This collaborative effort provided an exciting and important opportunity to teach students how information problem-solving can be applied to course assignments. The partnership between the Library and the Writing Program allowed for the sharing of information and expertise in the instructional design stages that led to the development of a research unit strong in both writing and information skills instruction. The librarians on the project team appreciated the opportunity to play a significant role in the design of a two-week unit that impacted hundreds of students.

Learning from the experience and the feedback from students and instructors, the Library hopes to revise the Web guide for future projects with the Writing Program and to work with other academic departments as well. Using the Big6 and other information problem-solving models as a framework, the Library can work with faculty to help prepare students to be successful researchers in any discipline, and ultimately, in all learning opportunities within and beyond the classroom.

The BIG6™

CHAPTER 12

Kids and the Arts

The Big6 and Music

By Ferdi Serim / vE4, no2

Students at EJ Martinez Elementary school, where I teach in Santa Fe, New Mexico, are exploring the world of music by creating, recording, arranging and performing music for a variety of purposes. We are using technology to help us in every aspect of our projects. We are also using the Big6 Information Problem Solving Skills to guide us through the challenges we find along the way. This means we are learning how technology contributes to developing Contemporary Information Literacy Skills (Big6), as well as learning how technology (hardware and software) can help us to create better musical performances.

Until you think about it, you may not see the connection between a process for solving any information based problem and the act of creating music. Musicians, however, recognize that almost every step along the way presents challenging problems that can benefit from a reliable, flexible process, especially one that provides us with a set of tools for approaching these problems. Additionally, musical artists seek to combine music with words and images, using technology to create a combined live/multimedia performance. We will use music we create ourselves, if it is of high enough quality (otherwise, we'll seek permission to use recorded music within the Fair Use copyright guidelines (http://www.musiclibraryassoc.org/Copyright/guidemed.htm)

The Big6 provides us with tools to meet both the Contemporary Literacy and Music Performance challenges. See how each skill reinforces the other.

First, it helps to know what the Big6 skills are:

Big6 Skills		
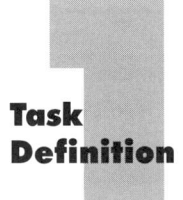**Task Definition**	**Contemporary Literacy Big6 #1 - Task Definition:** What's our goal, and what information do we need to accomplish this goal? Our goal is to create a multimedia presentation that combines music, words and images. We need to know how to digitize and create such a presentation.	**Music Performance Big6 #1 - Task Definition:** What's our goal, and what information do we need to accomplish this goal? Our goal is to create a good recording of a good performance of a good original composition. We need to know how to record, how to play well and what to play (and not to play).
**Information Seeking Strategies**	**Contemporary Literacy Big6 #2 - Information Seeking Strategies:** Determine all possible sources, and select the best source. We searched in the library, record stores, the Internet, personal CD collections, original artwork, and student performances to find appropriate music, words, and images for our multimedia project. We read the software manual and tested a sample program to learn how to create a multimedia presentation.	**Music Performance Big6 #2 - Information Seeking Strategies:** Determine all possible sources, and select the best source. We searched equipment manuals, the Internet, music stores, and interviewed our music teacher. We decided that our music teacher, Mr. Serim, would be the best musical artist and Mr. Serim would be the most available expert with experience to help us record music for our project.
**Location and Access**	**Contemporary Literacy Big6 #3 - Location and Access:** Locate the sources and find the information within the sources. We digitized original artwork from Mr. Towle's third grade class, and selected music that complemented the moods of the abstract art.	**Music Performance Big6 #3 - Location and Access:** Locate the sources and find the information within the sources. The multitrack digital recorder is a real-time database of musical "information" represented in the performances on each sound track. We need to learn how to navigate the hardware and software to store and retrieve our performances (find information within the source).
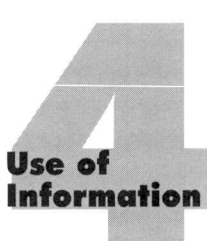**Use of Information**	**Contemporary Literacy Big6 #4 - Use of Information:** Engage (read, hear, view) and extract relevant information. We decided to focus on specific areas of the artwork, and have the images change with the music.	**Music Performance Big6 #4 - Use of Information:** Engage (read, hear, view) and extract relevant information. Since we save every "take" (recording attempt) we need to know which musical "information" is the best for this project, and which musical "information" was not up to our standards, or not relevant for this project.

Synthesis

Contemporary Literacy **Big6 #5 - Synthesis:** Organize the information from multiple sources, and present the result. We selected iMovie as the medium for organizing and presenting our creations. We used a soundtrack from Mr. Serim's "Mirrors, Echoes, Bridges" CD, and used the "Ken Burns" effect to zoom in and out on each student's artwork as the music played.	**Music Performance** **Big6 #5 - Synthesis:** Organize the information from multiple sources, and present the result. Here we combine literacy, artistic and technology skills. We must defend our choices about which performances are best by using music vocabulary, and we must use computers to publish our work on the Web as well as store on videos and CDs.

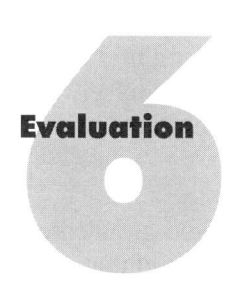

Evaluation

Contemporary Literacy **Big6 #6 - Evaluation:** Judge the result and the process. We were pleased with the results, which included an iMovie of Mr. Towle's third grade students' original artwork, as well as a multimedia accompaniment for Mr. Padilla's fourth grade students' performance of his original story "Orchard Bees" that was read by students, while digitized original artwork was projected as they played an original score.	**Music Performance** **Big6 #6 - Evaluation:** Judge the result and the process. Evaluation is constant - we always must decide whether to try again, or keep the current "take" as our best effort. Students evaluate each other's performance and ultimately decided which compositions would be performed at our Spring Arts Fling on May 2. We are noting along the way tips and traps to make our work easier the next time.

To see how it all fits together, see the EJ Studio Lessons Flowchart. at (http://oii.org/ferdi/EJStudioLessonsFlow.gif)

For more information and context, view the EJ Studio Lessons webpage at http://oii.org/ferdi/EJStudio.html

Big6 Rap Contest

By Sheryl Fullner / vE4, no4

Big6 No. 1 Task Definition

I got to ask
What is my task?
Can I define
What problem's mine?
I'll go online.
I'm gonna shine!
Rock me! Shock me!
Research talk me.

When the ancient librarian hobbled back from the convention dragging two book bags filled with the Big6 and even bigger ideas, it did not bode well for 450 unsuspecting middle school students. Soon a bright purple and orange one-foot by two-foot step exerciser platform had been installed as a stage in the library media center and contest banners were strung from the suspended ceiling.

The first batch of eighth graders found themselves unprepared when their library media specialist Mrs. F. ditched her cane, jumped on the miniscule stage, and growled out six stanzas of rap. Grins, groans and clapping greeted her efforts. She explained that when she was a girl (during colonial times, of course) students memorized a hornbook rap called "In Adam's fall, we sinned all." Mrs. F. was certain that the kids of Nooksack Valley Middle School could top that by writing one rap each week for each of the research strategies of the Big6 Research Model.

The contest wasn't voluntary. No rap=no exit. Mrs. F. read the first tentative efforts with considerable drama. Then kids started jumping up on the platform themselves. Pretty soon there were back-up rappers making strange noises in unison while the M.C. extolled the virtues of information seeking strategies.

Each week a different step of the Big6 Research Model was printed in the daily announcements, reminding the students of the task ahead. Because middle school teachers usually have more subject matter than time, Mrs. F. took advantage of classes with substitutes and wrung the rap out of them in the absence of their teachers. As an incentive, the impecunious Mrs. F. found a mug emblazoned with the school mascot at a thrift shop and filled it with chocolate candy — a rap-contest prize at a bargain.

Soon, the library media center began to show the results of the students' hard work. Mrs. F. decorated the space with the students' rhymes, typed up in fancy fonts and printed on large paper. Bright construction paper was trimmed to photocopier size for great banners. Free glossy book covers from odd companies were reversed to create slick banners.

Immortality began to beckon the budding rap artists. Students performed with the aid of costumes, and video cameras recorded the whole affair. The resulting rap video went on the road to stir up the elementary schools. Let's see, that would bring us to "6.2: Judge the efficiency of the problem solving process." Definitely "A" for Awesome.

Here for your delectation are Mrs. F.'s other five stanzas. She used these as seed posters along with a Big6 and Little12 display, and arranged the kids' raps around the edges.

Big6 #2 Info Seeking Strategies

Where do I look?
Show me the book.
No, wait, I'm cool.
I'll mesmerize
this rockin' school.
The information's here someplace.
I gotta find a database.
Join forces:
Brainstorm sources.
Births, murders and divorces.
Don't forget those primary voices.
Print or online: gobs of choices.

Big6 #3 Location

I don't do reports "off the cuff"
I dig until I've got enough.
I use the index to locate stuff.
My project info's really buff.
A Boolean search is not too tough
As long as I get off my duff.

This brother is able
To read a spine label.
And a catalog card
Is not too hard.
I'm totally stoked to navigate.
I even know that Reference books
don't circulate.

Big6 #4 Use of Info

I'll take some notes,
Jot down some quotes.
Write down which dude
Got all the votes.
Read, hear, touch, view.
I'll cook me up a data stew.
I'll gather facts that are running loose
And squeeze 'em til I've got the juice.

Big6 #5 Synthesis

I'll write a 'zine.
I'll paint a scene.
My facts will hit
The silver screen.
I'll be this town's
Most righteous teen.
Forget obscene.

This brain is lean:
I'm Mr. Clean.
A walking, talking
Problem-solving machine.

Big6 #6 Judge

Don't flap your jaw.
Bring in the law.
Finest work they ever saw.
My product even
Please my Ma.
I did it smooth
And so complete.
My end result
Is really sweet.

Big6 #6 Evaluate

How can I tell
If I've done well?
Is it long enough?
Did I find good stuff?
Is my style animated?
Are my facts gold-plated?
If the answer's YO,
Then I've evaluated.

Choreography Assignment: Dance II (Grades 7-12)

By Cindy Powell-Skelley and Julie Webb / vE4, no2

Based on information from the book:*We Interrupt this Broadcast* By Joe Garner, Foreword by Walter Kronkite, CD Narrated by Bill Kurtis (http://www.amazon.com/exec/obidos/ASIN/1570719748/qid%3D1056047812/ sr%3D2-1/ref%3Dsr%5F2%5F1/102-7442825-8995312)

Overview

This instructional unit provides dance students with the opportunity to tie the creativity of movement to factual, historical, "events that stopped our lives." Through instruction, library research, collaboration and rehearsal, students analyze and interpret a variety of reactions to these major historical events and translate those reactions to dance movements. Historical events are taken from the book *We Interrupt this Broadcast* which focuses on major historical world events that have warranted an "interruption" of regular programming on radio or television. CD's that play the original broadcast of the event accompanies the text. Students present their dance/movement to the actual broadcasts from these CD's.

Subject Area Objectives

1. Students will choreograph a dance/movement using social, historical or literary themes.

2. Students will analyze choreography.

3. Students will demonstrate knowledge of movement, improvisation skills and choreographic form.

4. Students will utilize elements of dance in their movement and their paper.

5. Students will defend their choice of movement in a written piece.

6. Students will learn to identify and analyze primary sources to gain ideas for movement choices.

Scoring Guide for Analysis Paper

Analyze your Dance Movement and Defend your Position

The following information should be included in your paper:

1. Description of the project

2. Description of the movement (use dance terminology)

3. What are you trying to say through your movement?

4. Is your meaning literal or conceptual? Describe why you made this choice.

5. How did your movement represent the person in your primary source? Describe the person's feelings.

6. Defend your choice of movement in your representation.

7. How did your movement fit with the movement of the other people in your group? Did you discuss one style of choreography over another?

8. In what way would you improve your movement if given the opportunity?

Correct grammar
Correct spelling
Variety in sentence structure
Transitions to help paper flow
Vivid adjectives and color words
Clear purpose

Big6 Objectives

Task Definition: Students will be able to accurately, in their own words, explain the assignment and the desired outcomes. They will also be able to identify what information needs they have based on the assignment.

Information Seeking Strategies: Students need instruction about what primary sources are and where they may be found. Videos, magazines, newspaper articles, books, websites etc… potentially contain information that might be helpful. Students must be able to locate primary documents by using a variety of search strategies involving the Internet, the vertical file, the card catalog.

Location and Access: The school library is the primary location for information, but family members with first hand experience would be helpful.

Use of Information: Once materials have been located, students must compare the reactions of the different authors, analyze the range of emotions and interpret those emotions as they apply to dance movements. They must also document their resources.

Synthesis: Students, in groups, will draw from the information gathered during their research to create a dance that interprets the emotions felt as America learned of the tragedies or celebrations that make up our history. Students must also create a paper that explains and defends the choices they made regarding their movements. Documentation of primary sources used is also required.

Evaluation: The dances will be videotaped so students can reflect upon their work. Part of the reflection will include whether or not the information they found in their primary sources was helpful, or if they needed "better" information. Their papers will also be evaluated to see if they were effective in explaining and defending their choices of movement, and citing their sources.

Activities

1. Choose an event from the book *We Interrupt this Broadcast* and read about it.

2. Present Big6 (librarian) and discuss documentation.

3. Have each individual (in the library) find a primary source that explains one person's feelings or views about the historical event.

4. Share primary resources with group members.

5. Groups listen to the actual broadcast and make notes, comparing what they found in their primary resources to what is being broadcast.

6. Based on prior instruction in dance class, begin planning movement according to emotions and facts taken from the broadcast and primary documents.

7. Write paper analyzing and defending movements. Include documentation.

8. Perform for the class while being videotaped for evaluation.

Products

1. A dance reflecting the feelings of the American people during a given historical event.

2. A paper analyzing and defending your choice of movement for your dance.

3. Documentation to show your use of resources.

Instructional Sequence

Day 1

A. Students are introduced to the Broadcast project, including review of notes on lyrical, geometric, jazz and comical choreography.

B. Librarian presents Big6, discusses primary resources, use of information and documentation.

C. Students (in groups)* choose topics from the book and begin research in the library.

Day 2

A. Review project criteria

B. Continue research in the library, take notes and begin choreography paper

C. Return to the theatre to share primary documents

Day 3

A. Groups begin choreography

B. Warm up

C. Move, creating "Broadcast" movement/dance

Day 4

A. Students share analysis of movement papers

B. Discuss movement with their group

C. Rehearse

D. Finalize dance/movement project

Day 5

A. Warm up

B. Rehearse with groups and prepare to present

Grouping

In order to differentiate, grouping students is very important. Gifted students can be grouped in a variety of ways. Because this assignment incorporates history and writing as well as dance, students that are gifted in dance can be paired with students that are gifted in history or writing. They can also be grouped according to ability. Because of the broad scope of the assignment, students at all levels should be able to succeed.

Reflection/Adjustments

Quality of primary resources is vital to the success of the assignment. Students overwhelmingly agreed that if they did not have a good primary source, they struggled with the assignment. It is important for the librarian to determine what materials are available before students make their choices.

■ Big6 Step #2 Information Seeking Strategies was particularly helpful because students were not sure where to go to get primary documents and did not know what was available.

■ Depending on the size and personality of the class, 1 day in the library may not be enough time to find and compare resources.

■ Students expressed that an example would have been helpful. Because dancing to words is different than dancing to music, they were forced out of their comfort zone and would have liked to see an example.

■ Students commented on the importance of grouping. One student stated that it is important to group students based on individual talents and ability to move. Each member of the group is able to bring something different to the dance.

We Interrupt this Broadcast Movement Evaluation

_____ Movement demonstrates emotions from primary source (20 points)

_____ Movement demonstrates force (20 points)

_____ Dancers demonstrate effective use of space (20 points)

_____ Dancers demonstrate effective use of time (20 points)

_____ Dancers demonstrate teamwork (20 points)

Total _____ 100 points

Super3 and Costume Planning Tips! (Grades K-2)

By Michelle S. Wurster, Susann L. Wurster
From the Big6 website: www.big6.com

#1 - Plan:

What (or who) would you like to be for a costume party?
Make a list of choices.
Choose your favorite character!

#2 - Do:

Draw a picture of yourself dressed in your costume.
Ask a grown up to help you make or buy your costume.
Wear your costume for fun!

#3 - Review:

How did your costume work out?
Were you happy with your costume?
Was it fun to be that character?

Instructor's Guide: Super3 and Costume Planning Tips!
By Susann L. Wurster

Let's dress up! Great idea! What will I be this year?

Your students are making decisions about their costumes! Use this unique moment to introduce the Super3 Plan-Do-Review concepts in a real-life situation—costume planning.

The Super3 process can help students make creative decisions about what to wear for costume party fun. Use the following prompts to ask your students to think about their costume ideas:

#1 - Plan:

What (or who) would you like to be for the costume party?
Make a list of choices.
Choose your favorite character!

#2 - Do:

Draw a picture of yourself dressed in your costume.
Ask a grown up to help you make or buy your costume.
Wear your costume for fun!

#3 - Review:

Did your costume work out?
Were you happy with your costume?
Was it fun to be that character?

The**6**BIG

CHAPTER 13

Special Education

The Big6 and Special Needs Students:
My Personal Experience

By Laura Robinson / vE4, no3

C hildren with special needs often have difficulty completing class work and school
assignments, particularly complex assignments such as book reports, science projects
and end of the unit projects. These tasks that may appear "easy" for some students can be
overwhelming and challenging for special needs children. This is true because the directions
are often hard to process and the specific steps are hard to break down. Special needs
students often have trouble understanding the specific assignment requirements and what is
expected of them. In addition, these children can experience difficulty with the
organizational skills required to complete a large assignment. From a Big6 perspective, the
problem is clear: these students need help with Task Definition, Big6 #1. The remainder of
this article shares some of my personal experiences of using the Big6 with special needs
students. In a future issue, I will offer a more detailed explanation of the scope of special
education and how the Big6 can make a positive difference.

The Big6™: A Special Needs Perspective

As a special education resource room teacher of fourth and fifth grade children, I see too
many students give up, become discouraged and frustrated, and appear unenthusiastic about
their work. I have tried different methods of helping these children, such as outlining the
assignment for them, working on one piece of the assignment at a time, even reducing the
assignment requirements. These strategies still presented my students with difficulties. Despite
these modifications, the students became uninterested in the work, confused about the task,
and unmotivated to complete the assignment. Clearly, I needed my students to take ownership
of their learning and to become motivated and excited about their work and learning.

The Big6 helped me to do this with my students. The same students who once showed
little interest in producing quality work are now eager to undertake a project, can create a
dazzling science project or compose an amazing book report, all while feeling confident and

positive about themselves as learners! My students love taking ownership of their learning and use Big6 #2 Information Seeking Strategies to determine what resources they need to get the job done, and Big6 #3 Location and Access to find those resources and the information within the resources. This helped to build confidence and allowed my students to realize that they CAN do the work and complete the assignment…with a little help from the Big6! With Big6 #4 Use of Information, and #5 Synthesis, the children were a direct part of their learning as they used the appropriate resources to complete the actual task.

Using The Big6™ with Special Needs Students

How did I achieve such success with The Big6? To begin with, I was energized and animated as I introduced my students to the world of Big6. I was extremely excited and enthusiastic when we embarked on the journey of learning the Big6 Skills. My students picked up on this and in turn, became excited themselves. The children and I first learned the Big6 #1 Task Definition and the individual steps of the process. We went through each step with real life situations over and over until the kids were confident and comfortable with the Big6. As one child said, "We Big 6-ed inside and out. We breathed the Big6."

For example, using The Big6, we problem solved situations that were meaningful and relevant to each child's life: what to buy your best friend for her birthday, what movie to see, what to do over the summer. With my help, the students went through each step of the Big6 to solve the problem. The students loved doing this! Each child made a Big6 reference guide "cheat sheet" for their folders with the steps outlined on it. They gave presentations on the Big6 to the younger students and to their parents and sang the Big6 song at a school-wide assembly. Moreover, my students became responsible for their learning and were an active part of the learning process. Therefore, they became excited and motivated to use the Big6 in a curricular context.

Show me the Big6 song! See page 185.

After a few weeks, I decided to try using the Big6 with school assignments. I spent a few class hours showing the students how the Big6 can help with school work. We talked about this and I did an example project for the children using the Big6. My kids were surprised to see that they could manage their assignments, complete the work, and feel good about themselves while using the Big6. This changed the dynamics of our special education program. The children were able to complete the same assignments as their classmates just by using the Big6 Skills. Big6 # 6, Evaluation, helped my students to reflect on their work and the process of completing the project. They were able to reflect on what worked, what didn't work, and what they would change in the future. In this way, I know that The Big6 will help them achieve ever-greater success in school.

When working with students with special needs, it is important to remember that these children learn differently. It is often difficult for these children to organize and plan their work, understand directions, and complete tasks. The Big6 allows my students to stay organized, take control of their work, and complete classroom tasks in an orderly and easy to understand manner. We now use the Big6 every time a classroom teacher assigns a book report, project, or lengthy assignment. The students come into the resource room and know that it is "time to Big6!"

Big 6 Song!

Words by Barbara A. Jansen
(Sung to the tune of B-I-N-G-O)

There is a process I can use and Big6 is its name-o

B-I-G S-I-X, B-I-G S-I-X, B-I-G S-I-X,
And Big6 is its name-o.

Big6 One will help me find out just what I should do-o.

B-I-G S-I-X, B-I-G S-I-X, B-I-G S-I-X,
And Big6 is its name-o.

Big6 Two will help me choose those things that I should use-o.

B-I-G S-I-X, B-I-G S-I-X, B-I-G S-I-X,
And Big6 is its name-o.

Big6 Three will help me get those things that I will need-o.

B-I-G S-I-X, B-I-G S-I-X, B-I-G S-I-X,
And Big6 is its name-o.

Big6 Four helps me to take out words that I can use-o.

B-I-G S-I-X, B-I-G S-I-X, B-I-G S-I-X,
And Big6 is its name-o.

Big6 Five helps me finish the work that I must do-o.

B-I-G S-I-X, B-I-G S-I-X, B-I-G S-I-X,
And Big6 is its name-o.

Big6 Six helps me to know if I did my best work-o.

B-I-G S-I-X, B-I-G S-I-X, B-I-G S-I-X,
And Big6 is its name-o.

Special Education and The Big6

By Laura Robinson / vE5, no1

As a special education teacher of upper elementary students, I have first hand experience using the Big6 skills with students with special needs. These children often experience difficulty with basic school skills: completing homework and assignments, learning new content material, remembering important facts and information, preparing for tests, and carrying out research projects and reports. These tasks that are often "easy" for some students can present quite a challenge for children with basic learning disabilities. This is where the Big6 comes in. The Big6 allows students to learn and remember new material, complete school and homework assignments, and prepare for tests in a systematic, efficient, and orderly manner. This article will discuss each Big6 stage and how the Big6 is a valuable tool when teaching students with special needs.

Big6 #1, **Task Definition**, allows children to define their specific schoolwork and assignments. It helps them to identify the work requirements and to determine what information is needed in order to complete each task. This stage is particularly helpful when my students have to complete a research project, book report, or prepare for a test. We always use Big6 #1 to define the task and organize the assignment requirements. When students receive an assignment or project, we first talk through it and then they individually restate the task in one or two sentences. In addition, students are instructed to reflect on the task and answer the following questions:

- What is the task or assignment?

- What do I need to do to complete the assignment?

- What is my job in the assignment?

From answering these questions and reflecting on the task, children will gain a deep understanding of the assignment and will know what is expected of them, helping them to meet success. By using Big6 #1, the children are able to outline the assignment requirements in an orderly and logical manner. This is crucial for students with special needs!

Let's look at **Big6 #2, Information Seeking Strategies**. After making sure that the students know what they have to do and what is required for the assignment, we need to help them to determine where they can get the resources that they need in order to complete the assignment. Big6 #2 allows students to brainstorm, evaluate, and select the best resources for the job at hand, again, by a systematic approach. We often do this as a whole group activity, brainstorming and creating a large web or map of the possible resources that will help with the assignment. For example, when working with fourth grade students who are required to write a report on a country, we brainstorm where we can get information about each country. The students all share their ideas and we create a list of resources to use ranging from the Internet, encyclopedias, National Geographic and travel magazines, books from the library, travel agents, and actual people from their chosen country. From this list, each child selected the resources that worked best for them and began to gather information about their country. Each child was organized, accurate in their research, and efficient at gaining information. By engaging in Big6 #2, my students are able to recognize that information can be gathered from many sources—a skill that will help them throughout life.

Location and Access, Big6 #3, helps children to actually locate the sources and find the information within the sources. Children with special needs may have trouble with finding and organizing materials and information due to lack of organization and overall processing difficulties. This is where Location and Access comes into play. With this stage, children with learning disabilities are able to gather sources for the job at hand.

Big6 #4, Use of Information helps students to actually extract the information from the source. This is part of the active stage, where students are engaged in the assignment; they are reading, hearing, viewing, and touching to acquire information. For research projects and reports, students are required to site the sources they used as part of the project. This step is critical for students with learning disabilities. All children learn in different ways and Big6 #4 allows for each child to find and use the information they need in the way that works best for them.

Synthesis, Big6 #5, is when students organize and present the information for the task or assignment. Again, this is another crucial stage for children with special needs given their difficulty with organizing information. In my class students are able to present their information in a way that works best for them, whether it's in the form of an oral report or presentation, diagram, poster, chart, or written report. When third graders recently had to complete a book report, some students orally presented the book, others wrote a song about the book and shared it with the class, while others created posters advertising the book. With synthesis, students are able to organize information in ways that works best to match their specific learning styles while presenting the information according to the assignment directions. This step allows children with special needs to use their learning strengths when organizing and presenting content information.

The last step, **Big6 #6, Evaluation**, allows children to judge their product and judge the process of completing the task. This is a vital stage for my students. They need to be able to evaluate their work as well as the process in which they completed the task. My students are continuously self-evaluating and determining ways to become better learners. This evaluation takes many forms, including self-assessment, teacher conferences, and peer evaluations. The students sometimes use scoring webs and grading charts (see sample rubrics – Mathematics Rubric (see Rubric 1) and Story Writing Rubric (see Rubric 2)) to evaluate their own work. At other times, I have each child write a short paragraph about their project or work, the manner in which they completed it, and the strengths and challenges of the assignment. In pairs or small groups, students will offer "compliments or suggestions" to their peers in a comfortable and non-threatening manner. By doing this continuous assessment, the children are able to take an active role in their learning and recognize their strengths and weaknesses as a learner. In turn, this motivates my students to always strive to do their best work. Big 6 #6 ensures that children with special needs are able to reflect on their work habits in a positive and non-threatening manner.

The Big6 Skills have become a routine in my special education classroom. It is a familiar process that my students use to "tackle" their schoolwork, whether it's studying for a test, completing a book report, or answering reading comprehension questions. The Big6 allows my special education students to be organized, efficient in their time management, and thorough in completing assignments.

Mathematics Rubric: Problem Solving Activities

Name: _____   Date: _____

Category	4 Excellent	3 Good	2 Satisfactory	1 Needs Work
Mathematical Concepts	Work and explanation shows complete understanding of the mathematical concepts used to solve the problem.	Work and explanation shows substantial understanding of the mathematical concepts used to solve the problem.	Work and explanation shows some understanding of the mathematical concepts used to solve the problem.	Work and explanation shows very little understanding of the mathematical concepts used to solve the problem.
Completion	All problems and questions are completed.	All but 1 of the problems and questions are completed.	All but 2 of the problems and questions are completed.	Several of the problems and questions are not completed.
Mathematical Terminology	Correct terminology and notation are always used, making it easy to understand what was done.	Correct terminology and notation are usually used, making it fairly easy to under-stand what was done.	Correct terminology and notation are used, but it is sometimes not easy to understand what was done.	There is little use, or inappropriate use, of terminology and notation.
Strategy and Procedures	Typically uses an efficient and effective strategy to solve the problems.	Usually uses an efficient and effective strategy to solve the problems.	Sometimes uses an efficient strategy to solve the problems.	Rarely uses an efficient strategy to solve problems.

Story Writing Rubric

Name: _____   Date: _____

Category	4 Excellent	3 Good	2 Satisfactory	1 Needs Work
Ideas	My story makes complete sense. Writing is clear and easy to understand.	My writing is pretty understandable. One idea may be out of place.	My story is hard to follow and my story is somewhat confusing.	The reader will not be able to understand this writing. My ideas do not make sense.
Organization	My beginning creates interest, my middle is well-developed, and the end is unifying.	My story has a clear and interesting beginning, middle, and end.	My story has a clear beginning, middle, and end but needs details to make it interesting.	My story does not have a clear beginning, middle, or end. My story is hard to follow.
Word Choice	My writing has a lot of powerful and exciting words to enhance the meaning.	My writing has some powerful and exciting words.	My writing has a few powerful and exciting words.	My writing has no powerful and exciting words. It is boring to read.
Fluency	I used complete sent-ences that are varied in style and length. My sentences flow together.	I used complete sent-ences that are varied in length. Some of the sentences flow together.	I used only short complete sentences. My story does not flow together in places.	I used incomplete sentences. My story does not flow together at all.
Conventions	I edited my writing and it is free of spelling, punctuation, and capitalization errors.	I edited my writing and it still contains some errors.	I edited my writing and it contains a lot of spelling, capitalization, and punctuation errors.	I still have many spelling, capitalization, and punctuation errors in my writing. It is hard to read and understand my writing

Part III:

Big6™ and Technology

The BIG 6

CHAPTER 14

Technology Tools

The New Toy: Tablet PC

By Ru Story-Huffman / vE4, no1

*J*ust as you begin to feel the world of technology is leveling off and you are comfortable with the technology you're using in the classroom, something new comes knocking at your door. Such is the case with the Tablet PC. In my everyday technological life, I use a computer and my personal organizer, and often will use a laptop and video projector for instruction. Now, I'm beginning to dream of a Tablet PC, as I see possibilities for this little gem that are astounding, exciting, and just plain fun.

The Tablet PC prototype was introduced by Microsoft in 2000, and is essentially a full Windows computer with the ease of pen and paper. The Tablet PC's primary advantage is that you can have your email, Internet connection, all Microsoft applications such as Word, PowerPoint, Excel, and complete databases with you at all times. About the size of an 8 1/2" x 11" paper pad or notebook, the Tablet PC is smaller than a laptop. It's also more portable, and because you can write on the screen with a stylus, you can use the Tablet PC as a note-taking device in a meeting, parent/teacher conferences, or for the weekly grocery list.

Computers in the classroom, and technology in general, are busy paving the way for current education reform and curriculum advances. The Tablet PC could be a major factor in the success of the connected classroom, providing a single device for note-taking, connecting to the Internet for web access or email, and for organizing and managing work and schedules. The Tablet PC provides a range of new functions as well as access to the same tools and applications as on a regular desktop or laptop computer. For students, a Tablet PC is a natural component to learning, as it can help meet the needs of multiple intelligences, takes up less space than a conventional PC and provides a convenient method of managing data, information and homework. Classroom management, here we come!

The Tablet PC can function as a digital writing pad, since it allows those of us who prefer taking notes the old fashioned way (by writing instead of typing) to still benefit from technology advances. The Tablet PC captures the full images of handwritten notes, but its handwriting recognition capability converts to digital text. This text is now searchable—that's right, we can now search in our notes for key words, topics, or dates. In addition the digital text is now available for word processing, database or other applications.

Described as the "next step" for laptop computers, the Tablet PC also has the potential to be a powerful teaching and presentation tool. With a wireless connection to a projection unit, the Tablet PC can replace the chalkboard or whiteboard. Furthermore, teacher presented images and notes can be shared electronically with students, and they can add their own ideas, thoughts and observations. In addition, when classes do experiments or take field trips, students can use Tablet PCs to bring information with them and to take notes for later use.

Many of these Tablet PC capabilities are still in developmental stages (see news and reviews on www.tabletnews.com, http://tabletpc2.com as well as almost all computer magazines), offering more promise than reality. Also, current Tablet PCs are expensive—about the same price as a laptop. But, the software is expected to improve and the price will drop. So, while I don't necessarily recommend early adoption, we are excited about the potential for new functionality, portability, and ease of use.

Tablet PC and the Big6

"So, how might the Tablet PC be used with the Big6?" Well, I have a few ideas to suggest, each one of which can be adapted, revised or refined for specific situations. With each Big6 stage, technology plays an important role in the success of mastering the learning outcomes. The Tablet PC can aid each student with the entire process of information problem-solving, and the little technology wonder known as the Tablet PC will aid educators in their quest to guide students on the road to informational success. For each Big6 stage, I offer a few ideas that you may find useful when considering the choice of a Tablet PC for personal or classroom use. Sometimes, a decision to purchase a major appliance is easier if one has some uses in mind, although a PC is not necessarily an appliance like a refrigerator, but it can be considered a major purchase.

1. Task Definition
1.1 Define the information problem
When asked to define the information problem, a student could begin brainstorming using the writing stylus of the Tablet PC. When faced with a new research problem, I find myself reaching for pen and paper to graph the problem and all sub-problems or to brainstorm words and questions. The Tablet PC would take the place of my pen and paper and allow me to save my work and transfer it to text.

1.2 Identify information needed in order to complete the task (to solve the information problem)
Once again, the Tablet PC would be a great asset when it comes to identifying information needed. The note taking application and capabilities of a Tablet PC would greatly ease the stress one experiences when multiple pieces of notebook paper get lost, misplaced, or eaten by the dog, as the case may be!

2. Information Seeking Strategies
2.1 Determine the range of possible sources (brainstorm)
Asking myself "What are the best possible resources for locating my information?" can be a breeze when I make notes of my brainstorming ideas using the Tablet PC. Just jot down all the ideas that you think of when waiting for the school bus or standing in a long line at the grocery.

2.2 Evaluate the different possible sources to determine priorities (select the best sources)
Once you've got all your ideas in a file on the Tablet PC, you can take your stylus pen, refine your choices, prioritize and begin to move to the next step in the Big6 process.

3. Location and Access

3.1 Locate sources (intellectually and physically)

After the information in your Tablet PC is finalized from step 2, beside each possible resource, write the location. Do you need to make a trip to the library, access the Internet from home or school, or locate information using an Interlibrary Loan system at the local public library? Developing a "To Do" list with your Tablet PC would greatly aid in time management and help those of us who really need daily reminders!

3.2 Find information within sources

After the sources are located, the file on your Tablet PC will begin to grow. Make notes of each source, including relevant bibliographic information, and perhaps a short summary or list of pertinent information.

4. Use of Information

4.1 Engage (e.g., read, hear, view, touch) the information in a source

Deciding how to best use the information from each source can be a major accomplishment toward the completion of the information-seeking task. When using the Tablet PC, one could develop a database of each source to organize the information, its relevancy and importance, or download electronic information from the Internet or electronic databases. Compilation of all source information into the Tablet PC and the ability to carry the information electronically is a good method of engaging information.

4.2 Extract relevant information from a source

Specific information from each source can also be highlighted in the Tablet PC, or footnotes could be formed using a word processing application. In addition, if the Tablet PC was used in a wireless environment, quick and easy access to relevant information could be obtained and stored using the applications provided in the Tablet PC.

5. Synthesis

5.1 Organize information from multiple sources

Organization is a major step in the process of information gathering and use. When using the Tablet PC, one can organize information sources using citation methods desired by the teacher, rank relevant sources and information or make notes based on readings.

5.2 Present the information

Using the Tablet PC, the student or teacher can determine the audience and method of delivery. Perhaps the student wants to make an outline of important information, or develop a PowerPoint presentation. Maybe the teacher needs to email the finished product to a collaborating teacher. Whatever the method of arrangement, the Tablet PC can aid in the presentation of information and allow the user to fully implement the assigned task.

6. Evaluation

6.1 Judge the product (effectiveness)

Any refining or revising of the information sources can be done during this step in the Big6 process. Using the Tablet PC to more fully integrate information or organize sources is a great method of problem solving. One of the jewels in the Tablet PC crown is its portability, so while you are waiting for the students to return from recess, you can revise information you processed for the latest curriculum initiative in your content area or even the entire school system.

6.2 Judge the information problem-solving process (efficiency)

If you use a rubric to evaluate effectiveness for assignments or tasks, you could have a template on your Tablet PC, and instantly determine your process. The Tablet PC could also provide you the means to develop new rubrics based on new information, just by cutting and pasting information gained during the process into a new assessment rubric.

So, even though some may deem the Tablet PC a new, technological gizmo, that only the "nerdiest" would appreciate, the reality is the Tablet PC has great potential for use in education. Educators will appreciate the ease of use, portability and wide range of applications. Students will like the fact they can write on an electronic screen and their words will be transformed into type. In a wireless network world, the ease of reading email while waiting for the students to finish the latest geometry quiz will be a great asset for educators. Librarians will appreciate the Tablet PC for the ease of developing bibliographic citations, web links or instruction methods. And all users of the Big6 will appreciate its ease in making the information seeking process just a little bit easier. Have fun, enjoy and don't forget your Tablet PC!

The Tablet PC is worth the time to investigate, and if funds allow, purchasing for use in the home, school or even office. As with all new toys, each one of us has a favorite, and who knows, the Tablet PC may become one of yours!

From Chalkboard to Storyboard: Using the Big6™ to Harness the Power of Digital Video

By Ru Story-Huffman / vE3, no1

When I was a student in elementary school, too many years ago for me to readily admit, the chalkboard was a masterful tool. I can remember in first grade being intrigued as Mrs. Kent wrote spelling words on the chalkboard. I thought the chalkboard was a neat tool. Yes, it looked messy, as I could see chalk dust floating in the air while I sneezed my way through spelling class. And yes, there was the necessary task of cleaning the board and erasers. But the chalkboard offered me another avenue of learning that enhanced my education, although I did not realize it at the time. I just thought it was cool. But I must confess I did not enjoy working Math problems on the chalkboard in front of the entire class! When I was in school, the chalkboard was "technology."

So much for a trip down memory lane—fast-forward to 2002. Students in our world today expect more of technology than just a chalkboard. They have been raised with technology, and the Internet is commonplace in schools, numerous homes and perhaps even the local coffee shop, public library or bank. Technology standards exist in many states, and local school systems are adopting existing standards and developing innovative means to meet and exceed those standards. One way to enhance learning, meet technology standards and incorporate Big6 learning, specifically number 5, Synthesis, is to use digital video and editing as an educational tool.

Digital video and editing can be a very simple production that details a classroom visit or fieldtrip, or it can be more involved and include numerous settings, characters and scenes. No matter the method, digital video and editing can offer opportunities for improved learning and understanding of the subject at hand. The use of multimedia can enhance creative thinking and problem solving and advance knowledge of technology for students. An added benefit will be the knowledge gained by educators as they learn to use digital editing and understand the impact it plays in learning.

So, you may be thinking to yourself, "Yeah, right. I can do that (in a million years)!" Well, yes you can. It is not as difficult as it may seem, and when combined with use of the Big6, it can become very understandable and educator-friendly. Not only will your students synthesize information learned, you the educator, will be able to synthesize your newfound knowledge of video as an educational tool. To create and manage video you will need access to video camera, computer, and computer software that allows you to edit your video. Even if you do not have access to all the above equipment in your classroom, there may be other avenues of locating the necessary tools. Try the technology coordinator, media center or even a willing friend. Once you have the equipment in hand, the rest is easy.

First Steps First: Planning for Curricular Success

The first step is to plan the video and tie it to stated curriculum or technology standards. Curriculum benefits can include development of higher order thinking through the production of video, collaboration between teacher and student, student and student, or student and the knowledge of the world. In addition, students and educators will learn technology skills that will be useful in "real" life. Each state has specific technology standards for education, and knowledge and familiarity with the standards will aid in the determination of the technology standards that would be met through the use of digital video and editing as a means of coursework delivery.

What's Your Purpose? Who Will See It, and How?

Next, you will want to determine the nature and purpose of your video and decide on a format. Are you going to view the video in VHS format on a television screen or will it become available via the Internet? Are you, the educator, going to make the video for the class to view, or is the video going to be produced by students? Having students produce a video containing information learned during a science workshop or language arts unit for example, would be an excellent way to work Synthesis (Big6, Stage # 50 into the curriculum. Once the students have organized the information, they can then present the information for use by others or to reinforce learning. A video that has been developed and prepared by students is an excellent example of Synthesis.

Show, Don't Tell

The next step should be to determine how you'll treat the subject you want to cover or highlight in your video. Conceivably, video could be used with any subject matter being studied in the classroom. For example, a middle school social studies teacher and students may wish to consider video to develop and produce a piece that outlines information on the fall of the Berlin Wall. Or, upon completion of a study of the Dewey Decimal System, the teacher librarian in an elementary situation could assist students in producing a video that outlines the Dewey Decimal System and would be then available for use by others. Other instructional topics or ideas that could benefit from being presented in digital format include career exploration, oral history projects, the learning of a second language, and interviews with school personnel, art history or mathematics. A digitized video that was edited and presented as a continuous clip on a computer of primary children in the classroom would be a great addition to the annual school open house evening. Once you become more familiar with digital video and editing, the educational opportunities become endless!

From Story to Storyboard

Once the subject decision has been made, progression to writing the story or determining an outline will aid in the development process. Having an idea of what is to be presented will aid in the overall production of the video. Students could develop a newscast situation where they report on the "news" of the fall of the Berlin Wall. Consultation between teacher and students can produce a storyboard in which each shot is developed, along with a script and other animation or audio enhancements to be incorporated. Once everything is ready, it will be time to shoot the video, and then edit. Editing can include "shifting" sequence, adding clipart, animation, sound or otherwise enhancing the finished product.

There are numerous computer programs available that can aid in the editing of video. Determination of your particular situation, budget allowances and computer knowledge will aid in the editing software selection process. A partial list, with Internet addresses includes:

- Avid Cinema (www.avid.com): Developer of a variety of products for animation, editing and production of video.

- Dazzle (www.dazzle.com): Create video productions, edit, organize and produce video for viewing on the Internet.

- iMovie2 (http://www.apple.com/ilife/imovie/): Produced by Apple, this application allows the user to shoot, edit, enhance with visual effects and sound and view via DVD, the Internet or videocassette tape.

- Adobe Digital Video Products (http://www.adobe.com/motion/main.html): Digital media, streaming video for the computer, editing products and visual effects are all offered through a variety of products developed by Adobe.

- MovieXone (www.aistinc.com): A downloadable application that offers video editing, animation and audio. The download is free, but no technical support is offered.

Coming Soon to a Screen Near (or Far From) You

For those who are a bit more adventurous, video can be developed which can be played on a computer or by way of the Internet. An educator in high school could develop a lecture that would be made available for students by logging on to the Internet. Students could then view the lecture in a manner that would fit with their schedule. With a little experimentation and a CD burner on your computer, you can even save video to a CD. Students understand, and in some cases expect, variety in their learning. Remember, these are the children who sometimes cannot believe that black and white television actually existed! (At least my teenage sons have that false belief!) Anyway, our students are accustomed to video, VCR's, CD, and now DVD's. Presentation of information in media format is a natural avenue to capture their attention, stimulate creative thinking and motivate learning.

How the Big6™ Helps

The Big6 is a wonderful avenue to aid in the development of learning. Not only will our students experience greater success by following the steps to information literacy as presented by the Big6, but educators can as well. In fact, you could use the steps of the Big6 when planning a video for classroom use. Once you have defined your task, determined the range of possible subjects and or curriculum goals to be covered by the video, located potential information, and use that information, you could be more than half way to a finished product. Synthesis, which is the Big6 component that fits well with presentation of media learning, is a great way to illustrate your final video project. Evaluation techniques could be student outcome, personal assessment, and other identifiers specific to your classroom, school district and state standards.

So the next time you seek a new way to present the "same old subject" or want to present a new topic in an exciting and stimulating manner, consider digital video and editing as an avenue for exploration. Who knows, we might even develop a new award where all the digital media educators of the world "walk the red carpet" for a gala evening of awards and accolades! Perhaps we could offer the Digital Apple Award for the most creative use of digital media in an information education society! Start planning your wardrobe now for the big event!

Inspired! The Big6 Symbol Library in Inspiration 7.0!

By Ferdi Serim / vE4, no3

As many of you probably know, Inspiration and its companion product, Kidspiration are tools to help students visualize, organize, brainstorm, plan, outline, diagram, and write. They are extremely useful for Task Definition as well as Synthesis and Evaluation. And now, thanks to Ferdi Serim, Inspiration will now include a full set of Big6 icons. Here's an introduction to the Inspiration and Big6 connection. - M.E.

*E*very *Inspiration* user who gets the new version 7.0 also receives a special gift for Inspiration's 20th Anniversary: a new symbol library containing Big6 Icons. This quiet synergy provides teachers, students and parents with incredible power, by making student's thinking and problem solving process visible. Many Big6ers are also *Inspiration* fans, and to us, this seems like prayers answered. But even if you are new to Big6 or *Inspiration*, there are many benefits you can begin to enjoy right away.

Research Into Practice

Both the Big6 and Inspiration (http://www.inspiration.com/) are based upon substantial research about how people learn and organize their thoughts. As Carrie Lowe writes in the Research Foundation for the Big6 Skills "The Big6 may be the most widely-known approach to information problem-solving, but it is not the only one. The Big6 is based on a rich foundation of research into how humans find and process information (information literacy), and this research basis has led to the development of similar and complementary approaches that create a more complete picture of ways people solve information problems."

The development of *Inspiration* tells a similar tale of creative problem solving. Two decades ago, systems analysts and programmers struggled to document the thinking that went into their designs. Their text-based terminals didn't provide much help, but with the appearance of the Macintosh computer, visual aspects were added to the human/machine interactions. Starting with symbols traditionally used in flow-charting and circuit diagrams, Inspiration soon added many more graphics, organized into symbol libraries, and soon took on a life of its own in the education market. Today, Inspiration notes that "research has shown that visual learning is one of the best methods for teaching thinking skills. Visual learning techniques—graphical ways of working with ideas and presenting information— teach students to clarify their thinking, and to process, organize and prioritize new information. Visual diagrams reveal patterns, interrelationships and interdependencies. They also stimulate creative thinking."

How Visual Learning Techniques Help Students

Brainstorm - Idea maps help students generate ideas and develop thoughts visually. They're great for brainstorming and prewriting exercises, and for producing plans and solving problems. (Big6 #1 - Task Definition)

Clarify thinking - Idea maps clarify thinking by helping students to see connections between ideas. Using fast, five-minute exercises in word and idea association, idea maps utilize keywords, symbols, colors and graphics to form nonlinear networks of potential ideas and observations. (Big6 #2 - Information Seeking Strategies)

Situating knowledge - A web is a visual map that shows how different categories of information relate to each other. Webs provide a structure for ideas and facts that help students learn to organize and prioritize information. Webs enhance learning by displaying concepts and the relationships between them in a visible, structured format. Major topics or core concepts are located at the web center. Outward links connect supporting details. (Big6 #3 - Location & Access)

Reinforce understanding - Students recreate, in their own words, what they've learned. This helps them absorb and internalize new information, giving them ownership of their ideas. (Big6 #4 - Use of Information)

Integrate new knowledge - Diagrams updated throughout a lesson prompt students to build upon prior knowledge and internalize new information. By reviewing diagrams created previously, students see how facts and ideas fit together. (Big6 #5 - Synthesis)

Identify misconceptions - Just as a concept map or web shows what students know, misdirected links or wrong connections reveal what they don't understand. (Big6 #6 - Evaluation)

To learn more about visual thinking, see this page from Inspiration.

http://inspiration.com/vlearning/suggestread/index.cfm?fuseaction=suggested

I asked Janet Murray, high school teacher-librarian, about my use of Inspiration to develop ideas among our team at the Online Internet Institute project. She replied, "Because I'm a visual learner, your use of it helps me to see the relationships between ideas and concepts that I don't always perceive easily from words alone. I think the Inspiration-produced diagrams also help students synthesize by encouraging them to express their ideas in a limited number of words." Janet has added links to Inspiration's "The Power of Visual Thinking" and their home page to step 1 on the Big6info matrix. (http://www.surfline.ne.jp/janetm/big6info.htm)

It soon becomes clear that with so many possibilities and so many implications, there is more going on in a student's Inspiration project than can be captured in a single label. That's why we've provided the Big6 Icons as a new symbol library in Inspiration 7.0!

A MultiPurpose, MultiDimensional Tool

Let's look at webs, as just one example of an Inspiration activity type. Linking concepts and labeling the relationships leads to a diverse range of activities, each with implications for one or more of the Big6. Literary webs help students analyze stories or novels so that they more fully understand the literary elements at play, as well as the composition of the story (Big6 #3 - Location and Access, Big6 #4 - Use of Information). Character webs represent one of the ways in which visual learning can support reading comprehension (Big6 #5 - Synthesis, Big6 6 - Evaluation). Comparison is one of the most basic and powerful forms of analysis in any discipline (Big6 #4 - Use of Information). Prewriting describes the brainstorming and organizing students do before writing a story (Big6 #1 - Task Definition, Big6 #2 - Information Seeking Strategies).

Big6™ Icons Make Inspiration an Information Problem-Solving Assessment Tool

We know that Synthesis is the hardest skill for students to master, and that cross-curricular research projects are one of the most popular and effective applications of the Big6. According to Art Wolinsky, Big6 author and middle school technology teacher, "When creating an overall Big6 Project map, some of the stages will be represented by a single bubble that acts more like a reminder on a storyboard, while others such as ISS (Information Seeking Strategies) would have many bubbles. As I look at the Big6 and Inspiration combo and think about how I would use it with kids here's what I see. The act of creating a Big6 web with Single item place holders will aid in the evaluation process."

Using the new Big6 icons, teachers can annotate student Project Maps that use Inspiration to document the Big6 process, as follows:

- Add a single item for Task Definition. The teacher can attach a note to the icon, making comments or suggestions to assist the student.

- Add multiple items with links that show how they relate to the information needed to solve the problem.

- Brainstorm the items to be sure all the bases are covered.

- Organize the items developed under 2.1 in order of priority.

- Add a single item to document sources that will be used.

- Add a single item to document the ability to find the information in the sources.

- Add a single item to demonstrate what happens when students engage the material. This item is perhaps the most important source of evidence when you are examining the comprehension parts of student literacies (reading, visual, information, etc.)

- Add multiple items in the form of notes. Although it's not likely that students will use Inspiration for this, the teacher annotation provides crucial feedback to complete the reading/comprehension/problem-solving process.

- When students and teachers use Inspiration for 4.2, they can organize the notes in this phase. Frequently, the mix of sources (print, Internet, CD/multimedia, interview) makes it challenging to remember what's been gathered, and how it best fits together.

- The act of organizing an approach through Inspiration can aid in Synthesis for the actual product.

- A single item "reminder" allows students and teachers to comment on the effectiveness of the process.

- A single item "reminder" allows students and teachers to comment on the effectiveness of the product.

This article can only scratch the surface of what appears to be a rich source of evidence for improving instruction and the quality of student work. In fact, I'm hard at work writing a new book on how to get the most out of combining Inspiration and the Big6. Stay tuned!

Product information:
Inspiration <http://www.inspiration.com/> offers a free 30-day software trial.

Technology as a Tool: Applications in a Big6™ Context

From the Big6 website: www.big6.com

Computer Capabilities and the Big6™

Technology	Big6™ Skill
Word processing, graphics, desktop publishing	Synthesis (writing) Use of Information (note-taking)
Spelling and grammar checking	Evaluation
Information Retrieval and Search Systems	Information Seeking Strategies Location & Access
Spreadsheets, Database management systems	Synthesis
Hypermedia	Use of Information Synthesis
Electronic resources (on CD-ROM, servers, WWW)	Information Seeking Strategies Location & Access

Internet Capabilities and the Big6™

Technology	Big6™ Skill
E-mail, listservs, chat, video conferencing, instant messaging)	Task Definition Information Seeking Strategies Location & Access, use of Information, Synthesis, Evaluation
Network navigation (www Netscape, Internet Explorer, Portals)	Information Seeking Strategies Location & Access
FTP, download/upload	Use of Information
Yahoo, Google, Yahooligans, Lycos, AltaVista, portals	Location & Access
Web Authoring	Synthesis
Web Sites	Use of Information

Adapted and reprinted with permission from Eisenberg, M.B. & Berkowitz, R.E. (1999). The New Improved Big6 Workshop Handbook. Worthington, OH: Linworth Publishing, Inc. p.43.

Compact Disk Re-Writable Drives

By Ru Story-Huffman / vE2, no1

D o you remember when you bought that computer with the 50-megabyte hard drive and you were so excited because you thought you'd never run out of space? Now computers routinely come with multi-gigabyte hard drives, and it is hard to think back about that 50-megabyte hard drive, isn't it? You may remember when 50 megabytes seemed like oceans of storage space. Funny thing—you ran out, didn't you? Now that files incorporate graphics, file sizes are large and management of storage space is an issue. Enter the Compact Disk-ReWritable (CD-RW) drive.

Advantages of CD-RW

The CD-RW has moved to the head of the class for computer storage devices, often replacing the use of CD-R, a write-only compact disk medium, and 3.5-inch floppy disks. If you need to increase storage capacity, but don't need to change information, a CD-R allows you to save information to a CD disk one time only, and is less costly. The cost for a CD-R drive for a computer can sometimes be less than $200. However, if you are interested in revising information, updating, and changing assignments or including pages from the Internet, a CD-RW is the way to go. Here are a few CD-RW facts today:

- Approximate storage capacity, 650 MB
- Can rewrite information up to 1000 times per disk
- Is perfect for storing text, graphics, video and/or audio
- Requires a CD-ROM drive to support the multi-read feature, or ability to read regular
- CD's, CD-R or CD-RW
- Is easy to install and operate
- Can be compared to a floppy or hard disk

Personal computer systems have routinely included CD-ROM drives for some time, but newer models can be purchased with CD-RW built into the workstation unit. For those who wish to explore the CD-RW technology, units may be purchased and installed on existing computers for a relatively low price. As with most technological inventions, prices continue to drop for CD-RW drives. The current price range is $200-$500 and the price per CD-RW disk is approximately $10.00. CD-RW drives in the higher price range provide increased speeds for writing, rewriting, and reading. Some CD-RW drives can write information at 1800 KB/second, rewrite at 1200 KB/second and read at 4800 KB/second, while other CD-RW drives have the ability to support more detailed software. Basically, the higher the speed per second, the faster you can save and read your information. Just as in a floppy disk, you can delete files, change information, and add new information to a CD-RW.

Check for Compatibility

Before purchasing a CD-RW for your computer, you will need to evaluate the age, speed, and memory of your existing computers to be certain that the CD-RW drive will work properly with your existing hardware. All of this information can be obtained from a CD-RW vendor or your school or library technology coordinator. Once you've decided to purchase a CD-RW, check the "software bundle" that accompanies the product. The "bundle" is the program that allows you to save your information to the CD-RW. For example, once you have created an assignment using a word processing program, you would then use the software bundle to "burn" or save your information. Investigation and research are the best tools to determine which CD-RW will meet your needs.

Uses for a CD-RW

A few of the great uses for CD-RW that come to mind immediately are: back ups, archiving, and portfolios. How many of us have been caught without a back up when the hard drive or network drive has crashed?

Backups and archiving. A CD-RW disk provides a quick and convenient way to back up your work and your students' work. If you have limited storage space on your school or home computer, using a CD-RW will allow you to archive various files for future use. The advantage of archiving to a CD-RW disk is that the disk can be read in any computer with a CD-ROM drive, provided that the programs that were used to create the files are also available on that computer.

Portfolios. For students completing portfolios, the CD-RW technology is a wonderful advantage. Each time the student adds to, or revises his or her portfolio work, the process of "reburning" would be completed and students can have a transportable copy of their portfolio. No matter the media being used, PowerPoint, word processing, or spreadsheets, students can save or backup their portfolio information on the CD-RW. Teachers and administrators could then have access to the material and students will have the added bonus of using technology to enhance their learning and presentation of knowledge.

Other uses: literary collections, review material. Make a collection of the school's newspaper or literary publication available in the library on CD-RW. Each new publication can be added to the CD-RW. Student projects could be archived on a CD-RW in the same way and added to the library for all to share and view. CD-RW disks could be created to help students review for exams. For example, an English teacher could ask groups of students in her class to create a HyperStudio presentation that would refresh students' memories of the novels and short stories that had been studied throughout the year. Once these projects have been checked for accuracy and approved by the teacher for publication, they could be made available to all students for review in the library.

Providing Assignments on CD-RW

Teachers can use CD-RW disks to store their assignments. Let's take the case of a middle or high school history teacher who wants to create an assignment focusing on the sixteenth president of the United States, Abraham Lincoln. The teacher wants to include print resources and Internet research. Once Internet and print resources are located, the teacher can place the assignment on a CD-RW disk for each child or computer station in the classroom, computer lab or media center. Here is an example of such an assignment:

1. **Task Definition**

    What am I to do? Abraham Lincoln was the 16th President of the United States. You will need to pick an event during his Presidency, from 1861–1865, and provide detailed information about that event. Possible events include certain battles during the Civil War, the Emancipation Proclamation, Gettysburg Address, or his death. You will need to provide information about your chosen event and Lincoln's role or his response.

2. Information Seeking Strategies

Much has been written about Abraham Lincoln, and he is well regarded as influential in ending of the United States Civil War. Many Web pages have been devoted to Abraham Lincoln and his life. It is up to you to determine which materials would best help in this assignment. You will want to use encyclopedias, a biography of Abraham Lincoln, or an encyclopedia of the United States Civil War. In addition, you will use selected Web pages.

3. Location & Access

The classroom teacher or school library media specialist will insert a bibliography of materials specific to the school or library. The teacher or library media specialist will list Internet resources that would be hot linked on the CD-RW, so students could go directly to the indicated Web pages using a browser.

Here are some great Web pages:

- The History Place: Abraham Lincoln, Timeline, Photos, Words (http://www. historyplace.com/lincoln/index.html)

- The History Place: A Nation Divided (http://www.historyplace.com/civilwar/index.html)

- The American Civil War Homepage (http://sunsite.utk.edu/civil-war/specific)

- Abraham Lincoln (http://www.whitehouse.gov/history/presidents/al16.html)

- Abraham Lincoln: Presidential Career Links (http://showcase.netins.net/web/creative/lincoln/education/presidential.htm)

4. Use of Information

Keep a journal to record information you have gathered each day you work on this project. Be certain to document your sources of information, including author, title, publication date, URL, etc. With each entry, highlight or otherwise indicate information that you believe will be most useful to you in this project.

5. Synthesis

Organize the information so that you can prepare a report on the topic you have chosen. Once you have prepared the report, be prepared to present it in class. In addition, develop a handout that you can provide to your class members that synthesizes and highlights main points from your research.

6. Evaluation

Consider and answer the following points:

- Did I find information to achieve my task?

- Was I able to find information that would assist my classmates in understanding my topic?

- Was I happy in the information gathering process?

- Did I like doing this activity using a CD-RW and Internet sources?

After developing the information for the Big6 activity, the classroom teacher or school library media specialist could use any type of word processing or Web authoring program to finish the page. Once the entire package is finalized, including photographs, graphics, or other visual effects, the product is then burned into a CD-RW disk using the software bundle that accompanies a CD-RW drive. At this point, the instructor can save multiple CD-RW if funds allow. Students are able to take the CD-RW to a school or classroom computer station, insert the CD-RW into a computer CD-RW disk drive and complete the assignment. Students are using Big6 to locate and utilize information, meeting educational goals, and getting practice using technology. Students who use selected Internet sites can practice using critical thinking and information seeking skills. An added bonus to the activity could be introduction of Internet Web site evaluation skills.

Following the completion of the assignment, the library media specialist and teacher should meet to evaluate the effectiveness of the assignment delivered via CD-RW. If a school district technology assessment plan is in effect, one could use this as a guide. Or, the teacher and school library media specialist could evaluate the curriculum goals and standards for the particular assignment. If the assignment is to be repeated, updating the assignment will be an easy task because the information is stored on a CD-RW. Checking links, replacing any non-existent Web pages, revising questions or learning outcomes can be easily done and then updated using the rewritable capability of a CD-RW.

Conclusion

Each day, classroom teachers and teacher-librarians have exciting opportunities for helping students learn. Education has gone beyond "reading, writing, and arithmetic," and includes a world of possibilities. That 50-megabyte hard drive computer, with monochrome monitor that you thought was wonderful, may now qualify for inclusion in the Smithsonian Museum. Well, perhaps not as drastic as the Smithsonian, but you understand the concept. The world is changing, and using the Big6 with technology such as the CD-RW is a wonderful opportunity to educate and enrich the minds of our students. Each new invention opens the doors to further enhancement of the information literacy skills stressed by the Big6, and allows teachers, librarians, and students to explore endless worlds of information.

The Internet/ World Wide Web

CHAPTER 15

The **BIG6**™

Big6 in Action: Big6 Web Sites by Practitioners

By Blythe Bennett / vE2, no2

Job Aids:

- The Big6 at Lufkin High School: (http://www.lufkinisd.org/lhshome/library/big6main.htm) In addition to sample projects and assignment organizers, this site has tools for note taking, evaluation forms, templates for creating multimedia projects, and ideas for using the Web with the Big6 process.

- The Big6 - Information Problem Solving Model: (http://www.auburn.wednet.edu/mtbaker/library/links/big6/index.htm) This site by John Lees has a set of checklists for student use including a homework helper, keeping track of resources, synthesis and evaluation checklists. Each Big6 step is also explained on the opening page.

- Big6 integration with curriculum, using graphic organizers: (http://collaboratory.nunet.net/nssd112/oakterrace/imc/big6.html) Have you been looking for examples of using graphic organizers for the Big6? Check out this site. There is a nice introduction reinforcing the need to teach information skills in context followed by a collection of graphic organizers for each of the Big6 stages. There is also a link explaining how to use graphic organizers with students and a demonstration of how to use the Big6 in real-life as Bob chooses a restaurant.

- Follow a Research Process: (http://wwwshs1.bham.wednet.edu/curric/cool/research.htm) Students will find a set of questions to guide them through the Big6 process, links to other sites and to internal school sites for more ideas. Be sure to check the Research Checklist (pdf) for a long list of ideas many students will find intriguing. There are also 30 suggestions of possible synthesis products. Evaluation rubrics are useful additions.

Teaching Aids:

- PowerPoint Demonstration on the Solar System using the Big6: (http://www.eastrock.org/powerpoi.htm) Librarian Paula Daitzman has posted a great PowerPoint presentation covering the Super3 and Big6 steps using an example of her students' Solar System project. While her presentation is specific to her school and students, it is a wonderful example that you might want to adapt for your own school.

Parental Involvement:

- Calvin Smith: (http://www.granite.k12.ut.us/CalvinS/bigsix/bigsix.htm) Elementary in Utah has a very attractive design for their Big6 pages and includes coaching tips for parents. The series of pages has information for teachers, descriptions of each step, and objectives for using the Big6 as a problem-solving model.

Academic Libraries:

- How to Get Started with Research: An Easy 6-step Approach (See page 212): (http://www.kutztown.edu/library/materials/research.html) This site has a short introduction to each stage and further explanations of each step. The keywords to clarify assignments and possible primary and secondary source suggestions are especially helpful.

- Coe College - Big6 Skills: (http://www.public.coe.edu/departments/Library/skills.html) A concise page that refers to "information-smart students," and describes what research skills such a student possesses. The positive outlook promotes a sense of confidence, "I can be an information smart student, too!"

Lesson Plans:

- Big6 Projects: (http://www.fortbend.k12.tx.us/library/big6.htm) Chemical elements, the Renaissance, Shakespeare, The Elizabethan Period, British Literature, Mythology, Victorian Era, American Camelot, and Contemporary Literature are all lessons created by teachers from the Fort Bend Independent School District, Sugarland, Texas. Teachers use a template to integrate the Big6 skills with curriculum related lessons. There is also a link to the template and a brief description of each step in the process.

- The Science Fair Page: (http://www.hpl.lib.tx.us/youth/science_fair_index.html)

- Cinco de Mayo Page: (http://www.hpl.lib.tx.us/youth/cinco_index.html) The Houston Public Library and local public schools teamed up to develop Big6 based lessons on science fairs and Cinco de Mayo celebrations. This example uses the same template as the Fort Bend School, and you'll find useful resources for these topics. This is a great example of public and school libraries collaborating on a project for children in the community. Talk to your own public librarian and consider a similar collaboration!

- Experimental Science Project: Selecting a Research Topic or Title Using the Big6 Skills Model: (http://users.rcn.com/schene.ma.ultranet/big6rakarruda.html) Many students have a difficult time choosing a topic for a science fair project but this site will help them through the selection process. When the student reaches the Evaluation stage, he or she is prompted to begin the six-step process to investigate the topic.

- Environmental Science lesson: "Who Will Survive?": (http://www.k12.hi.us/~mbarbosa/research.html) This elementary school in Hawaii has a lesson for students doing a project on the human impact on wetlands. The school librarian and teacher collaborated on a research project related to the curriculum and incorporated the Big6. Consider collaborating with a colleague and posting your own lesson ideas online.

- Vinland Explores Explorers, Big6 Style (http://207.149.11.2/vinland/Explorers/exbigsix.htm) Students are in the driver's seat with this Web site. The information is directed toward the student who is working on a project about explorers. A grading rubric allows the student to check if he or she has completed each objective. There is also a rubric for an evaluation essay using the Big6, which the librarian will grade.

Web Research:

- Darby Creek - Change and Pattern: (http://www.cyberbee.com/pattern/index.html) Using the broad topic of Change and Pattern in the Biological Sciences, this site from CyberBee works through the Big6 steps. Skill level, concept level, and application level are addressed. The evaluation includes self, peer, and teacher evaluation ideas. Internet searching and resources are the focus of this unit.

- In the Hollow of a Tree - Raccoon Babies: (http://www.cyberbee.com/raccoons/movie.html) Using the topic of raccoons, the site takes students through the six steps of the Big6 Skills and how to find resources on the Web. Each step has a short description, some examples and an activity to do as practice. Copyright and citations are addressed in the Use of Information step.

- Applying Big6 Skills™ and Information Literacy Standards to Internet Research: (http://www.surfline.ne.jp/janetm/big6info.htm) Related to an article written for the January 2000 eNewsletter (http://www.big6.com/showarticle.php?id=153) Janet Murray organizes the Big6 skills into a chart where basic and advanced activities reflect each Big6 skill. For example, Task Definition is illustrated by examples of concept mapping and graphic organizers.

- Effective Use of the Internet: (http://www.pcedug.vic.edu.au/eff_int.htm) Australian Computer Coordinator Roland Gesthuizen uses the Big6 in his presentation "Digging for Gold." He has adapted and used the steps to break up the information management task. The exercises he has included for most of the six steps are especially useful. Users receive some guided practice in using the information problem-solving model and searching online for relevant resources.

How to Get Started with Research: An Easy 6-step Approach (http://www.kutztown.edu/library/materials/research.html)

*Based on the Big6 Skills Approach to Information Problem-Solving
devised by Michael B. Eisenberg and Robert E. Berkowitz*

Step 1:
Task Definition: Define the assignment and decide what information you need to complete it.

Step 2:
Information Seeking Strategies: Brainstorm a list of possible sources, evaluate the list, and choose the best ones.

Step 3:
Location and Access: Locate your sources and find the needed information within them.

Step 4:
Use of Information: Examine all the information within a source and extract what you need.

Step 5:
Synthesis: Organize the information you gained from all the sources and present it according to the assignment.

Step 6:
Evaluation: Judge your final product for effectiveness, and determine the efficiency of your problem solving skills

Further Explanations of Each Step

Step 1:

Task Definition: Define the assignment and decide what information you need to complete it.

- Look at the information your teacher or professor gave you concerning the assignment and decide what you are expected to do / what is required as an end result (paper, speech, presentation, etc.).

- Pay attention to key words (see key words below) like "assess" or "compare" or "explain," and make sure you complete your task based on these words.

- Based on the assignment, determine what information you need or what you will need to do in order to complete it.

- Consider the due date and create a timeline for completing the assignment.

KEY WORDS
Assignment clarification words:

Assess: To rate or evaluate something.

Compare: To decide how things are the same and different. Tell about both the similarities and differences.

Contrast: To find differences between things and tell about them.

Define: To explain what something means. Tell how it is like some things and different than other. Give examples when appropriate.

Describe: To tell all that you can about something in an organized way.

Discuss: To determine what the different sides are and tell about them. Discuss is similar to describe.

Evaluate: To give the positive and negative points, advantages, and disadvantages, pros and cons. Also, give your opinion of something.

Explain: To clearly tell the details about something or the reasons or causes for something.

Illustrate: To describe specific examples. Usually, the more examples you give, the better.

Relate: To tell how things are connected or what they have in common.

Summarize: To present your information in your own words and in as few words as possible

Step 2:

Information Seeking Strategies: Brainstorm a list of possible sources appropriate for your assignment, evaluate the list, and choose the best ones.

- Determine where you can find the information to complete your assignment. What sources (books, periodicals, web sites, indexes, etc.) will have information you need?

- Decide which resources would be the best ones to use, and what kind of information each one might provide.

Possible Sources

Primary Sources:

1. Eyewitness
2. Experiment
3. Observation
4. Historic Document

Secondary Sources:

1. Books (fiction / nonfiction)	6. Yearbook	11. Audio tapes
2. Dictionary	7. Indexes	12. Slides
3. Encyclopedia	8. Vertical file	13. Filmstrips
4. Atlas	9. Newspapers	14. Online sources
5. Almanac	10. Video tapes	

Step 3:

Location and Access: Locate your sources and find the needed information within them.

- Look up resource locations using an OPAC (computer catalog) system, a card catalog, web directory, or other method so you can get the needed sources.

- Flip, search, or surf through the item to find the information you need within it.

Step 4:

Use of Information: Examine all the information within a source and extract what you need.

- Read, view, examine, or digest the information from each source and write down what pieces of knowledge you need to complete the assignment or solve your problem.

- Write down the citation information you will need for each source while you are extracting information from it. Keep the source data and the extracted information together for when you compose your bibliography or works cited page.

Step 5:

Synthesis: Organize the information you gained from all the sources and present it according to the assignment.

- Use all the pieces of information along with your own ideas to create your paper, video, speech, presentation, or whatever the assignment calls for you to create. Using transitional words and phrases will create a smooth flow to your writing or to other presentation formats.

- Don't forget to create a bibliography/works cited page and give credit to your sources within the text.

Transitional Words and Phrases

above	beside	further	next
accordingly	beyond	furthermore	on the other hand
additionally	consequently	however	outside
after	contrary to	in addition to	rather than
also	different than	in fact	similarly
although	due to	inside	so
another	during	instead of	such
as a result	earlier	just as	therefore
at last	finally	later	through
because	first	moreover	thus
behind	for instance	much as	under
below			

Step 6:

Evaluation: Judge your final product for effectiveness, and determine the efficiency of your problem solving skills.

- After you are all done and your assignment has been turned in or presented, determine how you did.

- Did you complete all the requirements?

- Did your research methods work?

- What was the quality of your final product?

Follow a Research Process

(http://wwwshs1.bham.wednet.edu/curric/cool/research.htm)

Don't begin a research process without considering these steps first!

☐ 1. Task Definition: What is my question? Is it a good question? How can I make it meaningful to me? (define the problem, find your focus, explore, get an overview, form focused questions)

☐ 2. Information Seeking Strategies: What are some sources of information? Which are the best sources?

  ☐ Read descriptions of the subscription tools on the Sehome Networked Resources list. (http://wwwshs1.bham.wednet.edu/curric/cool/resource.htm)

  ☐ Peruse the Research Checklist (pdf) (http:wwwsh1.bham.wednet.edu/curric/cool/researchchecklist.pdf) to other possible sources of information.

  ☐ Consult NoodleTools (http://www.noodletools.com/) for some guidance on Internet research

  ☐ After you've investigated all possible sources, prioritize them—which do you think will yield the most information for the time you are willing to spend? Not all will be equally useful.

  ☐ By what criteria will you assess your success? How will you know when or if you have answered the question or solved the problem?

  ☐ What kind of a product will you create to show what you've learned? - see section 5 below for ideas.

☐ 3. Location and Access: Where are the sources and how do I tap them?

  ☐ Develop your search strategy to access the information (determine key words to enter into electronic databases, learn the program, develop questions to ask your interviewee)

  ☐ Locate the sources (go find resources, make a phone call, access via computer, schedule an appointment)

☐ 4. Use of Information: How can I use the information?

  ☐ Engage the information (read, hear, view)

  ☐ Extract usable part (take notes, make sketch, conduct an interview)

  ☐ Record your sources in MLA format (http://wwwshs1.bham.wednet.edu/curric/cool/MLA5thed.doc) (download the Word document)

☐ 5. Synthesis: What can I make to show what I learned? How can I show my insights?

  ☐ I've determined my end product

Questionnaire	Survey	Research paper (see sample paper) wwwshs1.bham. wednet.edu/curric/ cool/respaper.htm	Report	Conclusion	Pamphlet or brochure
Chart	Graph	Outline	Diagram	List	Research paper
Plan	Summary	Category	Demonstration	Database	Magazine feature article
Enjoyment	Food to eat	Videotape	Photography exhibit	Tape recording	Service project
Formula	Invention	Poem	Story	Prediction	Experiment
New game	Media	Written music or song	Dramatization	Model	Recipe

☐ I have organized my presentation in a interesting way.
(some ideas: imagined, composed, made inferences, hypothesized, invented, created, estimated, produced, forecast, designed, predicted, concluded, panel, opinion, verdict, scale, value, recommendation, investigation, summarized, abstracted, classified, dissected, compared, contrasted, deduced, ordered, investigated, differentiated, categorized)

☐ 6. Evaluation: How will I know I did my job well?

Digital Media Services and the Big6

By Carrie Lowe / vE4, no4

Use of rich media such as video, interactive Web resources and digital versions of primary sources in the classroom can enrich student learning and sharpen information problem-solving skills, but it can also create massive headaches for teachers and library media specialists. Integrating these resources into the curriculum requires not only planning time, but also a great deal of legwork. Videos must be checked out of the media center and cued to the appropriate segments. Web sites need to be carefully reviewed and bookmarked, and all these resources must be smoothly integrated into lessons and units. Not to mention any technology training needed so that teachers and students know how to use these tools.

Digital media services – the future of video in the classroom?

A new technology beginning to make waves in schools across the country shows a great deal of promise in terms of relieving some of the time and logistical constraints associated with use of media in the classroom. What's more, this new tool will suggest ways to incorporate even more interactive tools into student learning, and provide a comprehensive library of resources for students of all levels. These resources go by many different names, but all can be considered together under the label *digital media services.*

At essence, digital media services add value to Web and broadcast resources by combining and packaging them in a way that makes them most useful for educators. The service is essentially a searchable, on-demand media library collection, which indexes program segments, contextualizes them with supporting multimedia, and delivers them to the classroom. This content can be used in a variety of ways—one to one as a student at a machine does research or works her way through a topic, one to many as the teacher demos the content to the class using a projector, and so on.

Digital media can be delivered to the classroom in a variety of ways. One method is via **broadband**—a content provider such as a local PBS station holds all of the information on a server, and the school streams what they need on-demand. While this method presents the resources in a Web site-like format teachers are very comfortable with, it is extremely bandwidth-intensive and can quickly tie up the school's network. Another method is the **datacasting** model. This requires the school to maintain a server that is equipped with a special broadcast antenna. The school's datacast equipment pulls digital data from the PBS station's digital terrestrial broadcast signal and stores it locally, making it available to all computers on the school network. The final model is the **offline** model, where schools receive content on a pre-populated storage device like servers, hard drives, data DVD's or CD-ROMs which they hold and distribute locally.

Developing a digital media service – a research-based approach

Broadcasters, like the Public Broadcasting Service (PBS) (http://www.pbs.org/), face a number of challenges as they look toward designing digital media services. While these resources provide an excellent way to repackage and distribute existing educational multimedia, as well as guide the development of new resources, specific aspects of such a service are still unclear. In order to try to clarify the best course to take in developing a digital media service, PBS recently undertook a pilot study to test different options for such a service. The study provides not only a fascinating case study of the integration of radically new technology into the classroom, but also hints at future opportunities for library media specialists and applications for The Big6™.

The PBS pilot study was designed to meet some lofty but vital goals. These include:

- identifying the issues related to school-based delivery and utilization of digital media,

- developing a strategic vision for educational digital TV programming, and

- testing models of interactive digital programming that enhance teaching and learning.

These goals were accomplished by designing three different model digital media services—one for each of the three delivery methods outlined above—and collaborating with seven local PBS stations and partner school districts to pilot test them for a limited time in several schools.

The pilot content included a very focused sample of PBS programming—Ken Burns' "The West" and "Lewis & Clark," combined with local station resources (such as germane local programming and Web sites), some digital versions of primary source materials and the existing PBS.org companion Web sites for both programs. These sources combined to create a searchable multimedia library collection on westward expansion. This content collection was delivered to participating schools via broadband streaming; digital datacast to networked school receiver; and on sets of CD-ROM's.

The teachers who participated in the study were given professional development workshops in the use of the new technology, a print guide with suggested user scenarios, and ongoing professional and technical support. They were asked to integrate the digital media resources into the curriculum as they would any other source.

Findings

In general, the classroom teachers who participated were very pleased with the tool and excited about the promise of the new technology. They underscored the importance of providing more than just video clips as part of the service, but rather contextualizing the clips and weaving them with online resources like images, interactive features, primary sources, etc. Additionally, they requested more personalization features, such as the ability to bookmark and annotate favorite resources.

When we compare various delivery methods, each presents its own strengths and weaknesses. Datacast brings excellent image quality, high speed and large volume, while it requires additional training for teachers and information technology staff who are required to maintain and use the school's media server. Broadband brought a familiar Web interface that nearly all the teachers felt comfortable using, but it also brought serious bandwidth problems and occasional firewall issues. CD-ROM was the most reliable method, but also the most cumbersome as teachers negotiated distributing discs to a class of busy students.

The study was also able to measure professional development issues related to technology integration. Perhaps the most fascinating finding was that the new technology didn't impact the teachers' existing pedagogical approaches—those who like to lead the class continued to do so with the new technology, while those who like project-based teaching found that the technology enhanced that approach. Another interesting observation was that pedagogy also predicted the preferred format; teachers who lecture liked the traditional CD-ROM delivery system, while constructivist educators were most excited about the newer technologies. Additionally, the study found that collaboration with other teachers positively impacted use of pilot content, for as we know multimedia resources can enhance an interdisciplinary approach to learning and teaching.

Big6™ implications

So where does this promise of new technology leave those of us who have dedicated significant amounts of time and effort to improving the information literacy and information problem-solving of those in our school buildings? To put it succinctly, the future looks bright.

First, digital media services, when created to maximize their potential to bring together many different kinds of resources, model Big6 #5, Synthesis for students and teachers. These services combine different kinds of media, contextualize the information presented, and even cite their sources. This may be one of the first media resources to bring together such radically different materials in a way that makes sense.

Second, the study's findings indicate that the integration of digital media services into the curriculum does not dramatically alter the teacher's and students' behavior. This points to effective Information Seeking Strategies and Use of Information, Big6 #2 and #4. The teachers who participated in the study were not forced to awkwardly insert the digital media resources into the curriculum—instead, the resources suggested their own use in ways that were natural and comfortable.

PBS's pilot study of digital media services gives us an indication of the types of educational technology resources currently in development by many different content providers. These resources will present many new challenges for classroom teachers and library media specialists, but if they are carefully designed, they will also help us to continue to develop better information problem solving skills in our students.

Insights Through Web Sites

By Bob Berkowitz / vE1, no2

As we all know, the Internet can be a wonderful research tool. We also know that the information found on the Internet is generally unedited and that its nature is dynamic; it is there one day and gone the next. When students access information on the World Wide Web we want them to be able to decide if the information is useful, reliable, and appropriate for their assignment.

One way to achieve this instructional goal is to teach students to "test" the Web site and information by using a set of criteria. Asking a series of general questions provides a strategy that is transferable to a full range of web-based and other information sources. Some sample questions follow:

- Who is the author or which institution sponsors this Web page?

- Who is the audience?

- What is the purpose of the information?

- How current is the information?

- Is the content accurate and objective?

John DonVito, a social studies teacher at Wayne Central Schools (Ontario Center, NY), and I developed an activity that would focus on social studies content and essential World Wide Web skills. The activity, "Insights Through Web Sites," was prepared for a course titled "Participation in Government" and focuses on information found on Presidential candidates' Web sites.

Students were asked to complete a Web Site Analysis Worksheet (see following pages) that was designed to review and refocus students' attention on the key questions to consider when assessing information found on web sites. These considerations had been introduced and taught previously in other integrated units. The Web Site Analysis Worksheet features a series of generic Big6 Skill # 2-Information Seeking Strategies, Big6 Skill #3-Location & Access, and Big6 Skill # 4-Use of Information questions. A simple idea? YES. An idea that teaches transferable skills? YES. An instructional idea that can act as a springboard for your own creativity? ABSOLUTELY!

Insights Through Web Sites

The Internet has made information dissemination easier now than at any other time in history. For example, the Internet's impact on politics is profound. No longer do political candidates, political parties, and special interest groups depend exclusively on print media or television to deliver their messages. The Internet is an instantaneous information medium. While the Internet may allow voters to obtain more information more rapidly, it provides no safeguards for the accuracy and dependability of the available information. As consumers of information, it is the responsibility of each of us to be concerned with the quality of the information that is available to us, especially on the Internet. A large amount of information that impacts our daily lives is, in fact, misinformation.

To be good information consumers, and good information-based decision-makers, we need to evaluate web-based information and its sources.

The goal of this assignment is to:

1. Provide a guided approach to Web site evaluation.

2. Analyze the information retrieved from various Web sites.

Your task is to:

1. Access the Web site that is assigned to your group.

2. Review the Web site based on the criteria below.

3. Complete the Web site evaluation "Check-list."

4. Complete the Issues Chart based on information found on the website.

5. Share the information your group gathers with the entire class.

The following is a list of Web sites for presidential political candidates:

1. http://www.algore2000.com/

2. http://www.georgewbush.com/

3. http://www.mccain2000.com/

4. http://www.billbradley.com/

5. http://www.keyes2000.org/

6. http://www.gopatgo2000.org/

The following is a list of election Web sites (compiled by: Blythe Allison Bennett):

1. Federal Election Commission (http://www.fec.gov/)

2. Project Vote Smart (http://www.vote-smart.org/)

3. Gore 2000 (http://www.AlGore2000.com/)

4. George W. Bush election site (http://www.georgewbush.com/)

5. Democratic National Committee (http://www.democrats.org/index.html)

6. Republican (GOP) National Committee (http://www.rnc.org/)

7. C-Span Campaign 2000 (http://www.c-span.org/campaign2000/)

8. C-Span's links to other candidates and political parties (http://www.c-span.org/campaign2000/links.asp)

9. Democracy Network from the League of Women Voters (http://www.dnet.org/)

10. electionSearch 2000 (http://www.electionsearch2000.org/)

11. Opensecrets.org (http://www.opensecrets.org/home/index.asp)

Insights Through Web Sites: Evaluating Information

Site name: _____

Site address: _____

Author: _____ **Date Visited:** _____

Directions: There are no editorial review boards responsible for information published on the Internet. It is essential that you learn to review Web sites critically. Below are some questions that will help you evaluate Web sites and information found on them.

Look at each Web site carefully and answer the following questions with a yes or no and then add your own comments.

Design	Yes / No	Comments
Is the site visually appealing?		
Does the site use features like sound and video that maxamize the internet's potential?		
Do the graphics enhance the site's content?		
Do both the internal and external links work properly?		
Is the material well organized?		
Navigation		
Is it easy to understand how to move around the web site?		
Are there clear choices about how to find more information?		
Can you navigate within the site without getting lost?		
Does the site have an inernal search engine?		
Authority (Author)		
Is it easy to determine the author or authors of the web site?		
Are sources sited?		
Is there a link to contact the authors with questions or feedback?		
Content/accuracy		
Does the page title reflect the content?		
Do the authors clearly state their objectives?		
If so, did the authors clearly meets their objectives?		
Is the material updated frequently and is the last revision date visable?		
Is the information unbiased and balanced?		

Comparing the Presidential Candidates' Views

Directions: Each political candidate has taken a position on the issues listed on this chart. Be prepared to present your findings to the class in a discussion that compares the candidates' positions on the issues.

Issue	Canidate 1	Canidate 2
Gun Laws		
Environment		
Abortion		
Trade		
Taxes		
Social Security		
Medicare		
Foriegn Policy		
Education		
Defense		
Affirmative Action		

Teachers and Class Web Pages: A Winning Combination

By Ru Story-Huffman / vE2, no3

Now that you've mastered getting online from your classroom or library, or have learned successful Internet searching tips, you're ready to tackle the "Big One!" You wish, or perhaps have been encouraged, to build your own course pages and post them to the Web! Publishing on the Web – that's Big6 #5 - Synthesis.

"What?" you say. "I can't do that," or "I don't have the time to do that," "I am afraid to do that," or "I don't know how to do that." I was once in your "technology" shoes. I too, admired educational pages that I saw on the Web. The instructional value was amazing, availability was unique and all the little "do-dads" and technical frills that appeared on some of the pages added to my desire. I really wanted to learn how to build a Web page for myself; to organize and present (again, Big6 #5) and to contribute my ideas to the world (Big6 #1 – Task Definition).

The Web can be seen as the largest publishing house in the world, and we are the authors. You too can be an author of a Web page on the World Wide Web. Not only can you be an author of a valuable educational Web page, you can do so in a very easy manner. As long as you have a connection to the Internet, you can be published.

When I first began to build Web pages, I used one of the numerous Web-authoring programs that can be purchased (e.g., DreamWeaver, FrontPage). I struggled with some of the technology and would get frustrated when a page did not appear as I wanted it to. Soon I discovered with a little patience and time, I could make Web pages that were useful to my students. As the Web has grown, so has the number of commercially available Web authoring programs. But, why pay for something when you can get it free? This is an important question in education, as often our budgets will not allow for the purchase of expensive programs.

There are a number of free Web hosting sites designed specifically for educators (see list at the end of this article). Do it yourself Web pages, built and maintained by these free programs, can be a dream come true for the busy teacher or librarian. Plus, not all schools have the technology available to build and host Web pages, so the free sites can be an added bonus to educators. Most of these sites require some type of registration; some may have advertisements on the page, or templates that you can customize for your classroom use. Sometimes the pages become "public," which means that anyone with an Internet connection can view your pages. Whatever the situation, these free Web pages have potential, and if used in an educational setting can enhance the learning process for our students.

Getting started

First, you must always consider the target audience for your pages (Big6 #1 – Task Definition). This can be students, parents, or fellow teachers. Busy parents may not have time after work to dig through a child's backpack to discover notes from school. By posting parent announcements or reminders on your Web pages, you have the ability to communicate with many parents who have Internet connections. Of course, for those who do not, you will still need to use the paper message method and trust the students to get the information safely home. As a parent, I know what this is like! Web pages for students can provide updates on homework, tips on using the Big6 to accomplish assignments, announcements, links to additional Web pages, and contact information for you, the teacher. If you team-teach in your school, the Web pages can become a joint project, which allows both classrooms to be on the same page, so to speak. Another idea is to make a combination page so that all three audiences can find the information they need.

As a precaution, before registering for any of the programs available, you should check your school district technology plan or outlines. You would not wish to go against policy. Once that hurdle has been cleared, the fun can begin. The next step is Information Seeking Strategies and Location and Access (Big6 stages #2 and #3)—to find and locate several of these Web-hosting sites and investigate the requirements, intended audience, and look at pages that others have published, if possible. Check with other teachers in your school or school district to find out what Web-hosting sites they use. They may know some sites that work well and perhaps, some to avoid. Again, see the end of this article for links to a selection of these free sites. The list isn't inclusive as more appear each day, but this list will give you a good place to start.

Once you have investigated the possibilities and have chosen a site you would like to use, then plan what type of pages you wish to include (back to Big6 #1 - Task Definition, then to Big6 #4 – Use of Information, then on to #5 - Synthesis). The Web-hosting site that you choose may limit you because some offer templates that may not be customizable. If your site is for a specific class or subject, begin the planning stage by developing a list of all information you would like to include on your Web page. Develop an outline, and as you do this, you will be able to delete those items that become unnecessary. A paper outline can help you remember to include everything you want on your Web pages, clarify your thoughts and keep you on task. With the paper outline finished, you are now ready to begin the actual building of your Web page. This task is simpler than it sounds, but you will need to consider some guidelines for the pages themselves.

Some of the free Web hosting sites in this article provide you with the choice of background color, font size and color, and graphics. It is important to consider some design criteria when building and developing Web pages. Pages should be pleasing to the eye and easy to read. Don't include too much information on each page if possible, and make sure that your font size, color, and background are all compatible. Graphics are an important part of any Web page, but too many graphics can be distracting or may lead to long loading time for the pages. Once you've determined the background and layout of the pages, you are ready to begin.

Feedback From Teachers (Big6 #6 – Evaluation)

What do teachers say about using Web pages for their classes? How do they use them? To prepare for this article, I asked for thoughts on the concept of offering instruction via the Web using the Web hosting programs. I polled a small group of teachers and received the following answers to my questions.

- **What is the best advantage of the program you use?** "Ease of use." "Great for homebound instruction. A wonderful contact service between teachers and parents, also teachers and students…Parents can 'see' what we are currently working on." "This program makes the student accountable. The parents can see up-to-date assignments, activities, or events."

- **What are the drawbacks?** "Students without computers at home are at a disadvantage…this is less than 25% of my class." "Keeping it updated." "No capacity for uploading PowerPoint presentations or other formats."

- **Has delivering information via the Web enhanced your teaching in any way? If so, how?** "Absolutely – students have access to class materials, missed assignments, and background information in or out of school." "I tell the students if they do not have a computer at home, they can access this at the public library, our school library, or on the computer in their homeroom…they have enjoyed using this site. The first day of class I give the students a label with the Internet address on it and they place it in their planner. If they are out of school for any reason they can pull up the class assignment for the day and work at home."

- **What has been the reaction of your students? Parents? Administration? Fellow teachers?** "They (the students) love it…(parents) very positive." "Student reaction has been very positive – not much feedback from parents or administrators however." "Students like it…keeps them current…don't have as much trouble getting assignments in." "Parents are very impressed and think it a wonderful tool." "Administration is very supportive."

- **Was this the first time you've used a program to offer curriculum or information via the Web? Would you do it again?** "Fall 2000 is the first semester I used it. I only used it for one course. This semester I use it for all courses. It is wonderful."

As you can tell from the above testimonies, success has been achieved with the use of the free Web hosting programs. You can do the same in your classroom, with a little patience, planning, and perseverance. In my situation as an academic librarian, I have used the Web to communicate with students, colleagues, and to deliver library instruction modules. I have built Web pages using the free Web hosting programs and have found some that I like, and others that I like better. The best advice is to continually explore, determine your goals and educational objectives, and find the program that works best for your situation.

Web-Hosting Sites for Teachers

To prepare for this topic, I began a search on the Internet for free Web hosting sites that assist teachers. There were plenty to choose from, and more are probably being developed as you read this article. The following list of sites does not cover all that are available. Presented as a starting point, the list will help you to investigate and determine which site would be best for your needs and the needs of your classroom. I encourage you to find the site that works best for you and fulfills the goals you have established for the project.

- **QUIA** (http://www.quia.com)
  QUIA stands for Quintessential Instructional Archive, and provides a vast variety of services. Unlike most of the sites investigated for this article, QUIA offers neat activities that the educator can build in a few short steps. We've all seen the wonderful games and activities that are available on the Web, including Java games. Well, with QUIA, you can make your own games and activities using the provided tools and templates. Your games can include hangman, matching, jumbled words or an Internet scavenger hunt. The templates are useful, easy to use, and provide you with step-by-step guidance. Another option with the use of QUIA is to build class Web pages where you can post information about yourself, your school, or class and homework assignments or announcements. You can link to any activities that you have built with QUIA from your class home page. The registration is free, the Web pages are hosted on the QUIA server, (you'll receive notification of the specific URL for your pages) and it is easy to complete. Of all the pages investigated for this article, I found QUIA to be the best value for your money…even if it is free! By the way, QUIA does offer Premium Service, which provides Ad-Free Web pages for a fee, based upon class or school size.

- **Scholastic** (http://homepage.scholastic.com/classpages/start_hp.cfm)
  Scholastic, well known for children's books, teacher journals and curriculum support, has moved to the world of the Web. With their class home page builder, educators have the opportunity to build nice class Web pages. Upon free registration, you can include information for parents and students, photographs of classroom activities, and educational links appropriate for topics of study. You will also find a section titled "Editor's Picks," which provides links to various books and characters that are a portion of the Scholastic "collection." A nice feature of the Scholastic home page builder is that you can make your page private. Students must know the classroom user name and password to gain access to your pages.

- **MySchoolOnline.Com** (http://myschoolonline.com/golocal)
  Part of the "Learning Network," My School Online bills itself as the "Web's largest community of local education sites." The site offers free hosting in a template style, with turnkey, or ready to use website building tools. Upon registration, you can build a class website, create and maintain an electronic grade book, or sign up for professional development. As with many of the free Web hosting sites, advertising banners are located on the pages built by educators. Corporate and private sponsorship is sometimes necessary for these programs to be offered free to the Web community.

- **TeacherWeb** (http://www.teacherWeb.com)
  This is a nice site that provides a good opportunity for school-to-home communication. You can customize your pages to include announcements, homework, links, frequently asked questions, a calendar, and teacher information. When completed, the students are presented a clean looking page with links for each option available to them. Content updates are secure and easy, and your students and parents will receive instant information. Educators who use this site will find it a good place to communicate with students and parents.

- **HighWired** (http://www.highwired.com/HomePage/)
  The HighWired Network offers free Web hosting for a wide variety of educators. With this site, other school support services can participate online too! The school nurse can post office hours or the cafeteria manager can publish the lunch menu. The HighWired Network is a bit more customizable than some free Web hosting programs, and you have the opportunity to upload photographs to your pages or create an online newspaper for your school. The pages are stored on the HighWired server, and you can put your school name or initials in the actual address to make it a bit more representative of your school. The HighWired Network may not be for the novice, but with a bit of practice and patience, you too can have a nice site hosted on the HighWired server.

The above sites represent just a few of the numerous sites that are available for educators. I urge everyone to investigate the options for developing a Web page for the school or classroom. Do a search on the Internet for free Web hosting sites that have been developed for educators, students, parents or administration. Talk with other teachers who have used free Web hosting programs, and look at their pages. Look at each free Web-hosting site with a critical eye and know your goals, capabilities and needs. Soon you'll be on the way to publishing on the Web. Hey, if I can do it…anyone can!

The World Wide Web Is Just One Evaluation Away

By Ru Story-Huffman / vE4, no3

The World Wide Web has changed our lives in many ways, most profoundly in the way we access and retrieve information and knowledge. Before the availability of the Web, students relied primarily on books and journal articles to locate information for assignments and curriculum. With the Web now available in the classroom, library or home, information is simply a few keystrokes away, with graphics, audio, video and games to enhance the learning process.

Web Information: The Promise and the Challenge

The Web can provide information that is useful, interesting, entertaining and full of educational benefits. A teacher can locate lesson plans, curriculum extensions, technology standards, bulletin board ideas and even math problems for use in the classroom (e.g., see www.thegateway.org). Students can use the Web to locate information on a topic, learn about other countries, look at a dissected frog or play games that develop learning and knowledge. Parents can use a school web site to check on homework for missed school days, communicate with a teacher or check for tomorrow's school lunch menu. The possibilities for information, resources, ideas and new experiences are as varied as the Web itself.

As wonderful a tool as the Web can be, it is necessary to realize that not all information found on the Internet is trustworthy. Some Web sites are purposely false and misleading. Others may contain information the Web page author or publisher does not realize to be untrue. Complicating the issue is the fact that the Internet is not a static resource; it is constantly changing and growing. Currently, the Web is estimated at 6 billion pages and the Google search engine indexes more than 3 billion Web pages. (Jefferson Graham, "The Search Engine That Could," (http://www.usatoday.com/tech/news/2003-08-25-google_x.htm) *USA Today,* August 25, 2003).

With this many Web pages, and more developed every day, the choices for finding information are almost unlimited. With so many choices, how can one be certain the information from a particular web site is correct and will meet the needs of the user? One word will answer that question, one word that is an essential component of every stage of the Big6—EVALUATION.

The Importance of Evaluation – Big6™ Style

Although there is a separate Big6 stage for Evaluation - #6 – evaluation of information actually pervades every Big6 stage. For example, in Big6 stage #1, Task Definition, students evaluate the nature and type of information needed to complete a task. In Stage #2, Information Seeking Strategies, evaluation takes the form of considering all possible sources and then selecting the most appropriate source. Determining key words that will represent a source when searching is evaluation of information in Stage #3, Location and Access. When students interact with a source and extract relevant information, that's evaluation of information in Stage #4, Use of Information. For Synthesis, Stage #5, students evaluate which information to discard and which to include in their final presentation. And obviously, there's evaluation in Stage #6, Evaluation, as students judge the product and the process.

Assessment of information is crucial for students and educators. When considering the Web, evaluation of information mostly centers within Stage #2, Information Seeking Strategies and #4, Use of Information. For example, when teachers decide to use a Web page as an information source, that's Information Seeking Strategies. After locating the website, they must be certain the information presented is factual, correct and addresses stated curriculum goal—Use of Information.

Students do the same thing. As an Information Seeking Strategy, they decide to use a Web site. They should do so with a critical eye, thinking about the pitfalls and limitations of the Web. Then, during Stage #4, Use of Information, students apply even more critical evaluation indicators to determine if the information is accurate and trustworthy.

Below, you will find a list of evaluation criteria that can be adapted for use in evaluating websites and web information in a classroom or library setting. The age, reading and comprehension levels of the audience are important considerations when teaching Web page evaluation to students. For example, younger children may struggle with determining validity of a source, yet they can understand if the page looks bad or if the information deviates from your teaching and their learning.

Things to Consider when Evaluating a Web Page:

1. Is there an author or publisher listed on the web site?

a. Looking for the name of the person responsible for the web page or hosting organization (publisher) can help determine if the information is true. A person who develops a Web page may include their professional affiliation, such as school or university, and an email contact. If necessary, email the author of the Web page to obtain information about their qualifications or to help locate the source for information.

b. Sometimes it is hard to determine who published the Web page. Look for an identifying logo, graphic, "about us" or "contact us" section on the page. This information may be located on the left side of the page, near the top in a banner, or toward the bottom of the page. Another method of locating information about the publisher is to use the URL or web address of the web page. Typically, the part of the address that is after the http:// and before the first "/," will lead you to the publisher of a web site. For example, if you find the following Web address while you are looking for information about books: http://www.rustoryhuffman.com/books, backspace and delete "books" and you would then be directed to http://www.rustoryhuffman.com, or the homepage of the Web site you had just visited. From there, you should be able to determine the publisher and make a connection between their mission and the Web site you are using.

2. Is there a date listed on the web page that tells you when the page was last updated?

a. It is very easy to publish a web site, but harder to keep the page updated and current. Look for a date of creation and/or update to help you decide if the information is recent and practical for stated curriculum. You would not want to encourage children to write a report on the latest methods to control diabetes using a web site from 1997, now would you?

3. Is the information presented factual? Is it objective?

a. Especially when using statistics, biographical or scientific information, students need to be sure the information is correct. When writing a research paper, students must cite their resources. The same is true for a good Web page. Is biographical information or a references list available on the Web site? If statistics are present, can the readers tell where they come from? If you cannot find any information to back up the Web site's content, it is best not to use the site for research.

b. Sometimes an organization will develop a web page to support their causes or beliefs. This information may be biased, depending upon the views of the organization and/or the reader. A Web site that presents objective information is a Web site that gives differing views on a subject. For example, a Web site that said the only way to cook a chicken was to fry it is not providing information on grilling or roasting a bird!

4. The way a Web site looks can also influence learning. Other factors when evaluating a Web page include design, readability and ease of use.

a. A Web page that has a black background, orange text and numerous graphics is a site that is difficult to read. A good Web page design features a white, or light colored background, black text in Ariel or Times New Roman font, and minimal use of graphics. Too many icons, singing bears or musical chairs can distract from learning, comprehension and slow the load time for a page, especially when using a dial-up modem.

b. A critical factor, especially for educators when looking for pages to use in a classroom setting, is readability. You do not want to use a Web page with a child that has content and reading level designed for adults. Not only will they be frustrated, as they will be unable to comprehend and read the information, but you will too.

Conclusion

The evaluation criteria and questions presented in this article are designed to provide you with a starting point. Each class is different, and each Web page experience is different as well. The evaluation techniques are designed to be adapted for use with all ages, situations, curriculums and standards you may encounter during your educational career. You can even adapt the evaluation criteria and questions to make a rubric exercise for students. Older students can participate in creating a class- or subject-specific rubric that can be used over and over. While the evaluation criteria are important, it is even more important for students (and teachers) to learn the necessity for evaluating information on the Web critically.

Evaluation Sites for Use in the Classroom

The following Web sites are just a few of the choices available on evaluating Internet information. Some of the sites provide additional links, worksheets and are part of well-known Internet sites for educators.

WWW CyberGuides for Evaluation
http://www.cyberbee.com/guides.html
Developed in 1996 as part of the "Adventures in Cyberbee's" web site, this evaluation site features a ratings guide for evaluation of Internet information and ratings for Web site design. The CyberGuides for evaluation site has been used in classrooms as a curriculum tool to enhance the learning process.

Kathy Schrock's Guide for Educators – Critical Evaluation Information
http://school.discovery.com/schrockguide/eval.html
Kathy Schrock maintains an excellent resource for teachers through her Web site. The Critical Evaluation page offers evaluation surveys for use with elementary, middle and

secondary students, PowerPoint presentations and articles on Web page evaluation, and links to information by other experts in the field.

Evaluating Web Pages: A WebQuest
http://mciunix.mciu.k12.pa.us/~spjvweb/evalwebteach.html
Designed for use with 9th through 12th grade students, this WebQuest activity teaches critical evaluation of information from the Internet. Students are presented with resources from the Internet and they are to determine the authenticity of the pages. While an exercise in critical thinking and evaluation, it may also address information literacy and technology standards.

The Quality Information Check List (QUICK)
http://www.quick.org.uk/menu.htm
Designed for use with middle school students, but adaptable for all ages, this nicely designed site features a quiz on evaluation resources, a checklist of evaluative points and resources for teachers.

2Learn – Evaluating Internet Web Sites
http://www.2learn.ca/evaluating/evaluating.html
The information found on this Web site is concise and features printable forms designed for use with different grade levels. Additional links to evaluation resources make this site a useful tool for educators.

Yahooligans: Teachers' Guide to Internet Literacy
http://www.yahooligans.com/tg/activities.html
The Student Activities section of the Teachers' Guide to Internet Literacy provides exercises on comparing Web sites, Internet and non-Internet resources, learning about Web sites and a form for student analysis of Web sites.

Ed's Oasis Evaluation Center
http://www.classroom.com/edsoasis/evaluation.html;jsessionid=YVMIY25RIC0VVQFICQ FCUYQ
Part of the Classroom Connect Web site, Ed's Oasis Evaluation Center is a great site for teaching Web page evaluation techniques to children. General guidelines are presented, as are teacher and student evaluation worksheets that can be used to grade Web sites using various assessment criteria. The worksheets contain a section where specific questions are answered and a scoring guide to aid in determination of the Web site.

Web Page Evaluation
http://www2.cumberlandcollege.edu/library/Li/evaluati1.htm
This Web site is maintained by the author, and is used to teach Web page evaluation to college students. The evaluative points and illustrations can easily be adapted for use with high school students who need to learn Web page evaluation.

CHAPTER 16

Technology and All

Conversations with Timber Drive Elementary School's I&T Team

By Ferdi Serim / vE4, no1

While researching my new book *Information Technology for Learning: No School Left Behind*, I received a midnight e-mail from Mike Eisenberg, sharing an e-mail he'd just received. Jean Koch, Certified Big6 Trainer and Library Media Specialist (LMS) in VA, wrote "I live near NC and receive the PBS station from NC as well as our local PBS station. Monday evening, October 14, I saw a great program about Timber Drive Elementary School in Wake, County, NC. They use the Big6 and have implemented Mike's idea of Information & Technology (I&T) Teams. This elementary school has two full time Library Media Specialists, one computer teacher and a network administrator who is also a certified teacher. They do regular planning with the grade level teachers, and the administrators attend and support this approach completely. The entire culture of the school supports using the skills of this team to help students learn and improve. They seem to be living out what you just wrote about and it was so exciting to see."

Jean continued, "I mention it because it seemed to be a great example of what we can become. My system, Virginia Beach City Public Schools, has gone through a job redefinition project and we (LMS and the Computer Specialist) are now called an Instructional Technology Team. We are encouraged to collaborate with the teachers and we have been meeting regularly. We are just getting this off the ground, and so we're looking for models and practices that work well for the students and staff. I was encouraged by the program I saw Monday."

Applying the Big6™ Skills to This Task

It was midnight, and already the Big6 was working for me:

My Task Definition: Tell the story of this incredible school.

Information Seeking Strategies: Find the school website, get some e-mail addresses to make the initial contact.

Location and Access: I found the site, found pages about the Library/Technology program and the e-mail addresses of Steven Moore and Ted Fillhart.

Use of Information: I sent e-mail inquiries, received replies the next morning, and we set a time for a conference call. During this 90-minute phone call, I gathered the information that forms the basis of the conversation you see below.

Synthesis: I pulled my notes from the interview together into a summary, which I provided to the Timber Drive team for corrections and comments. Following several e-mail exchanges, these became three different pieces: a white paper for CoSN on Data Driven Decision Making, "I&T Team Snapshots" for the new book; and this eNewsletter article.

Evaluation: The members of the Timber Drive I&T Team feel that our products accurately reflect their experience, meet Jean's original desire to help schools who are "just getting this off the ground so are working out some kinks" and hope you are "encouraged" by what you read here.

Meet the Timber Drive I&T Team

Timber Drive Elementary School is a year-round school in Garner, North Carolina. In a year-round elementary and middle school, the traditional 180-day school year is divided into nine-week quarters with a three-week break at the end of each quarter. Students are in school the same number of days as their counterparts in traditional schools. Their days are simply redistributed throughout the year. The reorganized schedule is called a 45/15 calendar - 45 days in school, 15 days off.

However, what distinguishes Timber Drive from most other schools is the way in which collaborative planning and teaching embrace technology to reach every child. It is a "living, breathing" model for what a powerful I&T program can achieve.

Our call began with introductions of the I&T team: Mrs. Sue King (principal), Nancy Finger and Sue Ellen Ott (Library Media Specialists), Steven Moore (Instructional Technology Facilitator), Ted Fillhart (Network Administrator), Frank Creech and Susan Boyer (Assistant Principals). The team had asked me to send questions in advance, and I provided them with the Introduction to IT for Learning, which breaks down the challenges into four areas:

- Accountability (Making IT Work for Assessment and Growth)

- Learning (Making IT Work for 21st Century Learning)

- Leadership (Making IT Work for Sustained Support)

- Technical (Making IT Work for Everyone)

History of Timber Drive Elementary School and its I&T Team

Ferdi: "How did you get started on this path?"

Nancy Finger replied, "I was excited by the first articles about Flexible Access in *School Library Journal* in 1989. By 1992 I'd attended every conference I could to learn more about putting the concepts into practice. In 1993-94, Wake County was one of several districts awarded a Library Power grant, which opened doors to the best thinkers and doers in the information literacy world. Through these doors came Mike Eisenberg, who introduced the Big6 to our district in 1996. That was the same year that my principal, Sue King, opened a new school, Timber Drive elementary. Mrs. King left nothing to chance. She developed a leadership team that applied the many lessons learned in their previous schools, making collaboration, trust and teambuilding a part of Timber Drive's DNA before the doors even opened, before any teacher was hired."

Mrs. King remembers, "Nancy really did educate me. I was a classroom teacher, but I hadn't experienced the technology or the media. I was open to finding new and better ways to help children learn, so this was great to discover. At our previous school, we'd developed a model of collaborative planning and teaching, so with this model in place, we set about building our new school. This model embraces the integration of technology as a key tool for learning, a tool with incredible resources embedded. We constantly speak of the Library/Media Center as the hub of learning for the school, and for us, that is more than just words."

Mrs. King added, "It is so rewarding for us as administrators, because we know it works. When we're in budget planning time at the school, we get to decide on how we will add to our staff (when enrollment goes up, we are allocated more personnel). Our leadership team, supported unanimously by our 55-60 teachers has added three key positions over the years (two full time Library/Media Specialists, a media assistant and one full time Network Administrator) beyond those that the state will provide us. This shows that the staff understands the vital contribution to the educational well being of the entire school, as a learning community, that our I&T team makes."

The Path to a Successful I&T Team

Ferdi: "What do you see as the primary requirement for the success you've experienced?"

Frank Creech: "It is crucial that an appropriate culture be in place. The culture must support professionalism enough to set a standard for being innovative and willing to change methods in order to improve."

Ferdi: "It seems that you've enjoyed such success because you've taken years to put down roots that have staying power. What do you say to schools and leaders who are looking for a quick fix?"

Mrs. King: "We've worked our way on this path every day for the past five years, and we will never stop. Once you get over the illusion that you may someday 'arrive' at technology integration, and realize that improvement is forever, it becomes quite exciting. We all say 'this is a work in progress' and I hope we never stop saying it."

Using the Big6™ Skills

Ferdi: "What role does the Big6 play in your integration efforts?"

Frank Creech: "The kids who come to us at or below grade level grow the fastest. Students near the top require support in problem solving, to build higher order thinking skills. That's where the Big6 has been so helpful. A tremendous number of curriculum goals can be addressed in a single project when we can differentiate instruction in such ways."

Meeting the Accountability Requirements of No Child Left Behind

Ferdi: "What you've done for higher order thinking and collaboration is incredible. But what about the schools that have put the brakes on those types of learning as a response to *No Child Left Behind*? Does the need to examine data and meet accountability requirements derail efforts for integrated learning?"

Frank Creech responded, "Using data to guide instruction is nothing new to us in North Carolina. We've been doing this for the last five or six years with data from the North Carolina ABC's of Public Education (our State-wide standardized testing). Looking at data and changing what we're doing on the basis of needs the children are showing only makes sense. The NCDPI and our district research department provide us with disaggregated test data. We work with teachers to analyze this data. The flexibility of our team approach enables us to break large classes down into smaller groups, targeting on skills and individual student needs."

Steve Moore added, "Too often when people focus on data and test scores, they lose sight of the primary resource for improving achievement: building relationships and community. Our administrators took a risk, in allowing us to devote extra resources to building our team. It is a risk that has paid off. Of the 78 elementary schools in our district, Timber Drive is one of eleven schools that has met both Expected and High Growth standards for five consecutive years. This didn't happen through remediation. It happened by strengthening learning for all students."

Mrs. King explained how it works. "Each year, when the state testing data arrives, we hire subs and spend time with teachers, looking at the data, child by child. A team comprised of every professional who works with any child who's having difficulty confers about patterns we see in the data. We do not focus on remediation: we believe that an invigorating experience of learning is good for every child. There are multiple opportunities for each child to learn a concept: they may learn it with Steve in the lab, with Nancy in the media center, in class. We have such abilities to differentiate instruction, to use different media and modalities to get the concepts across (through the Big6 and WebQuests) that we provide opportunities for all to grow."

Sue continued, "An example is our Write Point project. When this school opened, we drew from 13 sending schools. That first year our scores on the 4th Grade NC writing assessment left us no doubt we had a problem! Children came to us with 13 different levels of preparation. We experimented with a program of concentrated writing instruction. We brought in all the specialists (media, technology, administrators, and special ed) and created a cadre of writing coaches. We took the entire fourth grade population and divided them, by ability, among the staff, which resulted in groups of about eight students per staff. We zeroed in on the needs for each specific group, using this approach: what is our problem, what do we want to happen, what can we do to get there? The results were incredible, and set us on our path for continuous growth."

Collaborating to Integrate Technology Across the Curriculum

Ferdi: "How do you get past the staff reluctance and difficulty so commonly reported when we work to integrate technology across the curriculum, throughout the school?"

Sue Ellen Ott replied, "Trust is crucial. The trust level must be deep enough that we can focus on teaching **how** to learn, not **what** to learn. Collaboration at this level is not tied into planning periods, where kids come to the lab or media center to provide teachers with a break. We're in there together, working together for the benefit of the kids. Teachers come to us, suggesting topics, and we help them to design lessons, many times teaching the lessons with them. Word soon gets around, and other teachers want to know if we can teach those lessons with their classes. Soon, these good practices spread throughout the school."

Providing Professional Development - Flexibly

Ferdi: How do you make the staff development work? What roles do teamwork and flexibility play?

Ted Fillhart replied, "Our staff development happens before school. In my position as network administrator, I am able to offer staff development during the teacher's planning time as well - one on one or small group instruction. Although Steven has a schedule, and can't be as flexible as I can in working directly with teachers and students, we do find ways to work with them, in the lab, in the media center, in classrooms, in the TV studio. With the recent addition of LCD projectors for each grade level we are able to support teachers as they integrate technology into their classrooms and their lessons in ways they couldn't do before. It takes lots of the pressure and fear off of them when we're able to be there, alongside teachers in preparation for their lessons."

Choosing Software

Ferdi: "Some schools seem to think they can buy products to do what your team does, perhaps because they think the requirement of collaboration is beyond their grasp. How do you decide about software to support your efforts?"

Frank Creech: reports, "We constantly evaluate the worth of available software. Our students are very active with multimedia presentation. We're finding that focusing on a minimal number of programs that allow kids to produce (*Inspiration/Kidspiration, HyperStudio, Office*) along with certain web-based programs is a better fit for methods of supporting student growth. The value comes from what the students can create with the software they use, not what's been built into the programs when they are purchased."

Ferdi: "This seems to fly in the face of other districts, who take pride in the vast number of programs they have available on their servers."

Steve and Ted agree: "We prefer to focus on what students are doing with the software rather than how many types and kinds of programs we own. We do our best to keep up with what's available. However it is tragic to see how many other schools and districts are wasting time and money, as if software were a magic bullet. The North Carolina DPI guidelines for software help inform our decisions. The state, county and district also make available district wide resources, including Gale, Search-a-saurus and Encarta, so that all students have access to high-quality, evaluated, vetted and organized resources, in addition to what they can find on the Internet through teacher provided links and search engines."

Making IT Work for Everyone

Ferdi: "What are the "nitty gritty details of your work in supporting technology at Timber Drive?"

Ted answered, "It's no secret that I have a unique position as a network administrator (system operator) at an elementary school. It is so important for someone who's hired for a position like mine to be a certified teacher. I was a classroom teacher for 14 years before taking on this position 3.5 years ago. Why is being teacher in my position so crucial? I am able to relate to teachers and understand what their needs are. Those needs range from what needs to be fixed to who needs to be trained, what application would work best, and so on. Not only do I work with the network, but as a certified teacher I can actually teach a 5th grade language arts class, or lead a 4th grade small group in microscopic organisms or share a book talk with kindergartners."

Ted continues, "Having over 1000 logins and over 300 PCs means that the file servers must be maintained and routine directory service repairs need to be made. Other responsibilities of my job include maintaining the school's Internet site and Intranet sites, on-site equipment repairs, trouble shooting, following up on staff work orders (in house or reported to county tech), technology related purchases, providing staff development, assisting in Internet searches for teachers, video taping requests and editing and the morning WOLF TV broadcasts that are led by 5th grade students. So, there you have it, and yes I LOVE MY JOB!"

Teamwork: The Bottom Line for Learning

Ferdi: "In conclusion, what advice do you have for schools who feel they must choose between No Child Left Behind and a vibrant Library Media/Technology program?

Sue King: "No Child Left Behind is certainly proving to be a wake up call for many districts. They are being challenged to *do something different*. My message to these districts is this: a school's media/technology staff helps ensure that no child will be left behind. Schools that have decreased or dropped their Media programs are depriving themselves of just the resources they need to succeed. Our Media/Technology team is composed of the leaders of our instructional program. That is why we constantly speak of the Library/Media Center as the hub of learning at our school.

The FITness Report: Being Fluent with Information Technology

By Kathleen L. Spitzer / vE2, no3

Information technology has increasingly become a part of our everyday lives and work-places. Not only is information technology pervasive, but it is ever changing. How can individuals cope? Being Fluent with Information Technology, a report published in 1999, is an attempt to answer the question: "What should everyone know about information technology in order to use it more effectively now and in the future (Committee on Information Technology Literacy, p. 2)?"

*I*n 1997, the Computer Science and Telecommunications Board (CSTB) of the National Research Council formed a committee chaired by Dr. Larry Snyder, Professor of Computer Science and Engineering at the University of Washington to study the subject of information technology literacy. The committee, which considered input from a range of computer and information professionals, decided to use the term fluency rather than literacy noting that "fluency connotes the ability to reformulate knowledge, to express oneself creatively and appropriately, and to produce and generate information (rather than simply to comprehend it) (Committee on Information Technology Literacy, p. viii). The committee's report, *Being Fluent with Information Technology*, considers information technology from a comprehensive perspective.

FITness

Fluency with Information Technology, or FITness, "requires that persons understand information technology broadly enough to be able to apply it to their everyday lives, to recognize when information technology would assist or impede the achievement of a goal, and to continually adapt to the changes in and advancement of information technology (Committee on Information Technology Literacy, p. 15)." FITness requires knowledge in three areas:

- **Intellectual capabilities** - having the ability to solve problems by reasoning, test possible solutions, anticipate and adapt to change, and troubleshoot.

- **Fundamental concepts** - knowing about computers and information systems, being aware of how they work and how they impact society.

- **Contemporary skills** - being able to manage a personal computer and use common software applications such as e-mail, word processing, spreadsheets, and databases.

Each of these areas contains ten suggested elements that experts identified as the top ten capabilities, concepts and skills needed for FITness. By integrating these capabilities, concepts, and skills, a person should be able to solve problems and apply technology appropriately. However, due to the evolutionary nature of information technology, FITness cannot be considered as a goal to reach only once, rather it needs to be a commitment to lifelong learning.

Implementation

The committee chose to focus on implementation at the college level since colleges and universities already have existing models for such efforts and would likely have an existing information technology infrastructure. Possibilities for implementation include offering courses that focus on FITness or infusing information technology projects throughout the curriculum. A number of sample projects are described in the report.

The University of Washington used the report as the basis for a new course co-developed by the Department of Computer Science and Engineering and the Information School. Now offered every term to undergraduate students, Fluency with Information Technology (CSE100/INFO100), is a course designed to develop fluency through lectures, lab work, and by involving students in a number of projects. One such project, "Website of Misinformation" requires students to create a Web page featuring a photograph that they have altered accompanied by text that provides information about the altered photograph. Students are encouraged to make their Web pages believable and to field test these pages with other students to determine if the desired affect has been achieved. Among the objectives for the assignment are:

- To design and implement a Web site using HTML

- To manipulate a photograph in *PhotoShop*

- To experience first hand the ease with which "misinformation" can be made available online

- To become aware of and systematically explore the "cues" that users may use to assess the content of a Web site

- To conduct user testing to evaluate your Web site

- To reflect on the challenges for misinformation online

- Ultimately, to become an appropriately cautious user of online information (Snyder, 2001).

- Students completing this project would use all three components of fluency; problem-solving, creating a Web page, and learning about the societal impact of technology.

The Big6™ Connection

How can students use the Big6 to develop FITness? As an information problem-solving process, the Big6 provides students with a roadmap for developing their problem-solving abilities. Following is an analysis of the project described above which requires students to find a photograph to be altered, alter it, create a Web page on which to display it and provide text about the photograph that is believable.

- **Big6 #1: Task Definition:** Find a photograph to alter and then provide believable text about the photograph.

- **Big6 #2: Information Seeking Strategies:** Search news Web sites such as CNN, NBC, Associated Press, and browse through magazines to find text.

- **Big6 #3: Location & Access:** Find a photograph and text currently associated with it.

- **Big6 #4: Use of Information:** View the photograph and read the current text that is associated with the photograph or other text about that topic.

- **Big6 #5: Synthesis:** Use *PhotoShop* to alter the photograph and compose fictional but believable text to accompany the photograph. Prior to composing the text, analyze the current information available about the topic to think of something that will be believable. Put together the Web page featuring the altered photograph and the text.

- **Big6 #6: Evaluation:** Test the Web page to determine if the website is believable. Think about the process used to complete the assignment. What did you do well? What would you change?

Conclusion

Being Fluent with Information Technology points out, not all individuals are capable of achieving FITness but all are capable of achieving some level of FITness. As we work with students to develop their information problem-solving capabilities, we are developing the building blocks for FITness.

Note: Being Fluent with Information Technology is available for purchase from the National Academy Press or may be read online for free.

Bibliography

Committee on Information Technology Literacy. (1999). *Being fluent with information technology*. Washington, DC: National Academy Press.

Snyder, L. (2001). "Web of misinformation." (14 July 2001). [On-line]. http://www.cs.washington.edu/education/courses/100/CurrentQtr/labs/Project1.htm

The Importance of Contemporary Literacy in the Digital Age: A Response to Digital Transformation: A Framework for Information Communication Technologies (ICT) Literacy

By Ferdi Serim / From the Big6 website: www.big6.com

*T*echnology is the Big Bang that has propelled literacy into an expanding universe. Scientists, no longer able to keep up through printed journals, now understand each other's work online, through sophisticated visualizations and simulations made possible by supercomputing. Economists, unable to process the volume and complexity of financial transactions, employ armies of programmers to deploy powerful tools for real-time visualization of the flow of wealth. Visualization extends literacy by enabling people to perceive relationships hidden below the surface of vast amounts of data, and to synthesize meaning from these relationships. The challenge to "everyday people" to keep up with this expansion can only be met through development of a framework for Information & Communications Technology (ICT) Literacy, such as that proposed in Digital Transformation, and the resulting research based interventions. Information "thinking skills" are the true essential skills for the 21st Century.

Literacy has always been at the heart of the education enterprise. From the time of the 3Rs to now, being literate has been a consistent yet evolving foundation for citizenship in each cultural era. Literacy has also been used as a wedge, from the times of slavery (when teaching slaves to read was a felony) until the civil rights era, when literacy tests relied upon the inequality of schools to recreate a disenfranchised population by proxy.

In January 2001, Educational Testing Service (ETS) convened an international panel to study the growing importance of existing and emerging Information and Communication Technologies (ICT) and their relationship to literacy. Their report, Digital Transformation, has just been released, putting forth a framework for ICT Literacy that provides a foundation for the design of instruments including large-scale assessments intended to inform public policy and provide diagnostic measures to test skills associated with information and communication technology.

Published by Educational Testing Service's Center for Global Assessment, Digital Transformation states a definition of ICT literacy as "using digital technology, communications tools, and/or networks to access, manage, integrate, evaluate, and create information in order to function in a knowledge society." A free PDF copy of this report is available at http://www.ets.org/research/ictliteracy/ictreport.pdf.

In Digital Transformation, Educational Testing Service (ETS) gathered a distinguished panel of international researchers, who find that "ICT literacy cannot be defined primarily as the mastery of technical skills. The panel concludes that the concept of ICT literacy should be broadened to include both critical cognitive skills as well as the application of technical skills and knowledge. These cognitive skills include general literacy, such as reading and numeracy, as well as critical thinking and problem solving. Without such skills, the panel believes that true ICT literacy cannot be attained."

Such a definition heightens the importance of the work of IT Teams at every level. Only when the people responsible for curricular, instructional, management and technical aspects of the school operate from a shared understanding of the importance of ICT Literacy can their actions align to make contemporary literacy possible for all students. Fortunately, such initiatives are already underway, and reporting significant success.

In December 2000, e-Learning: Putting a World Class Education at the Fingertips of All Children, the second National Technology Plan ever devised was released. In addressing ICT Literacy, the plan states "A meaningful, unified approach to providing students with the skills they will need for their futures must be more than a checklist of isolated technology skills, such as knowing the parts of a computer, writing drafts and final products with a word processor, or searching for information using a CD-ROM database."

"Rather, technology skills are only a first step in assuring all our children become proficient information and technology users. Also necessary are information literacy skills such as:

- **Task definition**—The first step in the information problem-solving process is to recognize that an information need exists, to define the problem, and to identify the types and extent of information needed.

- **Information seeking strategies**—Once the information problem has been formulated, the student must consider all possible information sources and develop a plan for searching.

- **Location and access**—after students determine their priorities for information seeking, they must locate information from a variety of resources, access specific information found within individual resources, and evaluate the quality of resources.

- **Use of information**—After finding potentially useful resources, students must engage (read, view, listen) the information to determine its relevance and then extract the relevant information.

- **Synthesis**—Students must organize and communicate the results of the information problem-solving effort.

- **Evaluation**—Evaluation focuses on how well the product meets the original task (effectiveness) and the process of how well students carried out the problem-solving process (efficiency).

The plan described above is the Big6 Approach to Information Problem Solving, the most widely known and used approach to teaching information and technology skills. The Big6 is used in thousands of K-12 schools and higher education institutions, as well as in corporate and adult training programs. An estimated 84,000 teachers have been trained in the Big6 program.

The Bertelsmann Foundation and the AOL Time Warner Foundation have joined with experts from education, business and government, recently convening an international 21st Century Literacy Summit. The Summit demonstrated notable examples of 21st Century Literacy initiatives, and recommended to various institutions how they can support individuals in taking full advantage of the tools and resources of the Digital Age.

Cited as an exemplary practice in the Summit whitepaper, the Big6 (first developed in 1988) provides a systematic process based on six broad skill areas necessary for successful information problem-solving. This approach builds a set of skills and an organized strategy for effectively meeting information needs while developing critical thinking skills. Big6.org provides a complete library and information skill curriculum that can be used throughout a student's development.

The research basis for this approach is extensive. In her recent literature review of this research, Carrie Lowe writes "The existing body of research on information literacy can be considered in the context of three themes, which are the nature and scope of information literacy, the value of information literacy, and effective methods of information literacy skills instruction."

On the nature and scope of information literacy, Lowe notes "Kuhlthau's research contributions led to a much greater understanding of the importance of teaching information skills (such as individual steps in The Big6) in context and not as discrete tasks. Kuhlthau's (1993) research into the information seeking behavior of students contributed to her central philosophy of information literacy – that information literacy is not a set of individual tasks or skills, but rather a way of thinking that allows individuals to be the flexible thinkers and lifelong learners who will succeed in the information age."

Regarding the value of information literacy, Lowe notes that the cognitive aspects and related benefits are key. "Pitts' (1995) examination of the mental models of students engaged in the information problem-solving process found that they use different domains of knowledge to complete a task, including one responsible for information seeking and use and others related to the other aspects of the task, including subject knowledge. Pitts found that a lack of knowledge in one area (including information problem-solving skills) could limit learning and success overall."

The crucial importance of ICT Literacy heightens the value of successful implementations. Lowe reports "Eisenberg and Berkowitz (1988) found that the best way to teach information literacy skills (such as the Big6) in curriculum context is through the collaboration of classroom teachers and library media specialists. Brievik (1998) found that the same is true in higher education, as students succeed in integrated courses designed by faculty members and academic librarians."

Given the new national educational policy focus on improving student achievement, through research-based practices which document student growth, the work of the ICT is both timely and imperative. As noted in the 1999 National Research Council report Being Fluent with Information Technology, the "requirement of a deeper understanding than is implied by the rudimentary term 'computer literacy' motivated the committee to adopt 'fluency' as a term connoting a higher level of competency. People fluent with information technology (FIT persons) are able to express themselves creatively, to reformulate knowledge, and to synthesize new information. Fluency with information technology (i.e., what this report calls FITness) entails a process of lifelong learning in which individuals continually apply what they know to adapt to change and acquire more knowledge to be more effective at applying information technology to their work and personal lives."

The goal of developing measures of these skills needs to recognize both the context, as well as the nature of the process, and how this process differs from those typically measured in schools. The report notes, "Because FITness is fundamentally integrative, calling upon an individual to coordinate information and skills with respect to multiple dimensions of a problem and to make overall judgments and decisions taking all such information into account, a project-based approach to developing FITness is most appropriate."

This is precisely the approach taken by thousands of educators as they work with their colleagues in applying the Big6 Skills to their instruction and assessment. The cover story for *MultiMedia Schools* magazine May/June 2002 issue Moving Every Child Ahead: the Big6 Success Strategy describes how this powerful ICT strategy has resulted in improved student achievement for several years running. Instead of teaching to the test, scores are raised by improving student thinking skills. See *MultiMedia Schools,* May 2002 issue. http://www.infotoday.com/MMSchools/may02/berkowitz.htm

Conclusion:

The Digital Transformation report and resulting Framework for ICT Literacy could not come at a better time. As both national and international agendas begin to act on the implications of the digital age on the education, workplace and civic domains, the value of reliable measures and effective interventions is unsurpassed.

Learning and Teaching Information Technology–Computer Skills in Context

By Doug Johnson (www.doug-johnson.com), Mike Eisenberg
From the Big6 website: www.big6.com

There is clear and widespread agreement among the public and educators that all students need to be proficient computer users or "computer literate." However, while districts are spending a great deal of money on technology, there seems to be only a vague notion of what computer literacy really means. Can the student who operates a computer well enough to play a game, send e-mail or surf the Web be considered computer literate? Will a student who uses computers in school only for running tutorials or an integrated learning system have the skills necessary to survive in our society? Will the ability to do basic word processing be sufficient for students entering the workplace or post-secondary education?

Clearly not. In too many schools, teachers and students still use computers only as the equivalent of expensive flash cards, electronic worksheets, or as little more than a typewriter. The productivity side of computer use in the general content area curriculum is neglected or grossly underdeveloped (Moursund, 1995).

Recent publications by educational associations are advocating for a more meaningful use of technology in schools (ISTE, 2000). Educational technologists are clearly describing what students should know and be able to do with technology. They are advocating integrating computer skills into the content areas, proclaiming that computer skills should not be taught in isolation and that separate "computer classes" do not really help students learn to apply computer skills in meaningful ways. There is increasing recognition that the end result of computer literacy is not knowing how to operate computers, but to use technology as a tool for organization, communication, research, and problem solving. This is an important shift in approach and emphasis.

Moving from teaching isolated technology skills to an integrated approach is an important step that takes a great deal of planning and effort. Fortunately, we have a model for doing so. Over the past 25 years, library media professionals have worked hard to move from teaching isolated "library skills" to teaching integrated "information skills." They found that information skills can be integrated effectively when the skills (1) directly relate to the content area curriculum and to classroom assignments, and (2) are tied together in a logical and systematic information process model.

Schools seeking to move from isolated information technology skills instruction will also need to focus on both of these requirements. Successful integrated information skills programs are designed around collaborative projects jointly planned and taught by teachers and library media professionals. Information technology skills instruction can and should be imbedded in such a curriculum. Library media specialists, computer teachers, and classroom teachers need to work together to develop units and lessons that will include both technology skills, information skills, and content-area curriculum outcomes.

A meaningful, unified information technology literacy curriculum must be more than a "laundry list" of isolated skills, such as knowing the parts of the computer, writing drafts and final products with a word processor, and searching for information using the World Wide Web.

While these specific skills are important for students to learn, the "laundry list" approach does not provide an adequate model for students to transfer and apply skills from situation to situation. These curricula address the "how" of computer use, but rarely the "when" or "why." Students may learn isolated skills and tools, but they would still lack an understanding of how those various skills fit together to solve problems and complete tasks. Students need to be able to use computers and other technologies flexibly, creatively and purposefully. All learners should be able to recognize what they need to accomplish, determine whether a computer will help them to do so, and then be able to use the computer as part of the process of accomplishing their task. Individual computer skills take on a new meaning when they are integrated within this type of information problem-solving process, and students develop true "information technology literacy" because they have genuinely applied various information technology skills as part of the learning process.

The curriculum outlined on pages 2-3 of the ERIC Digest, "Technology Skills for Information Problem Solving," demonstrates how technology literacy skills can fit within an information literacy skills context (American Association of School Librarians, 1998). The baseline information literacy context is the Big6 process. The various technology skills are adapted from the International Society for Technology in Education's National Educational Technology Standards for Students (2000) and the Mankato Schools Information Literacy Curriculum Guideline. Students might reasonably be expected to authentically demonstrate these basic computer skills before graduation.

Some technology literacy competencies that may be relevant in some situations include: (1) knowing the basic operation, terminology, and maintenance of equipment, (2) knowing how to use computer-assisted instructional programs, (3) having knowledge of the impact of technology on careers, society, and culture (as a direct instructional objective), and (4) computer programming.

Defining and describing technology skills is only a first step in assuring all our children become proficient information and technology users. A teacher-supported scope and sequence of skills, well-designed projects, and effective assessments are also critical. Equally essential is collaboration among classroom teachers, teacher librarians, and technology teachers in order to present students with a unified and integrated approach to ensure that all children master the skills they will need to thrive in an information rich future (Eisenberg & Lowe, 1999).

Technology Skills for Information Problem-Solving

A Curriculum Based on the Big6 Skills Approach

1. Task Definition

The first part in the information problem-solving process involves recognizing that an information need exists, defining the problem, and identifying the types and amount of information needed. In terms of technology, students will be able to:

A. Communicate with teachers regarding assignments, tasks, and information problems using e-mail; online discussions (e.g., listservs, threaded Web-based discussions, newsgroups); real-time communications (e.g., instant messaging services, chat rooms, IP telephony); desktop teleconferencing; and groupware on the Internet, intranets, and local area networks.

B. Generate topics, define problems, and facilitate cooperative activities among groups of students locally and globally using e-mail, online discussions, real-time communications, desktop teleconferencing, and groupware on the Internet and local area networks.

C. Generate topics, define problems, and facilitate cooperative activities with subject area experts locally and globally using e-mail, online discussions, real-time communications, desktop teleconferencing, and groupware on the Internet and local area networks.

D. Define or refine the information problem using computerized graphic organization, brainstorming or idea generating software. This includes developing a research question or perspective on a topic.

2. Information Seeking Strategies

Once the information problem has been formulated, the student must consider all possible information sources and develop a plan for searching. Students will be able to:

A. Assess the value of various types of electronic resources for data gathering, including databases, CD-ROM resources, commercial and Internet online resources, electronic reference works, community and government information electronic resources.

B. Assess the need for and value of primary resources including interviews, surveys, experiments, and documents that are accessible through electronic means.

C. Identify and apply specific criteria for evaluating computerized electronic resources.

D. Identify and apply specific criteria for constructing meaningful original data gathering tools such as online surveys, electronic interviews, or scientific data gathering tools such as probes, meters, and timers.

E. Assess the value of e-mail, online discussions, real-time communications, desktop teleconferencing, and groupware on the Internet and local area networks as part of a search of the current literature or in relation to the information task.

F. Use a computer to generate modifiable flow charts, time lines, organizational charts, project plans (such as Gantt charts), and calendars which will help the student plan and organize complex or group information problem-solving tasks.

G. Use handheld devices such as personal digital assistants (PDAs), electronic slates or tablet PCs to track contacts and create to-do lists and schedules.

3. Location and Access

After students determine their priorities for information seeking, they must locate information from a variety of resources and access specific information found within individual resources. Students will be able to:

A. Locate and use appropriate computer resources and technologies available within the school library media center, including those on the library media center's local area network (e.g., online catalogs, periodical indexes, full-text sources, multimedia computer stations, CD-ROM stations, online terminals, scanners, digital cameras).

B. Locate and use appropriate computer resources and technologies available throughout the school including those available through intranets or local area networks (e.g., full-text resources, CD-ROMs, productivity software, scanners, digital cameras).

C. Locate and use appropriate computer resources and technologies available beyond the school through the Internet (e.g., newsgroups, listservs, WWW sites, ftp sites, online public access library catalogs, commercial databases and online services, and other community, academic, and government resources).

D. Know the roles and computer expertise of the people working in the school library media center and elsewhere who might provide information or assistance.

E. Use electronic reference materials (e.g., electronic encyclopedias, dictionaries, biographical reference sources, atlases, geographic databanks, thesauri, almanacs, fact books) available through intranets or local area networks, stand-alone workstations, commercial online vendors, or the Internet.

F. Use the Internet or commercial computer networks to contact experts and help and referral services.

G. Conduct self-initiated electronic surveys through e-mail, listservs, newsgroups and online data collection tools.

H. Use organizational systems and tools specific to electronic information sources that assist in finding specific and general information (e.g., indexes, tables of contents, user's instructions and manuals, legends, boldface and italics, graphic clues and icons, cross-references, Boolean logic strategies, time lines, hypertext links, knowledge trees, URLs, etc.) including the use of:

1. Search tools and commands for stand-alone, CD-ROM, networked or Web-based online databases and services;

2. Search tools and commands for searching the Internet, such as search engines, meta search tools, bots, directories, jump pages, and specialized resources such as those that search the Invisible Web;

3. Specialized sites and search tool commands that limit searches by date, location, format, collection of evaluated sites or other criteria.

4. Use of Information

After finding potentially useful resources, students must engage (read, view, listen) the information to determine its relevance and then extract the relevant information. Students will be able to:

A. Connect and operate the computer technology needed to access information, and read the guides and manuals associated with such tasks.

B. Know and be able to use the software and hardware needed to view, download, decompress and open documents, files, and programs from Internet sites and archives.

C. Copy and paste information from an electronic source into a personal document complete with proper citation.

D. Take notes and outline with a word processor, database, presentation or similar productivity program.

E. Record electronic sources of information and locations of those sources in order to properly cite and credit sources in footnotes, endnotes, and bibliographies.

F. Use electronic spreadsheets, databases, and statistical software to process and analyze statistical data.

G. Analyze and filter electronic information in relation to the task, rejecting information that is not relevant.

H. Save and backup data gathered to secure locations (floppy disk, personal hard drive space, RW-CD, online storage, flash memory, etc.).

5. Synthesis

Students must organize and communicate the results of the information problem-solving effort. Students will be able to:

A. Classify and group information using a word processor, database or spreadsheet.

B. Use word processing and desktop publishing software to create printed documents, applying keyboard skills equivalent to at least twice the rate of handwriting speed.

C. Create and use computer-generated graphics and art in various print and electronic presentations.

D. Use electronic spreadsheet software to create original spreadsheets.

E. Generate charts, tables and graphs using electronic spreadsheets and other graphing programs.

F. Use database software to create original databases.

G. Use presentation software to create electronic slide shows and to generate overhead transparencies and slides.

H. Create and use projection devices to show hypermedia and multimedia productions with digital video, audio and links to HTML documents or other programs. Convert presentations for display as Web pages.

I. Create Web pages and sites using hypertext markup language (HTML) in a text document or using Web page creation tools and know the procedure for having these pages loaded to a Web server.

J. Use e-mail, ftp, groupware, and other telecommunications capabilities to publish the results of the information problem-solving activity.

K. Use specialized computer applications as appropriate for specific tasks, e.g., music composition software, computer-assisted drawing and drafting programs, mathematics modeling software, scientific measurement instruments, etc.

L. Properly cite and credit electronic sources (text, graphics, sound and video) of information within the product as well as in footnotes, endnotes, and bibliographies.

6. Evaluation

Evaluation focuses on how well the final product meets the original task (effectiveness) and the process of how well students carried out the information problem-solving process (efficiency). Students may evaluate their own work and process or be evaluated by others (i.e., classmates, teachers, library media staff, parents). Students will be able to:

A. Evaluate electronic presentations in terms of the content and format and design self-assessment tools to help them evaluate their own work for both content and format.

B. Use spell and grammar checking capabilities of word processing and other software to edit and revise their work.

C. Apply legal principles and ethical conduct related to information technology related to copyright and plagiarism.

D. Understand and abide by telecomputing etiquette when using e-mail, newsgroups, listservs and other Internet functions.

E. Understand and abide by acceptable use policies and other school rules in relation to use of the Internet and other electronic technologies.

F. Use e-mail, real-time communications (e.g., listservs, newsgroups, instant messaging services, chat rooms, IP telephony) desktop teleconferencing, and groupware on the Internet and local area networks to communicate with teachers and others regarding their performance on assignments, tasks, and information problems.

G. Thoughtfully reflect on the use of electronic resources and tools throughout the process.

The Big6 Skills Approach to Information Problem Solving
(c) Eisenberg and Berkowitz 1987

The Big6 is an information literacy curriculum, an information problem-solving process, and a set of skills which provide a strategy for effectively and efficiently meeting information needs. The Big6 Skills approach can be used whenever students are in a situation, academic or personal, which requires information to solve a problem, make a decision or complete a task. This model is transferable to school, personal, and work applications, as well as all content areas and the full range of grade levels. When taught collaboratively with content area teachers in concert with content-area objectives, it serves to ensure that students are information literate.

The Big6

1. **Task Definition**
   1.1 Define the task (the information problem).
   1.2 Identify information needed in order to complete the task (to solve the information problem).

2. **Information Seeking Strategies**
   2.1 Brainstorm all possible sources.
   2.2 Select the best sources.

3. **Location and Access**
   3.1 Locate sources.
   3.2 Find information within the sources.

4. **Use of Information**
   4.1 Engage in the source (read, hear, view, touch).
   4.2 Extract relevant information.

5. **Synthesis**
   5.1 Organize information from multiple sources.
   5.2 Present the information.

6. **Evaluation**
   6.1 Judge the process (efficiency).
   6.2 Judge the product (effectiveness).

References and Suggested Reading

American Association of School Librarians. (1995). Information literacy: A position paper on information problem solving. *Emergency Librarian*, 23 (2), 20-23. (EJ 514 998).

American Association of School Librarians. (1998). *Information literacy standards for student learning. Chicago: American Library Association.*

American Association of School Librarians & Association for Educational Communications and Technology. (1998). *Information power: Building partnerships for learning. Chicago: American Library Association.*

American Library Association. (2000). Information literacy community partnerships toolkit. Available online: http://library.austin.cc.tx.us/staff/lnavarro/communitypartnerships/toolkit.html

Association of College and Research Libraries. (2000). Information literacy competency standards for higher education. Available online: http://www.ala.org/acrl/ilintro.html

Bawden, D. (2001). Information and digital literacies: A review of concepts. *Journal of Documentation*, 57 (2), 218-59. (EJ 632 998).

The Big6 skills information problem-solving approach. [Online]. Available: http://www.big6.com

Bruce, C. S. (1997). *Seven faces of information literacy*. Blackwood, South Australia: Auslib Press.

Bruce, C. S. (1997). The seven faces of information literacy in higher education. Available online: http://www2.fit.qut.edu.au/InfoSys/bruce/inflit/faces/faces1.htm

California Media and Library Educators Association Staff. (1993). *From library skills to information literacy: A handbook for the 21st century*. Englewood, CO: Libraries Unlimited, Inc.

Committee on Information Technology Literacy, National Research Council. (1999). Being fluent with information technology. Available online: http://www.nap.edu/books/030906399X/html

Doyle, C. S. (1994). *Information literacy in an information society: A concept for the information age*. Syracuse, NY: ERIC Clearinghouse on Information & Technology. (ED 372 763).

Eisenberg, M. B. (1999). *Essential skills for the information age: The Big6 in action*. Video, 38 minutes. Worthington, Ohio: Linworth Publishing.

Eisenberg, M. B. (2001). Beyond the bells and whistles: Technology skills for a purpose. *MultiMedia Schools*, 8 (3), 44-48, 50-51. (EJ 633 043).

Eisenberg, M., & Berkowitz, B. (1988). *Curriculum initiative: An agenda and strategy for library media programs*. Norwood, NJ: Ablex. (ED 296 731).

Eisenberg, M. B., & Berkowitz, R. E. (1992). Information problem-solving: The big six skills approach. *School Library Media Activities Monthly*, 8 (5), 27-29,37,42. (EJ 438 023).

Eisenberg M., & Berkowitz, R. E. (1997). The big six and electronic resources: A natural fit. *Book Report*, 16 (2), 15, 22. (EJ 550 884).

Eisenberg, M. B., & Berkowitz, R. E. (1999). *Teaching information & technology skills: The Big6 in elementary schools*. Worthington, Ohio: Linworth Publishing.

Eisenberg, M. B., & Berkowitz, R. E. (2000). *Teaching information & technology skills: The Big6 in secondary schools*. Worthington, Ohio: Linworth Publishing.

Eisenberg, M. B., & Ely, D. P. (1993). Plugging into the "Net." *Emergency Librarian*, 21 (2), 8-16. (EJ 471 260).

Eisenberg, M. B., & Lowe, C. A. (1999). Call to action: Getting serious about libraries and information in education. *MultiMedia Schools,* 6 (2), 18-21. (EJ 586 238).

Eisenberg, M. B., & Spitzer, K. L. (1991). Information technology and services in schools. In M. E. Williams (Ed.), *Annual review of information science and technology,* Vol. 26. (pp. 243-285). Medford, NJ: Learned Information, Inc. (EJ 441 688).

Fulton, K. (1997). Learning in the digital age: Insights into the issues. The skills students need for technological fluency. Santa Monica, CA: Milken Family Foundation. Available online: http://www.mff.org/pubs/ME164.pdf

Garland, K. (1995). The information search process: A study of elements associated with meaningful research tasks. *School Libraries Worldwide,* 1 (1), 41-53. (EJ 503 407).

International Society for Technology in Education (ISTE). (2000). *National educational technology standards for students-connecting curriculum and technology.* Eugene, OR: International Society for Technology in Education.

Johnson, D. (1995a). Captured by the web: K-12 schools and the World Wide Web. *MultiMedia Schools,* 2 (2), 24-30. (EJ 499 841).

Johnson, D. (1995b). The new and improved school library: How one district planned for the future. *School Library Journal,* 41 (6), 36-39. (EJ 505 448).

Johnson, D. (1995c). Student access to the Internet: Librarians and teachers working together to teach higher level survival skills. *Emergency Librarian,* 22 (3), 8-12. (EJ 497 895).

Johnson, D. (1999a). A curriculum built not to last. *School Library Journal,* 45 (4), 26-29. (EJ 586 404).

Johnson, D. (1999b). Implementing an information literacy curriculum: One district's story. *NASSP Bulletin,* 83 (605), 53-61. (EJ 585 576).

Johnson, D. (2000). Information power: Building standards that are useful. *Teacher Librarian,* 28 (2), 19-20. (EJ 623 553).

Johnson, D. (2001). What gets measured gets done: A school library media and technology program self-study workbook. (ED 450 809). Available online: http://www.doug-johnson.com/new.html

Kasowitz, A. S. (2000). *Using the Big6 to teach and learn with the Internet.* Worthington, Ohio: Linworth Publishing. (ED 449 781).

Klink, M.T. (1999). Resource-based learning. *Knowledge Quest,* 27 (4), 26-30. (EJ 588 282).

Kuhlthau, C. C. (1993). Implementing a process approach to information skills: A study identifying indicators of success in library media programs. *School Library Media Quarterly,* 22 (1), 11-18. (EJ 473 063).

Kuhlthau, C. C. (1995). The process of learning from information. *School Libraries Worldwide,* 1 (1), 1-12. (EJ 503 404)

Loertscher, D. V., & Woolls, B. (2002). *Information literacy: A review of the research* (2nd ed.). Hi Willow Research and Publishing.

Mankato Schools Information Literacy Curriculum Guideline. [Online]. Available: http://www.isd77.k12.mn.us/resources/infolit.html

McKenzie, J. (2000). *Beyond technology: Questioning, research and the information literate school.* Bellingham, WA: FNO Press.

McNally, M. J., & Kuhlthau, C. C. (1994). Information search process in science education. *Reference Librarian,* 44, 53-60. (EJ 488 273).

Minnesota Department of Education. (1989). *Model learner outcomes for educational media and technology.* St. Paul, MN: Minnesota Department of Education. (ED 336 070).

Moursund, D. (1995). Effective practices (part 2): Productivity tools. *Learning and Leading with Technology,* 23 (4), 5-6.

Nuts and bolts of the Big6: In search of information literacy. [Online]. http://www.kn.pacbell.com/wired/big6

Pappas, M. L. (1993). A vision of school library media centers in an electronic information age. *School Library Media Activities Monthly,* 10 (1), 32-34,38. (EJ469122).

Pappas, M. L. (1995). Information skills for electronic resources. *School Library Media Activities Monthly,* 11 (8), 39-40. (EJ 499 875).

Potter, C. J. et al. (2000). *Information and technology literacy standards matrix.* Madison, WI: Wisconsin State Dept. of Public Instruction. (ED 445 663).

Rader, H. B. (1994). Information literacy and the undergraduate curriculum. *Library Trends,* (44) 2, 270-278.

Spitzer, K. S., Eisenberg, M. B., & Lowe, C. A. (1998). *Information literacy: Essential skills for the information age.*

Syracuse, NY: ERIC Clearinghouse on Information & Technology. (ED 427 780).

Todd, R. J. (1995). Information literacy: Philosophy, principles, and practice. *School Libraries Worldwide,* 1 (1), 54-68. (EJ 503 408).

Todd, R. J. (1995). Integrated information skills instruction: Does it make a difference? *School Library Media Quarterly,* 23 (2), 133-138. (EJ 497 921).

Todd, R. J. (1999). Transformational leadership and transformational learning: Information literacy and the World Wide Web. *NASSP Bulletin,* 83 (605), 4-12. (EJ 585 570).

Wisconsin Educational Media Association. (1993). *Information literacy: A position paper on information problem-solving.* Madison, WI: WEMA Publications. (ED 376 817).

The BIG 6™

Part IV:

Teaching Information Problem Solving

Helping Young Researchers Assess the Usefulness of Their Success

By Ellen Heath / vE2, no1

*A*s students in the third, fourth, and fifth grades in the Orchard School (Ridgewood, NJ) begin to do their first formal research reports, the stages of the Big6 help them (1) to break down the process into understandable parts and (2) to produce successful reports. It is really quite easy to teach some of the stages to these young students. For instance, many students can develop useful questions about their topics and can find materials in the library or online.

However, other more subtle stages or sub-stages are often more difficult and are skipped or downplayed. For example, I find that the sub-stage of evaluating sources – after Location & Access (Big6 #3) but before intensive Use of Information (Big6 #4) – is one of those difficult skills to master.

Using a Chart to Evaluate Sources

After my students finish Big6 Stage #3 (Location & Access), they need to take an explicit action to evaluate the usefulness (not the validity: that's another consideration) of their resources before they proceed further in Big6 Stage #4 (Use of Information). Without this evaluation action, students seem to rove among their sources without getting to the main information in any source.

Figure 1 shows an Evaluation Chart that was developed to help students assess sources and decide the order in which they will view their sources.

Source	Can I read it easily?	Does it seem to have the information I need?	Does it have useful illustrations?	Did I enjoy using it?
Book Title:				
Book Title:				
Encylopedia _____ Vol. _____ Pages _____				
Internet Site				

This example is for the third graders working on animal reports. Students write "yes," "no," or a more specific comment in each box. Student are "using" the resources, but only to gain some insight into the value of the resource for later in-depth use.

For example, the students must actually read a portion of the text to tell if it's easy to read. Showing third graders a three-inch portion of text on a page or computer monitor helps them to gauge what should be a manageable but sufficient amount of text. The chart can be modified for older students and other topics. For instance, fifth grade students can consider, "Is this source well organized for my needs," but the fifth grade students probably do not need to consider the usefulness of illustrations.

Additional sources may be added to the left column, such as biographical dictionaries, subject encyclopedias, and CD-ROM reference tools.

When presenting this evaluation activity, demonstrate the process and give students lots of time to fill in the chart. As each student finishes the chart, ask him or her to rank the sources in order of apparent usefulness. If students are using the chart for the first time, model this process for them. Have students rank their choices with stars or a numbering system, and keep the chart with their materials for use throughout the project.

Extracting Relevant Information: It's Just Like Eating a Meal

Another part of Big6 #4 (Use of Information), is extracting relevant information—note-taking (Big6 Step #4). I use a metaphor that compares eating a meal to gathering information. The source students ranked #1 is similar to the main dinner meal. When you're hungry, you eat everything on the plate. When students are hungry for information they will spend lots of time with the source they've ranked as the best, and will glean all of the important information from it. The second source is like dessert. After the main meal, you're not famished, but you're still looking for something good—more information to add to what you've already learned. The third sources and beyond are like after-dinner mints. You're not really hungry, but you can't resist another tasty bite, or tidbit of good information.

Teachers report that students who follow these stages are more purposeful in their work and seem much more confident that they have found the information they want. Even though using this system adds time to the research process, it is actually fun for most young students and this approach smoothes the way for the final stages.

How to Write a Grant Application

By Rosemarie Granger / vE2, no3

*A*re you interested in writing a grant? Here are some tips to help you on your way to success:

Choose a Project

- Choose a project you like and one in which you are invested. If you don't get the grant, at least you'll be satisfied with your own work.

- Choose a project that your students are easily motivated to complete.

- You have a good grant idea if your class gets excited, demonstrates achievement, and the project fits your curriculum.

Write the Grant

- Allow plenty of time to write your grant. Applications written at the last minute tends to give that hurried impression to others.

- Follow the directions. Write the application based upon the key points suggested.

- Keep your responses concise and to the point.

- Answer all the questions using a word processing program. By doing so, you will be able to reflect and revise your answers. Cut and paste your answers into the application if it is in electronic form.

- Present your project in a way that is fairly easy to replicate or adapt to other classrooms and grades.

- Articulate how the project meets your state and national standards.

- If applying as a group, select one person to do the writing to ensure that the writing style will remain consistent throughout the application.

- Attend training or join online chats if they are offered. Ask questions if you are confused about the application process.

- Finish your grant application several days in advance. Take time to reflect on your writing and make final revisions.

And finally...

- Volunteer to be a reviewer for grants or various awards. This is the best way to gain firsthand experience about positives and negatives, do's and don'ts.

- Don't get discouraged. Apply for several different grants. Submitting a grant application is similar to a new job search. It may take time to find the right one.

Laugh About It!

By Kathleen L. Spitzer / *vE2, no1*

Do you wonder if you'll ever be replaced by a machine? If you do, read on and find out why our students need us!

Students in an 11th grade American History class had just received an assignment to find out about various Supreme Court cases and also locate and read a magazine article about the topic of the court case. For example, those studying Roe v. Wade were to find up-to-date information on abortion.

As I approached one student to see how she was doing, I heard her bemoan the fact that she couldn't find anything! I inquired what she was trying to find, and she replied that she was looking for freedom of speech articles. While I asked her where she had been looking, I noticed that she had typed the following URL into the Internet Explorer address bar: **freedomofspeecharticles.com**

Here's one for those who are familiar with searching the ERIC database:

Students were trying to find information about recent scientific achievements and I had reminded them of various search strategies for using Magazine Article Summaries which is part of our EBSCOhost online service. From the EBSCOhost beginning search screen it is possible to choose to search a number of databases besides Magazine Article Summaries. One of the other databases students can search is ERIC.

I overheard one student telling another that this was the stupidest assignment and the computer just wasn't working. I went over to see what was the matter and asked him where he was searching. He showed me his screen. The database he had chosen was ERIC. I stated, "Oh, I see, you're in ERIC." He stated, "Where should I be? **Bob**?"

Quick and Easy Big6™ Reinforcements

By Claudia Stephens / From the Big6 website: www.big6.com

The library media specialist at North Elementary School in Ozark, Missouri, uses issues of *Zoobooks*, the children's magazine, as a tool to introduce Big6 #3, (**Location & Access**) to third graders. To prepare for the lesson, the library media specialist placed several issues of *Zoobooks*, a sheet of notebook paper, and a pencil for each student on the tables in the library. The library media specialist explained to students that they would be doing research, and the task was to "find five surprising facts" about an animal and record those facts in their own words to share with their classmates. Students were asked to investigate the animal on the cover of the *Zoobook* issue in front of them.

Students were told that they would not need to read the articles in the magazine, but simply skim for details, a skill they had practiced the previous week. To be sure the students understood what they were to do, a student volunteer was called on to define the task (Big6 #1, **Task Definition**). Another student reinforced Big6 #2, (**Information Seeking Strategies**) by answering "How will you begin?" The student suggested that they could look at the pictures and skim the writing under them.

The children began to locate and record their findings. After only a couple of minutes, the library media specialist asked how many students had written one surprising fact. Hands were raised and most students were busy writing the second note. After giving the students 13 minutes to complete the task, the library media specialist called on volunteers to share one unusual or surprising fact from their list (Big6 #4, **Use of Information**). The students were pleased to make announcements such as "Koalas can spend their whole life in a tree," and "Ostriches can run 40 miles an hour."

The lesson was simple, easy, and enjoyable. Several information skills were reinforced using the Big6 model. The students gained experience they could apply to a number of related activities and they exhibited new confidence in their ability to locate and access information. *Zoobooks* is a monthly publication for children ages five to fourteen and is available at *Zoobooks*, P. O. Box 85384, San Diego, CA or call: 800-992-5034.

The Big6™ and TCR/NewsBank: Turning Information into Knowledge

By Christopher W. Cook, Ph.D. / vE1, no1

*N*ewsBank is well-known among educators as a company that offers unique collections of domestic and international newspapers. Teachers and librarians know that *NewsBank* collections provide students with multiple perspectives, opposing viewpoints and firsthand reporting taken from local, regional, national and international sources. During the past 30 years, *NewsBank* resources have been specifically designed to challenge critical thinking and develop analytical research skills.

But as all Big6-ers know, the Big6 isn't just about library-research skills. State and local learning standards increasingly integrate information problem-solving with core subject-area knowledge. High-stakes assessments now require students to analyze and respond to primary source documents. And, of course, the information explosion forces everyone to recognize the need to prepare students to be effective users of information.

In fact, "…teaching students how to find information rather than memorize information" was ranked highest in importance in this year's Association for Supervision and Curriculum Development (ASCD) Issues Survey (2000, p.8). Eighty-four percent of the more than 4,400 ASCD members who participated in the survey rated the statement 5 or 6 on a six-point scale (with 6 meaning "extremely important").

Announcing TCR…The Curriculum Resource!

Because we work with educators who share these common concerns, this fall marks the launch of TCR…The Curriculum Resource (http://www.tcrconnections.com). The TCR Connections program represents NewsBank's vision of using primary source information and information literacy to bring together instruction that is both standards-based and authentic.

Quite simply, *TCR/NewsBank's* expanded mission is to harness Internet technology to *improve student learning* by doing the following:

- Connect classroom topics to the real world

- Connect information technology with standards and textbooks

- Connect technology staff development with instructional staff development

- Connect core content with critical thinking, problem-solving and decision-making skills

- Connect school learning to home learning.

TCR offers hundreds of online interactive student activities organized by subject and links to more than 3000 primary source materials.

TCR's Big6™ ToolKit

This fall, *TCR/NewsBank* proudly introduced a collection of interactive graphic organizers that were refined in consultation with Big6 co-developer Bob Berkowitz. These powerful tools, delivered by the Internet, give students the structures and prompts to analyze, evaluate, organize and synthesize complex information and ideas. Designed as a groupware application, the graphic organizers in *TCR's Big6 ToolKit* are perfect applications to help teachers lead discussions, or for students to use in small group projects. Reading teachers treasure the graphic organizers as effective mental models, or schema, upon which to build critical reading comprehension skills.

When students use diagrams such as Fishbone (for cause and effect), Idea Web (for main idea and supporting details), and Venn Diagram (for comparing and contrasting), you'll likely hear them remark "Now I **see** what you mean!"

Staff Development

TCR/NewsBank also connects standards-based instruction and authentic instruction with our commitment to staff development. The Big6 problem-solving model is a powerful vehicle for integrating technology skills with subject-area content.

TCR's on-site and online workshops are based on research that indicates that effective staff development must be active and collaborative. Beyond mere product training, teachers who attend *TCR* workshops actively develop their own resource-based units that promote information problem-solving.

Instructional Technology in the Era of Accountability

Connecting schools to the Internet requires an enormous public investment. Naturally, such an investment prompts questions like the following:

- Is technology being effectively used?

- How would we know?

- What skills do teachers and students need to harness information technology for learning?

- Does information technology use align with required learning standards?

- As a charter Big6 Partner, *TCR/NewsBank* supports the use of the Big6 as a catalyst for linking information skills, technology skills, staff development, and standards toward one simple yet important end...*improved teacher effectiveness and student learning.*

Big6 and NewsBank: "Doing History" vs. Learning History

By Christopher W. Cook, Ph.D. / vE4, no3

The study of history is an important educational endeavor. Through a deep understanding of history we learn who we are as a people and develop our intellectual skills. Regrettably, many students do not engage themselves in history studies and thus are handicapped in fully understanding history and lose an opportunity to develop their natural interests and higher-order thinking skills.

NewsBank-Big6ers often compare these two contrasting ways of teaching/learning history. Note that the characteristics of "Doing History" are much closer to what actual historians do.

Learning About History Doing History

- "names and dates"
- learning about "old stuff"…not relevant
- memorizing already summarized information
- de-personalized, sanitized
- accepting single source (e.g. textbook) as truth
- real people, places, events
- connect to students' own experiences
- asking important questions
- drawing your own conclusions
- personalized, humanized
- critically evaluating multiple sources

Together, NewsBank and many talented educators have found the Big6 process to be a highly effective process for making history instruction engaging and authentic.

A key ingredient, according to Margaret Lincoln (Library Media Specialist, Lakeview High School, Battle Creek, Michigan), is that the Big6 "promotes a self-directed learning experience in which the student asks his/her own interesting questions, rather than being told what to do."

"We all face an enormous quantity of online information. Begin by sifting through and determining the best sources. Narrow down the broad topic by asking good questions."

Here are some examples of good research questions that engage learners and promote effective Big6 thinking:

- Why was MLK a great leader?
- What if Kennedy had not been assassinated?
- What will happen in Cuba after Castro?
- How would you have survived the Great Depression?
- Were the "good ole days" really good?

These types of questions not only add pizzazz to history assignments, they require students to do more than repeat back what they find in sources. The questions require students to engage in high level Synthesis – combining information, reaching conclusions, and presenting supporting evidence. Students must first understand the question (Task Definition), determine and find appropriate sources (Information Seeking Strategies and Location and Access), and then dig in to the content and extract information relevant to the questions (Use of Information).

Another major benefit of these types of questions is addressing concerns of plagiarism. While it's pretty easy to plagiarize (unintentionally or not) a report on Martin Luther King, Jr., it's not easy to do so for the first question (i.e., Why was MLK a great leader?). Same thing with the other questions—students can only complete these tasks by really thinking on their own!

Big6 Skills and NewsBank–
A Perfect Combination

vE4, no2

This issue features suggestions from Sarah Debbs, Librarian, Homewood-Flossmoor High School, Community High School Dist. 233, Flossmoor, Illinois.

Editor's Note: NewsBank is one of the world's premier information providers with resources used by students world-wide. NewsBank resources contain information from newspapers, newswires, business journals, historical and scholarly documents, periodicals and more. These resources support classroom instruction across subject areas, and are used by students and teachers to delve into contemporary issues and events. We at Big6 have a very special relationship with NewsBank, partnering on curriculum projects, promoting information and technology literacy, and offering Big6 tools through NewsBank and its unique curriculum-focused program, TCR (The Curriculum Resource).

In our library we teach critical thinking skills through the research process. NewsBank's Big6 is a great format for students to type their responses to questions—key to effective library research. I particularly like the **Topic Chooser** section. It pulls the students into really thinking about their topic, especially when they have to recall what they already know about a topic and what they need to know about the topic.

The use of the Big6 feature to brainstorm ideas for student projects is great. The student can move from the selection of a topic to NewsBank's School Library Collection and find information from the most current sources. It can be a "one stop shop" for gathering information.

I find NewsBank's new subject-oriented interface easy to use for both students and teachers. It can be an effective way for students to narrow their research topic as they browse subtopics under the general topics. We direct students to this feature when they talk in terms of general topics for research.

Some other practical suggestions for effective collaboration

- It is helpful when teachers share their lesson plans or activities with the librarian so that resources can be identified and made available to ensure that the students have a positive research experience.
- NewsBank's daily headlines with activity plans provide straightforward and manageable tasks for students. They can be adapted to most social science activities.
- NewsBank's Hot Topics generate good discussions on current issues. I forward these to the appropriate subject areas.

Part V:

Big6 and Content Standards in the Curriculum

Apply Big6 Skills to Incorporate History Content Standards in the Curriculum

By Janet Murray / vE4, no2

*I*dentifying state and national standards and linking them to our curriculum has become increasingly important to classroom teachers and schools. How can library media specialists help the teachers they serve locate appropriate and relevant standards, and apply the Big6 Skills to teach subject specific content as well as information literacy skills?

The task of comparing the wide variety of content standards in state and national documents seems impossibly overwhelming; fortunately, someone else has already done it. You can compare your own state standards to McREL's Content Knowledge: A Compendium of Standards and Benchmarks for K-12 Education (http://www.mcrel.org/topics/ topics.asp?topicsid=14) (3rd Edition, 2000) to locate parallels. McREL's Compendium "presents a coherent set of standards for primary, upper elementary, middle school, and high school in an easy-to-read and consistent format. The compendium synthesizes information from more than 137 documents, reports, and other materials compiled by professional education organizations in the following content areas: language arts, mathematics, science, geography, foreign language, history, arts, economics, civics, health, physical education, behavioral studies, life skills, and technology."

In this article, we focus on using the Big6™ Skills to enrich students' understanding of history in the context of standards related to multicultural awareness at different grade levels.

Multicultural Awareness: K-4

Grades K-4 history standards focus on families and communities, local history, democratic values and other cultures. Having spent the last six years in Japan, I am particularly sensitive to the superficiality of Americans' understanding of other cultures. We are all familiar with the type of elementary lesson that asks students to compare how different cultures celebrate Christmas. How can we use the Big6 Skills (or the Super3 with younger students) to broaden and deepen that activity so that students learn to appreciate the contributions other cultures have made to America and the world?

The McREL web site offers a detailed explanation of the procedure they used to synthesize standards and benchmarks from a wide variety of national documents; to understand how they constructed the compendium, consult http://www. mcrel.org/standards-benchmarks/docs/process.asp. McREL also provides links to state standards at http://www.mcrel.org/resources/links/state-index.asp.

Big6 #1: Task Definition

Our task is to help students develop critical thinking skills when they consider American culture in light of other cultures. We might ask them "How does the traditional celebration of Christmas in America reflect the influence of other cultures?" or we might broaden the question to incorporate other winter holiday celebrations such as Chanukah, Kwanzaa, Ramadan and the Chinese New Year. If we want students to develop deeper understandings, the way we define the task is critical. [See "Transforming Standards to a Big Idea and Essential Questions" (http://www.mcrel.org/topics/topics.asp?topicsid=14) for help with this process.]

Big6 #2: Information Seeking Strategies

Ask students where they will look to find information. Almost invariably, they will reply "on the computer" or "on the Internet." This is the ideal opportunity to introduce or reinforce concepts like "reliable information" or "evaluating web sites." Of course, you will also want to highlight the value of encyclopedias as well as those books you have been systematically collecting to support this activity over the years.

Big6 #3: Location and Access

The Google directory (http://directory.google.com/) has an ample selection of links to holiday resources under "Society." I try to discourage my students from entering a single term in a search engine, and recommend subject directories instead.

You can always count on Kathy Schrock's Guide (http://school.discovery.com/schrockguide/) to collect worthwhile resources useful to schools. Her "holidays" collection includes a pointer to the Diversity Calendar, (http://www3.kumc.edu/diversity/), which lists world and cultural holidays by month.

Again, you want to continue to encourage use of a range of sources – print, electronic sources other than the WWW as well as the WWW.

Big6 #4: Use of Information

This is the critical point at which your essential question influences how the students interact with the information they find. Help them avoid statements of fact (e.g. "the Christmas tree came from Germany in favor of reflections of understandings (e.g. "Most cultures celebrate the winter solstice because …" or "why did the Christmas tree custom develop in Germany").

Big6 #5: Synthesis

What product does the assignment require? This is another opportunity to help teachers grow beyond the traditional "research report." How can we engage students in the process of integrating new learning (about other cultures) into their personal knowledge framework (how their own families celebrate Christmas)? Classroom teachers and library media specialist can encourage non-traditional products that reflect the students' acquisition of new knowledge.

Big6 #6: Evaluation

Students should be able to evaluate their end product as well as their process of working. Key questions to ask students are "where did you have the most difficulty?" "What would you do differently next time?"

The classroom teacher will want to evaluate the students' products, and the library media specialist can help evaluate the process: how did this assignment differ from previous years? How did it help our students think about the relationship between American and other cultures?

Multicultural Comprehension: Grades 5-8

World History standards (http://www.mcrel.org/compendium/Standard.asp?SubjectID=6) are arranged chronologically on the McREL web site but the theme of multiculturalism persists. Each era features standards that expect students to understand major movements and cultural interactions throughout history.

For example, in Era 6, Global Expansion and Encounter, standard 27 (http://www.mcrel. org /compendium/Benchmark.asp?SubjectID=6&StandardID=27) requires students to understand "how European society experienced political, economic, and cultural transformations in an age of global intercommunication between 1450 and 1750." An associated benchmark expects students to "understand early influences on the Scientific Revolution and the Enlightenment (e.g., connections between the Scientific Revolution and its antecedents, such as Greek rationalism, medieval theology, Muslim science, Renaissance humanism, and new global knowledge; connections between the Enlightenment and its antecedents, such as Roman republicanism, the Renaissance, and the Scientific Revolution)." What a great opportunity to use the Big6 Skills to help students make these important connections!

Big6 #1: Task Definition

What can we ask students to do to help them connect European history with its influences from other cultures and eras? What will be our essential question? Consider, "How did the expansion of trade change the culture of Europe in the sixteenth and seventeenth centuries?" Think ahead to the revolutions and colonialism of the late eighteenth century; anticipate the need to reflect on "how Eurasian societies were transformed in an era of global trade and the emergence of European power from 1750 to 1870." Although someone may have "taught" this in the schools I attended, I certainly never understood it until I lived in Asia.

Big6 #2: Information Seeking Strategies

World history texts produced in the U.S. have been criticized for the intensity of their focus on northern European history to the exclusion of other areas of the world. Can we use the power of the World Wide Web to contribute some balance to our students' knowledge? What about using magazine articles and non-fiction historical works?

Big6 #3: Location and Access

Similar to Kathy Schrock's Guide for Educators, Blue Web'n (http://www.kn.pacbell.com/wired/bluewebn/) provides links to web sites, lesson plans and activities appropriate for use in K-12 schools. However, I did not find a great resource with a global approach to this time period at a middle grade level in either place. The following web sites are more likely to provide starting points for your teachers than their students:

The Global History Sourcebook (http://www.fordham.edu/halsall/global/globalsbook.html) "is dedicated to exploration of interaction between world cultures. Specifically this means looking at:

- The ways in which cultures contact each other
- The ways they influence each other
- The ways new cultural forms emerge."

Discovery and Reformation (http://www.wsu.edu/~dee/REFORM/) "is designed as a learning module in the form of a 'research textbook.' … From a historical perspective, the module is written from a world systems standpoint. The module is designed to comparatively highlight the interactions between Reformation and discovery Europe and other cultures in Europe and the non-European world during this historical period and after."

Annenberg's Pages on the Renaissance (http://www.learner.org/exhibits/renaissance/exploration. html)(with links to hands-on activities) provide a more student-centered approach but their corresponding video series "The Western Tradition" is aimed at college, high school and adult learners.

Big6 #4: Use of Information

Remind students that they are looking for essential connections between different cultures in this time period, not just a rehash of exploration and trade routes. What happened when people of diverse backgrounds came together? What goods and stories did they trade?

Big6 #5: Synthesis

Since I did not find a great resource with a global approach to this time period on the World Wide Web, perhaps you and your history teacher will create a WebQuest worthy of inclusion in Tom March's "Best WebQuests" (http://bestwebquests.com/) to help your students understand the cross-cultural implications of the internationalism that arose in the mid15th to mid18th centuries.

Big6 #6: Evaluation

Whatever activity the library media specialist and classroom teacher design to address this standard, they will want to evaluate both the student product as well as the process of working together and working with students. As always, we believe in involving students directly in the evaluation process.

Multicultural Appreciation: High School

Among the World History standards listed on the McREL web site is one from the same time period above that expects grade 9-12 students to "understand the role of the Enlightenment in shaping European society (e.g., the impact of Europe's growing knowledge of other regions on the development of concepts of universalism, tolerance, and world history; the connection between the Enlightenment and the Scientific Revolution, and arguments supporting the notion that one was dependent upon the other)."

To start, ask yourself how well our students understand the concepts of universalism and tolerance. One would hope that by the time they reach high school, students have internalized the multicultural values reflected in the sample lessons above. I don't see it in my students, though. Perhaps, if we use the Big6 Skills to incorporate curriculum standards like these, both the knowledge students acquire and the approach to information problem solving they use will have more lasting effects.

Apply Big6 Skills to Integrate Content Standards in the Curriculum

By Janet Murray / vE4, no1

Increasingly, school districts are aligning the Big6 Skills with their state standards documents. The resulting charts and diagrams aligning standards with the Big6 Skills are helpful in designing integrated information literacy curricula. Potentially even more powerful, the alignments help classroom teachers and teacher-librarians to appreciate and understand how to use the Big6 to help their students achieve standards.

In this column, we will examine three different efforts that build on aligning the Big6 to standards.

Connecticut

In West Hartford, Connecticut, "all eighth grade students participate in the information and technology literacy course, which is part of the thirty-day unified arts rotation. This course completes the sequence that begins in sixth grade with thinking skills and continues in seventh grade with research strategies. Through this assured learning experience students will become efficient and effective users and producers of information, using the information and technology tools necessary for success in lifelong learning. ["Information and Technology Literacy Curriculum: Grade 8." 2002. West Hartford Public Schools. http://www.whps.org/library/ITL_Curriculum_Grade_8.htm]

Appendices align Big6 Skills with Connecticut's Learning Resources and Information Technology (LRIT) Content Standards as well as their Computer Technology Content Standards (which precisely mirror the National Educational Technology Standards for Students, NETS-S.)

New York

Clarkstown Central School District (West Nyack, NY) adopted a standards-based curriculum incorporating the Big6 Skills.

> "With information literacy skills, students will possess the capability to transfer their information knowledge to real-life information needs situations. With this curriculum, students will master the use of information, whether that information is obtained from a library or on a home computer. The intent of Clarkstown's library curriculum framework is to create consistency and momentum in the district's information literacy program. This intent is directing our plan to fully integrate information literacy curriculum into the subject curriculum district-wide." ["Philosophy." Information Literacy Curriculum. 14 Sep. 2001 (http://www.ccsd.edu/bardonia/CCSDLibraryCurriculum/)]

Clarkstown aligned the National Information Literacy Standards (ALA) with New York State Learning Standards in a wide variety of subjects and developed performance indicators and benchmarks.

Minnesota

The Mankato Information and Technology Literacy Curriculum developed by a committee led by Doug Johnson provides the foundation for many similar efforts across the nation. "The information skills curriculum is centered around large projects at each grade level during each school year. These projects:

- use a version of the Big6 (c. Eisenberg and Berkowitz) information processing model
- have clearly stated objectives from I.S.D. 77 Information Skills curriculum, which in turn supports the State Graduation Rule requirements
- are assessed in a complete and objective manner
- use technologies and identified productivity software
- and build cumulatively on skills learned the previous year.
- meet district benchmarks for each grade level, K-12"
  http://www.isd77.k12.mn.us/resources/infocurr/infolit.html
  The benchmarks refer to state standards in speaking, writing, inquiry and math.

Unique Features

Course Description

West Hartford's Information and Technology Literacy curriculum includes the course description and content, an invaluable guide to middle school teachers seeking a fully articulated plan. Students "create a WebQuest connected to a topic from one of the middle school curriculum areas" using the Big6 Skills and Connecticut standards as a framework. Goals, objectives, and content are all specified, with links to appropriate resources.

Appendices include web sites (with corresponding standards and grade levels) devoted to copyright, developing essential questions, Boolean logic, assessment, and graphic organizers (for teachers) and research guides, bibliography compilation and search skills for students. There is a template to organize the collection of bibliographic information, a rubric and self-reflection form to apply to the Big6 Skills (adapted from *Teaching Technology and Information Skills: The Big6 in Secondary Schools*), and a web site evaluation form. The glossary would be particularly helpful to those who may be unfamiliar with some of the vocabulary.

Scope and Sequence

The Clarkstown site includes a detailed list of grade level goals for each of the Big6 Skills that indicates at which grade each skill should be introduced, practiced and mastered. Another page identifies benchmarks at Grades 5, 8 and 12 for each of the information literacy indicators. This type of extensive detail can be helpful to library media specialists and teachers who grasp the concepts of the Big6 Skills and information literacy standards, but are unsure how to apply them in their own teaching situations.

The Clarkstown site also features more extensive alignment with subject area New York State Learning Standards than other sites that restrict their focus to information and technology literacy standards.

Benchmarks

Mankato identifies specific objectives for each of the "Little Twelve" and delineates benchmarks for each grade level, K-12, phrased as "I" statements in each of the following areas: Research and Inquiry Skills, Life-long Reading, Technology Skills, and Appropriate

Use of Resources. The Mankato curriculum includes an additional goal framed in terms of the information-based economy for which we are preparing our students:

> "Potential employers of Mankato public school graduates should be confident that their new employees will know how to identify information needs, locate relevant information in an efficient manner, understand and evaluate information, and use the information to solve a problem, complete a task, or be able to communicate that information clearly to others. Graduates will be able to use technology effectively in the information problem solving process."

Where the Rubber Meets the Road

So, how can you actually use these resources to improve your students' acquisition and mastery of standards? As Ferdi would say, "This is where the rubber meets the road." These are my ideas:

Imagine you are a library media specialist collaborating with a middle school science teacher working on a unit on biomes. I would use the Clarkstown site to help identify connections between information literacy standards and New York learning standards in science <http://www.ccsd.edu/bardonia/CCSDLibraryCurriculum/CurriculumCommittee/standard.htm>. For example, *"Learning Standards for Mathematics, Science, and Technology* Standard 7 [states that] Students will apply the knowledge and thinking skills of mathematics, science, and technology to address real-life problems and make informed decisions." Does your state have a similarly worded standard in science?

The preservation of biomes is certainly a real-life issue. What a great opportunity to introduce critical thinking skills and information problem solving based on the Big6 Skills. West Hartford's curriculum defines a student-created WebQuest as the final product. Good WebQuests incorporate roles that require multiple perspectives and require higher level thinking to construct new meaning. If your students aren't ready to create their own, consider using one or more of those listed on Tom March's new site, Best WebQuests.com, or apply his rubric to others you find. <http://bestwebquests.com/bwq/matrix.asp>

The Clarkstown site associates the following middle school grade level goals with the Big6 Skills (as I think they apply to this assignment):

- **Task Definition:** Create specific questions and use them to develop a thesis statement or hypothesis (P)

- **Information Seeking Strategies:** Determine what information is relevant (P)

- **Location and Access:** Analyze the timeliness, authoritativeness and reliability of the information (P)

- **Use of Information:** Read, view or listen for major ideas and keywords to identify relevant information from a variety of sources (P)

- **Synthesis:** Appraise the information gathered to see if it solves the information problem (I/P) and Make and support personal assertions (I/P)

- **Evaluation:** Inquiry Process: Scope of inquiry was relevant and authentic (P)

Use the web site resources listed in West Hartford's curriculum to help students develop essential questions and evaluate the web sites they plan to use. Use the Mankato objectives and benchmarks to help teachers focus their research assignments on standards and information problem solving. Use the templates from the Minnesota "Electronic Curriculum Repository" to guide the development of lessons or units integrating research skills and content standards.

Compare to Other States

Three of the states whose standards were featured in the previous column (Fall 2002 Vol. E-3 No. 2 http://fp3e.adhost.com/big6/enewsletter/murray.shtml) also have useful resources to consult. North Carolina's "Resources" page lists web sites for lesson plans, assessment (rubrics), web resources and activities. [http://www.ncpublicschools.org/curriculum/Information/resources.html] The Washington Library Media Association lists information literacy benchmarks aligned with each of the Big6 Skills for grades 4, 7 and 10. [http://www.wlma.org/Instruction/benchmarks.htm] Missouri's "Information and Technology Literacy Companion to the Show-Me Standards" includes a section of "sample learning activities that may be used to teach the various knowledge and performance skills" and emphasizes that "Many of the learning activities lend themselves to a cooperative instructional partnership between the teacher and the library media specialist." [http://www.dese.state.mo.us/divimprove/curriculum/literacy/]

Does your state have similar resources?

Big6 Skills and State Standards

By Janet Murray / vE3, no2

Since the establishment of the National Council on Education Standards and Testing (NCEST) in 1991, national standards have been adopted in virtually all curricular areas. "Currently, 49 states have adopted state standards and most districts are assisting schools in bringing standards-based reform to life in classrooms." Many states have developed information and technology literacy standards that extend across curricular boundaries to define skills important for 21st century students.

For example, North Carolina's "Information Skills Curriculum" explicitly connects to the national information literacy standards developed by the American Association of School Librarians (AASL) and the Association for Educational and Communications Technology (AECT) by quoting from the Information Literacy Standards for Student Learning: "Developing expertise in accessing, evaluating, and using information is in fact the authentic learning that modern education seeks to promote."

How can we help students acquire these skills? By using the Big6 Skills approach, of course! The Big6 information problem-solving process dovetails neatly with the information literacy standards as well as the National Educational Technology Standards for Students, as reflected in the matrix, "Applying Big6™ Skills, Information Literacy Standards and ISTE NETS to Internet Research." (http://www.surfline.ne.jp/janetm/big6info.htm)

In this column, I plan to explore four geographically dispersed states' information and technology literacy standards and demonstrate their connection to the Big6 Skills. (See the accompanying matrix) (http://www.big6.com/files/stdmatrx.pdf)

Purpose of State Standards for Information and Technology Literacy

- **Washington:**

  Washington state accompanied their 1996 publication of "Essential Academic Learning Requirements" with the following statement by the Commission on Student Learning:

  "Students need to be able to see patterns and relationships between facts and ideas, and to use facts as tools for understanding and organizing concepts and principles."

- **North Carolina:**

  North Carolina's "Information Skills Curriculum Competency Goals" observes,

  "In order for today's students to function in the 21st century, they must be able to acquire, evaluate, and use information effectively. . . . Information Literacy Skills emphasize the problem solving, critical and creative thinking, decision making, and cooperative learning that prepare students for the challenges in society."

- **Colorado:**

  Colorado's "Standards for Information Literacy" describe information literate students (http://www.cde.state.co.us/litstandards/infolit.htm) as ones who:
  - Are competent, independent learners
  - Actively engage in the world of ideas
  - Confidently solve problems

- Know what is relevant information
- Use technology tools to access information and communicate
- Operate comfortably in situations where there are multiple answers or no answers
- Have high standards for their work and use information ethically
- Create quality products
- Are flexible and adapt to change
- Are able to function independently and in groups.

Colorado's five guidelines describe students as knowledge seekers, quality producers, self-directed learners, group contributors, and responsible information users.

■ Missouri:

"Information and technology literacy skills empower the students to know how knowledge is organized, how to locate information, and how to evaluate and use the information in a way in which it can be communicated to others," according to Missouri's document, "Information and Technology Literacy: A Companion to the Show-Me Standards." (http://www.dese.state.mo.us/divimprove/curriculum/literacy/) It makes an important distinction between process / performance goals and content / knowledge standards, and connects components of information and technology literacy skills to both in a valuable matrix (the "component checklist").

The Missouri document further elaborates the connections between information and technology literacy skills and process / performance standards. For example, the first performance goal, "Students in Missouri public schools will acquire the knowledge and skills to gather, analyze and apply information and ideas," is expanded into ten performance standards elaborated with specific processes and benchmarks. Although these are the standards cited in the matrix accompanying this column, Missouri's other performance goals (2. communicate effectively, 3. recognize and solve problems, and 4. make decisions) also relate to information and technology literacy and are included in their matrix.

Integrate Information and Technology Literacy Skills Across the Curriculum

Each of these four state documents explicitly recognizes information and technology literacy skills as a process that needs to be integrated across the curriculum:

"Research supports the instruction of information literacy skills in an integrated approach, rather than taught in isolation." (Washington)

"A dynamic relationship exists between the goals and objectives identified in the Information Skills Curriculum and all other curricular areas." (North Carolina)

"Information literacy guidelines provide all students with a process for learning that is transferable among content areas and from the academic environment to real life." (Colorado)

"These skills are not meant to be taught as an isolated curriculum but are strands to be integrated throughout the school's curriculum." (Missouri)

Librarians and Big6™ Skills are Essential Partners

Traditionally, libraries have provided society's portal to the world of information, and librarians have been particularly well trained in research processes, including locating and evaluating information sources. All four state documents emphasize the importance of a collaborative partnership between teachers and library media specialists to help students achieve information and technology literacy skills:

> "This guide will be useful to both teachers and library media specialists as they work together in integrating these skills into all content areas, and in support of all the Essential Academic Learning Requirements." (Washington)

> "In collaboration with all classroom teachers, the library media specialist focuses on student involvement, activity and action." (North Carolina)

> "The library media specialist, teaching collaboratively with other teachers, is vital to student learning." (Colorado)

> "Indicator 10.1 C of the Missouri School Improvement Program (MSIP), [states] 'The library media staff, in partnership with the faculty, teaches information literacy skills or integrates these skills across the curriculum.'"

> The Big6 information problem-solving process helps teachers and library media specialists organize their approach to enabling students to acquire information and technology literacy skills. The accompanying matrix extracts a few of these state performance standards and aligns them with each of the Big6 Skills.

Other Resources for Exploring State Standards

Of course, these are not the only four states to have recognized the importance of information and technology literacy.

- **Wisconsin:**

    In 1998, the "Wisconsin Department of Public Instruction published standards that identify and define the knowledge and skills essential for all Wisconsin students to access, evaluate, and use information and technology. The conceptual framework of these standards details a progression from the physical access skills for the use of media and technology, to the intellectual access skills of information use, to skills and attitudes for learning independently, and finally to the skills needed for working responsibly and productively within groups." Wisconsin has developed a matrix of "Information and Technology Literacy Standards" (http://www.waunakee.k12.wi.us/DPI_Standards/matrix. htm) that explicitly relates these standards to the national information literacy standards, the national educational technology standards, and the Wisconsin state content standards.

- **Maryland:**

    Maryland describes "learner outcomes" in Library Media Skills that are measured in the statewide testing program, and cites the Big6 as "an information problem solving process model" to support outcome 3: "Students will demonstrate the ability to learn and apply reading, research and critical thinking skills to organize, and synthesize information in order to communicate new understanding." Maryland's School Improvement Site also supplies valuable links to national standards http://www.mdkiz.org.

- **Florida:**

    Mike Eisenberg and Sue Wurster aligned Florida state language arts standards (http://www.big6.com/showarticle.php?id=151) with Big6™ Skills.

- **Washington:**

  The Washington Library Media Association has compiled a valuable collection of information literacy (http://www.wlma.org/Instruction/infolit.htm) resources, from which I found many of those cited in this article. They also include practical ideas for teaching information literacy skills, with Big6 Lesson Plans at the top of the list.

Standards Collection:

Anticipating the need for a national database of standards, the Mid-continent Regional Educational Laboratory (McREL) began the "systematic collection, review, and analysis of noteworthy national and state curriculum documents in all subject areas" in 1990. McREL's Content Knowledge database (http://www.mcrel.org/standards-benchmarks/) is both browsable and searchable, as well as supported by activities and lesson plans. "Developing Educational Standards" (http://edstandards.org/Standards.html) provides links by subject and by state.

Why Use the Big6 Skills™?

Mike Eisenberg and Bob Berkowitz recognized the importance of information literacy skills as early as 1987, before the terminology was even adopted by AASL and AECT. Their Big6™ Skills model can help our students acquire information problem solving skills. Eisenberg and Doug Johnson made the essential connection between information and technology literacy in their 1996 collaboration, "Computer Skills for Information Problem-Solving: Learning and Teaching Technology in Context."

Therefore, there is a substantial body of research and practice to guide our efforts. By contributing to our developing database as requested in the sidebar, you can increase the value of these resources for yourself and your colleagues, wherever they live.

Big6 Skills™ Aligned with State Standards for Information and Technology Literacy

Big™ Skill	Washington Essential Skills for Information Literacy[1]	North Carolina Information Skills Curriculum Competency Goals[2]	Colorado Model Information Literacy Guidelines[3]	Missouri K-12 Curriculum and Integrated Information and Technology Literacy Skills[4]
1. Task Definition	recognize a need for information	4: The learner will EXPLORE and USE research processes to meet information needs	Determines information needs	1.1 develop questions and ideas to initiate and refine research
2. Information-Seeking Strategies	construct strategies for locating information	1: The learner will EXPLORE sources and formats for reading, listening, and viewing purposes.	Develops information-seeking strategies and locates information; Analyzes information relative to need	1.2 conduct research to answer questions and evaluate information and ideas
3. Location and Access	locate and access information	4: The learner will EXPLORE and USE research processes to meet information needs.	Acquires information	1.4 use technological tools and other resources to locate, select and organize information
4. Use of Information	evaluate and extract information	2: The learner will IDENTIFY and USE criteria for excellence to evaluate information and formats.	Organizes information	1.5 comprehend and evaluate written, visual and oral presentations and works (extract and organize)
5. Synthesis	organize and apply information	5. The learner will COMMUNICATE reading, listening, and viewing experiences	Processes information creates a quality product	1.8 organize data, information and ideas into useful forms for analysis or presentation
6. Evaluation	evaluate information process and product		Evaluates process and product	1.5 comprehend and evaluate written, visual and oral presentations and works (evaluate student process and product)

[1]http://www.wlma.org/Instruction/wlmaospibenchmarks.htm#skills
[2]http://www.ncpublicschools.org/curriculum/Information/preface.htm
[3]http://www.cde.state.co.us/cdelib/slinfoliteracy.htm
[4]http://www.desc.state.mo.us/divimprove/curriculum/literacy

More from Japan: Applying the Big6 Skills and the Information Literacy Standards for Student Learning to Internet Research

By Janet Murray / vE1, no1

"The new education must teach the individual how to classify and reclassify information, how to evaluate its veracity, how to change categories when necessary, how to move from the concrete to the abstract and back, how to look at problems from a new direction - how to teach himself. Tomorrow's illiterate will not be the man who can't read; he will be the man who has not learned how to learn." — *Herbert Gerjuoy*

Correlate Mike Eisenberg's and Bob Berkowitz' Big6™ Skills with the national Information Literacy Standards (http://www.ala.org/aaslTemplate.cfm?Section=Information_Power&Template=/ContentManagement/ContentDisplay.cfm&ContentID=19937) developed by the American Association of School Librarians (AASL) (www.ala.org) and Association for Educational and Communications Technology (AECT) (http://www.aect.org/) and the National Educational Technology Standards for Students (NETS) (http://cnets.iste.org/students/s_stands.html) to organize an introduction to research on the Internet.

Big6 Skill	Information Literacy Standards	NETS	Basic Activities	Advanced Activities
1 Task Definition	1.1 1.3	6.1	Concept Mapping Graphic Organizers	Ask Essential Questions
2 Information Seeking Strategies	1.4 2.4	5.3	Subject Directories Evaluating Web Sites	Web Site Evaluation
3 Location and Access	1.5 7.1	5.1	Keyword Searching Search Strategies	Advanced Search Strategies
4 Use of Information	2.1 2.2	2.2	Extract Information Analyze Sources Bibliographic Citations	Identify Point of View
5 Synthesis	3.1 3.4 9.1	3.2 4.2	Critical Thinking Appropriate Product	Classroom Applications
6 Evaluation	6.1	3.1	Assessment Rubrics	Information Power

1 Task Definition

1.1 Define the information problem.
1.2 Identify information needed in order to complete the task (to solve the information problem).

Information Literacy Standards

1.1 recognizes the need for information
1.3 formulates a question based on information needs

National Educational Technology Standards

6.1 Students use technology resources for solving problems and making informed decisions.

Basic Activities: *concept mapping*
Students often need guidance to refine their inquiry in terms appropriate to the assignment. They may try to tackle a subject that is too broad or too narrow. See "The Power of Visual Learning" (http://inspiration.com/vlearning/index.cfm) for techniques to help students organize their thinking process. Concept maps (http://www.surfline.ne.jp/janetm/concept.html) are a useful visual tool to establish hierarchical relationships.

Basic Activities: *graphic organizers*
There are many other graphic organizers (http://www.sdcoe.k12.ca.us/score/actbank/torganiz. htm) that will help students visualize their thinking (http://www.graphic.org/goindex.html) and brainstorming process. Consider using Inspiration software to facilitate the visualization of ideas. Big6 icons are now a symbol library (http://fp3e.adhost.com/big6/enewsletter/serim_inspiration.shtml) in Inspiration version 7!

Here's an interactive example of using a graphic organizer to enhance vocabulary and understanding of the relationship between words and their synonyms: The Visual Thesaurus (http://www.visualthesaurus.com/online/index.html)

Advanced Activities: *ask essential questions*
Ask essential questions to "promote deep and enduring understanding." See Use Task Definition to Achieve Standards. (http://www.big6.com/showenewsarticle.php?id=391)

2. Information Seeking Strategies

2.1 Determine the range of possible sources (brainstorm).
2.2 Evaluate the different possible sources to determine priorities (select the best sources).

Information Literacy Standards

1.4 identifies a variety of potential sources of information
2.4 selects information appropriate to the problem or question at hand

National Educational Technology Standards

5.3 Students evaluate and select new information resources . . . based on the appropriateness for specific tasks.

Basic Activities: *subject directories*
Students (and even adults) are often frustrated when a search engine retrieves overwhelming amounts of irrelevant information. Encourage new users to use a **subject directory** of

evaluated resources that organizes information hierarchically. Some good starting points for educators and students are:

Kathy Schrock's Guide for Educators (http://school.discovery.com/schrockguide/) focuses on web sites useful in K-12 schools.

Librarians' Index to the Internet (http://lii.org/) sponsored by the Library of California.

KidsClick! (http://sunsite.berkeley.edu/KidsClick!/) web search for kids by librarians.

Yahooligans (www.yahooligans.com) also works well for kids.

Use Google's (http://directory.google.com/) directory rather than its search engine.

Compare the results from trying the *same* search in a variety of subject directories. See

Basic Activities: *evaluating web sites*
Because anyone can publish on the world wide web, it is critically important that students learn to evaluate web sites for authority, accuracy, relevance, currency, and objectivity. Use Checklist for an Informational Web Page (http://www2.widener.edu/Wolfgram-Memorial-Library/webevaluation/inform.htm) to guide your evaluation.

Advanced Activities: *web site evaluation*
Experience the interactive exercise (http://www.lib.berkeley.edu/TeachingLib/Guides/Internet/Evaluate.html) evaluating web pages at the U.C. Berkeley Library.

Use the exercises at ICYouSee: T is for Thinking (http://www.ithaca.edu/library/Training/hott.html) with students.

See Kathy Schrock's presentation at NECC'99 (ABC's of Web Site Evaluation) (http://kathyschrock.net/slideshows/abceval/frame0001.htm) for a detailed summary of factors to consider. Use her 5W's of Web Site Evaluation (on page 288) with students.

3. Location and Access

3.1 Locate sources (intellectually and physically).
3.2 Find information within sources.

Information Literacy Standards
1.5 develops and uses successful strategies for learning information
7.1 seeks information from diverse sources, contents, disciplines, and cultures

National Educational Technology Standards
5.1 Students use technology to locate, evaluate, and collect information from a variety of sources.

Basic Activities: *keyword searching*
Help students improve their **keyword searching** skills by using a simple exercise (http://www.surfline.ne.jp/janetm/srchwk1.html) (on pages 289-290) that compares the results of a search using several search engines.

Introduce younger students to search engines designed especially for them:

Yahooligans (http://yahooligans.yahoo.com/)

Ask Jeeves (http://www.ask.com/)

KidsClick! web search for kids by librarians. (http://sunsite.berkeley.edu/KidsClick!/)

Basic Activities: *search strategies*

The OSLIS Elementary (http://oslis.k12.or.us/elementary/howto/index.html) Page introduces web research skills to younger students.

Teach students the rudiments of Boolean Logic. (http://www.surfline.ne.jp/janetm/boolean.html) see following chart on page 291

Use NoodleTools (http://www.noodletools.com/) with older students to explore search engine strategies, citation formats.

Advanced Activities: *advanced search strategies*

Try your earlier search in a metasearch engine (http://www.surfline.ne.jp/janetm/srchwk2.html) (one that searches using the results from several other search engines); evaluate the results.

Explore advanced features of search engines by reading their help screens or tips for searching. Use Alta Vista's Advanced Search (http://www.altavista.com/web/adv?qbmode=) to find information on very specific topics.

Examine a more detailed explanation of Boolean Logic. (http://library.albany.edu/internet/boolean.html)

Use Finding Information on the Internet: A TUTORIAL (http://www.lib.berkeley.edu/TeachingLib/ Guides/Internet/FindInfo.html) from UC Berkeley or Finding It Online: Web Search Strategies (http://www.learnwebskills.com/search/main.html) for more guidance on effective searching.

4. Use of Information

4.1 Engage (e.g. read, hear, view, touch) the information in a source.
4.2 Extract relevant information from a source.

Information Literacy Standards
2.1 determines accuracy, relevance, and comprehensiveness
2.2 distinguishes among facts, point of view, and opinion

National Educational Technology Standards
2.2 Students practice responsible use of technology systems, information, and software

Basic Activities: *extract information from a source*
Reading for Information: The Trash'n'Treasure Method of Teaching Notetaking (http://www.big6.com/showarticle.php?id=45)
Teach students to distinguish between summarizing, paraphrasing and quoting. (http://www.ohiou.edu/esl/help/quotation.html)

Basic Activities: *accuracy, relevance and comprehensiveness*
Analyze sources of information by evaluating traditional periodicals. (http://www.surfline.ne.jp/janetm/trad.html)

Analyze the use of statistics in "The Dangers of Bread. (http://www.geoffmetcalf.com/bread.html) "What is the relationship between the statistics and the author's conclusions? (See especially #12.)

Read Feline Reactions to Bearded Men. (http://www.improbable.com/airchives/classical/cat/cat.html) Who published this research Do the authors' data support their interpretations? What is your overall impression of the study?

Basic Activities: *bibliographic citations*

Make sure students understand correct bibliographical format. It is as important to correctly cite Internet sources as traditional print sources. OWL (Online Writing Lab) (http://owl.english.purdue.edu/handouts/research/r_mla.html) at Purdue University provides current updates to APA (American Psychological Association) (http://www.apastyle.org/elecref.html) and MLA (Modern Language Association) Style with detailed examples. Students like to use an interactive web tool: the Citation Machine (http://www.landmark-project.com/citation_machine/index.php) or Citation Maker. (http://www.oslis.k12.or.us/elementary/howto/cited/)

Advanced Activities: *identify point of view*

Compare two web sites about scientific research:
JunkScience: (http://www.junkscience.com/)"all the junk that's fit to debunk"
JunkScience from Disinfopedia: (http://www.disinfopedia.org/wiki.phtml?title=JunkScience.com) the encyclopedia of propaganda.
Both of these sites feature strongly worded opinions; what do you think?

5. Synthesis

5.1 Organize information from multiple sources
5.2 Present the information

Information Literacy Standards

3.1 organizes information for practical application
3.4 produces and communicates information and ideas in appropriate formats
9.1 shares knowledge and information with others

National Educational Technology Standards

3.2 Students use productivity tools to collaborate in constructing technology-enhanced models, prepare publications, and produce other creative works.

4.2 Students use a variety of media and formats to communicate information and ideas effectively to multiple audiences.

Basic Activities: *critical thinking*

Encourage the development of critical thinking skills in your Internet research projects. In addition to evaluating web resources, students should be engaged in evaluating their own thinking process and applying the information they gather to authentic challenging tasks.
New Times Demand New Ways of Learning
(http://www.ncrel.org/sdrs/edtalk/newtimes.htm)

35 Dimensions of Critical Thought (http://www.criticalthinking.org/resources/TRK12-strategy-list.shtml)

Basic Activities: *appropriate product*

Student presentations should be appropriate to their topics and their audiences. What will be the most effective format to demonstrate what they have learned? Examine Doug Johnson's "Designing Research Projects Students [and Teachers] Love" (http://www.infotoday.com/MMSchools/nov99/johnson.htm) for ideas. Consider the suggestions for successful Internet assignments (http://lib.nmsu.edu/instruction/evalsugg.html) at the New Mexico State University Library.

Look at NASA's Classroom of the Future Modules (http://www.cotf.edu/ete/modules/modules.html) for examples of problem-based learning. Adapt Project Based Learning (http://www.pblchecklist.4teachers.org/) checklists to guide your students.

Well-designed Web Quests (http://edweb.sdsu.edu/courses/edtec596/about_webquests.html) encourage collaborative learning, the thoughtful analysis of Web resources, and the creation of original products. Use Tom March's collection of "Best WebQuests" (http://bestwebquests.com/bwq/matrix.asp) to find quality examples.

Advanced Activities: *classroom applications*
Sample Teaching Strategies for K-12 Teachers (http://www.criticalthinking.org/resources/articles/#teaching) from the Center for Critical Thinking

6. Evaluation

6.1   Judge the product (effectiveness)
6.2   Judge the information problem-solving process (efficiency).

Information Literacy Standards
6.1   assesses the quality of the process and products of one's own information-seeking

National Educational Technology Standards
3.1   Students use technology tools to enhance learning, increase productivity, and promote creativity.

Basic Activities: *assessment rubrics*
Select from Kathy Schrock's collection of Assessment Rubrics (http://school.discovery.com/schrockguide/assess.html) to evaluate student projects, including web pages, research papers, multimedia and group presentations. Use RubiStar (http://rubistar.4teachers.org/index.php) to customize your rubric from a template.

Advanced Activity: *Information Power*
Information Power (American Library Association, 1998) includes an appendix describing assessment strategies for the **process** of information-gathering as well as the **products** of student synthesis.

The Five W's of Web Site Evaluation

Who

Who wrote the pages and are they an expert?
Is a biography of the author included?
How can you find out more about the author?

What

What does the author say is the purpose of the site?
What else might the author have in mind for the site?
What makes the site easy to use?

When

When was the site created? When was the site last updated?

Where

Where does the information come from?
Where can I look to find out more about the producer/sponsor?

Why

Why is this information useful for my purpose?
Why should I use this information?
Why is this page better than another?

Key Word Searching

Try this: Select a compound topic (at least two words). Use the diagram to help you choose the words you will use. Search in each of the search engines. Which one gave you the most useful results?

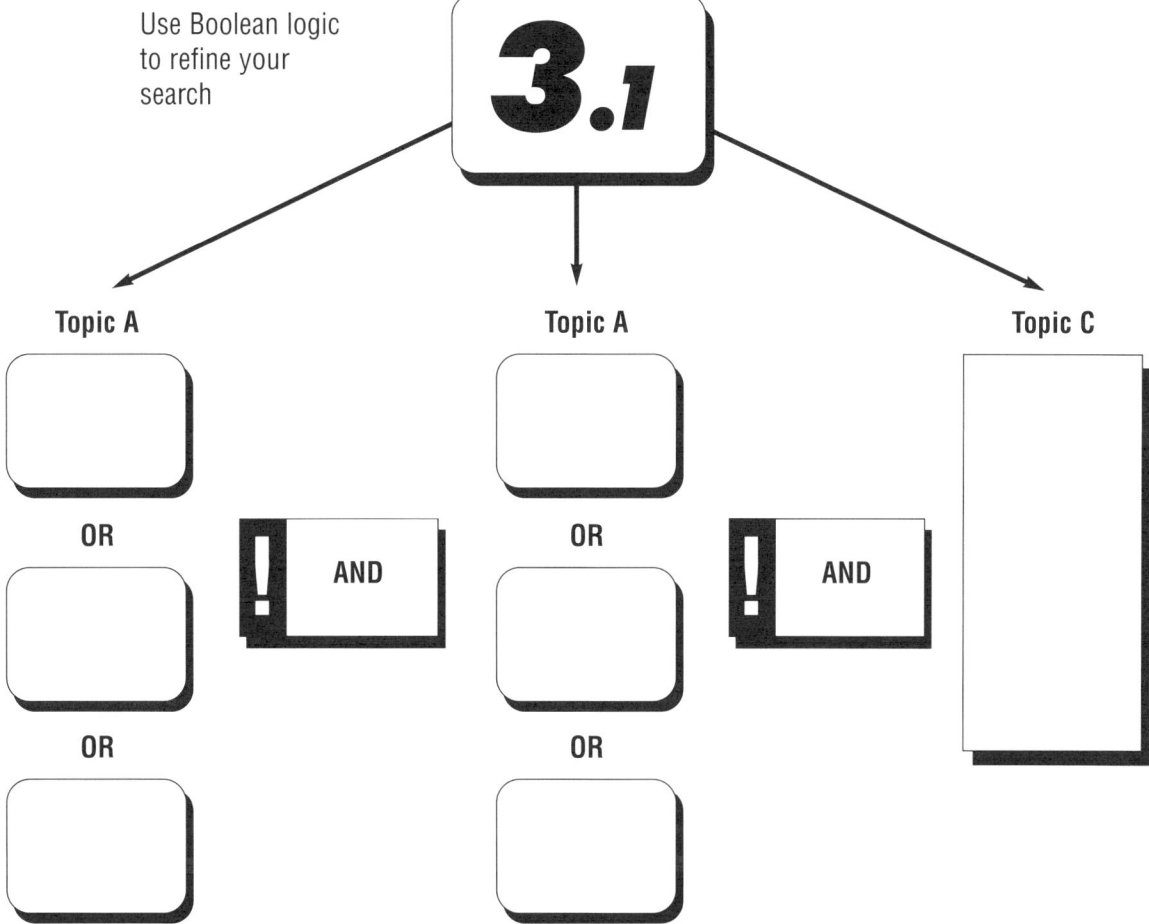

Use Boolean logic to refine your search

3.1

Topic A

OR

AND

OR

Topic A

OR

AND

OR

Topic C

Key Word Searching continued

Name: _____

Teacher/Period: _____

Use these search engines; while you're there, explore some of their features. Remember to write down not only the number of sites they retrieved, but also how many you think will be useful to you.

	Number of Sites	Useful Sites
Google		
Look at the list of sites you retrieved; just below each title is the "category" in which that site is listed. Click on a likely category; now how many sites did you find?		
Try a search "only in" your primary subject.		
KidsClick!		
Try an Advanced Search; now how many sites did you find?		
Yahooligans		
Look at the category matches; choose the one most closely related to your topic. Now how many sites did you find?		
Try a more specific search in "just this category" (your major topic.) Now how many sites did you find?		
Ask Jeeves		
Enter the two or three words of your compound subject.		
Try rephrasing your topic as a question; now how many sites did you find?		
Try a "metasearch" engine - one that compiles results from many search engines: **Dogpile**		
Now how many sites did you find?		

Boolean Logic

Computers can be very effective tools to locate information, but they are **ONLY** machines. It is important to understand that computer output depends upon human input, and is only as useful as the instructions we provide. Computerized search mechanisms are based on Boolean logic; the better we understand how it works, the better will be the results we obtain.

Boolean logic utilizes three primary operators: **AND**, **OR**, and **NOT**. It is helpful to diagram the effects of these operators:

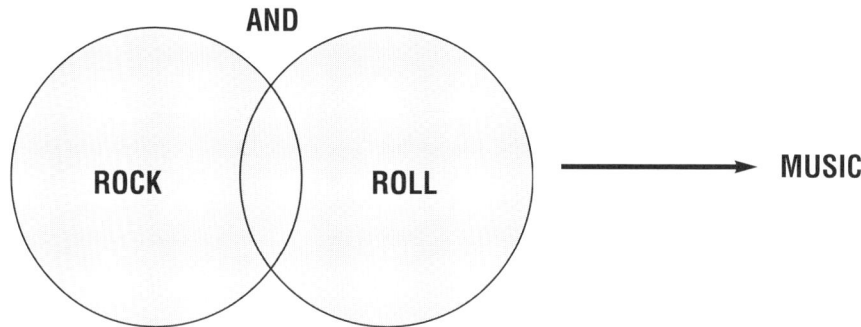

Using the word "AND" actually **narrows** the results obtained in a search, while using the word "OR" **broadens** the results.

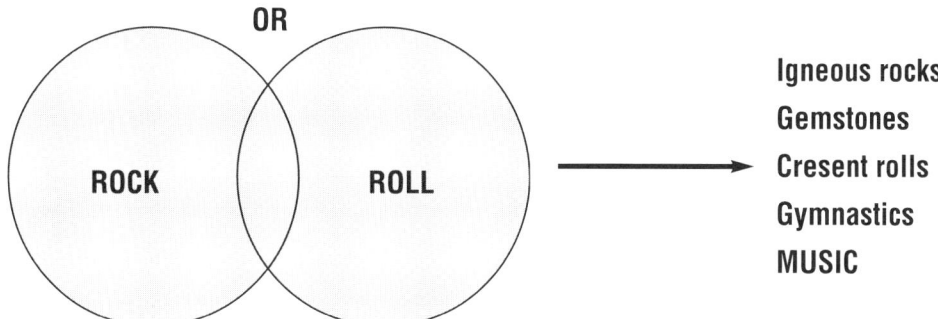

To see the difference, enter a search for acid rain on Metacrawler. Try the search once with "ANY" and then again with **"ALL"** by checking the appropriate boxes.

 Which search gave you the largest number of results?

 Which search gave you the most useful results?

The Boolean operator "OR" can be very useful when there are many synonyms for a concept, and we do not know which one might have been chosen by the author or indexer. For example, teenagers OR adolescents OR youth will yield many more citations than any of these words by itself.

We can also **limit** the results by using the Boolean operator "NOT."

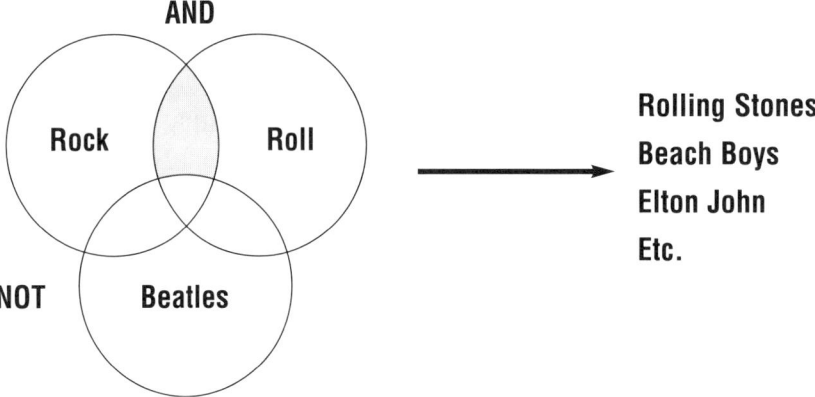

Different search engines incorporate Boolean logic in different ways. It is important to read the instructions for each search engine before entering your search terms.

Developing Information Literacy and Technology Standards Using the Big6

By Sally Lancaster / vE2, no3

The Everett School District is in the Seattle, Washington region. Seattle is widely recognized as a technology-savvy area, so it should be relatively easy to introduce a technology-driven curriculum into the local schools, right? After all, the region is home to Microsoft, Boeing, Amazon.com and the University of Washington. The use and acceptance of technology driven standards should be deeply imbedded into the psyche of Everett's students, faculty and administration, right?

Wrong! In spite of its location and technology-savvy population, the Everett Public School District faces the same challenges every school district faces in setting goals and developing strategies for information technology literacy. This article outlines the Everett Public School District's struggle to find a way to integrate technology into the curriculum and how the structure of the Big6 provided a practical framework for the everyday application of information technology.

National Technology Standards

Initial attempts at integrating technology into the curriculum led the Everett Public Schools' Technology Articulation Committee to the International Society for Technology Education (ISTE) National Educational Technology Standards (NETS). ISTE has developed six technology-learning standards for students. The committee reviewed each standard's viability for use, developed grade level indicators and initiated a pilot project to test ISTE standards at the classroom level. After months of committee work and educator feedback it was discovered that the ISTE standards, while wonderful targets, were not arranged in a way that would be easy for teachers to integrate into the teaching and learning process. Even the most technology-oriented teachers were not consciously pulling technology standards into their planning, even though there was evidence of technology use all around them.

Technology and Information Literacy

While the Technology Articulation Committee was working on integrating technology into the curriculum, the district teacher-librarians were working to adopt the Information Literacy Standards for Student Learning developed by the American Association of School Librarians (AASL) and the Association for Educational Communications and Technology (AECT) into the curriculum. These standards were to become the curriculum of the teacher-librarians in the district and provide a bridge for collaboration among teachers and teacher-librarians. Throughout the process there was much discussion around the redundancy of the NETS standards being proposed by the Technology Articulation Committee and the information literacy standards being proposed by the teacher-librarians. Concern was expressed about the ability of teachers to incorporate two more sets of standards into the curriculum when the pressure and stakes surrounding the implementation of content area standards were so high. Several unsuccessful attempts were made to collapse the two sets of standards into one document, but those efforts appeared to dilute both sets of standards. The challenge was to devise a way to assimilate the students' need to become literate users of information technology into the context of existing curriculum demands, without overburdening teachers.

How the Big6™ Structure Helped

Hearing of our frustrations, Mike Eisenberg suggested we use the Big6™ Information Problem solving process as a structure for organizing both sets of standards. This made sense when the district considered that virtually every classroom in the district engages in information problem solving of some type. Using the Big6 to organize the important technology and information literacy concepts all students should meet was a natural way to integrate them into the teaching and learning process.

With this new information, the teacher-librarians went back to work creating the Everett Public Schools' Information Literacy and Technology Standards. These standards were then shared with the Technology Articulation Committee and were piloted in classrooms throughout the district. Across the board, feedback was that combining both sets of standards made sense. Utilization of the Big6 provided teachers with a process for integrating technology in a way that did not seem like an added area to teach, but rather became a way to teach content using a variety of tools.

While the Big6 provides the structure for the first six standards, it was not inclusive of all the necessary technology skills. For that reason, a seventh standard was added to deal with basic skills necessary to utilize technology tools, with an emphasis on teaching these skills in context not in isolation.

Putting Standards to the Test

Testing the standards before adopting them was a critical step in this process. It was not until selected educators had the opportunity to put the standards to use in their classrooms that the core of the District's challenge in implementing these standards was unveiled. Everett still has many challenges to face regarding the implementation of its Information Literacy and Technology Standards. Training teachers about what the standards are and creating strategies for teaching the standards to students are the largest issues being confronted at this time. Recognizing that information literacy and technology are critical life skills for all of our students and connecting these skills to every class in our district is an important achievement for the Everett School District.

Big6™ Matrix: What's New?

By Janet Murray / vE3, no1

Integrating technology into student learning is a challenge for all of us. For a couple of years, I have been using a matrix that aligns Big6 skills with national information & technology literacy standards to help teachers see their relationship, improve their research project assignments, and guide students using the Internet for research. Indeed, I was privileged to share this matrix with attendees at the Big6™ Conference in August, 2001.

While most teacher librarians live and breathe national information literacy standards (e.g., the *Information Power standards* from the American Association of School Librarians and Association of Educational Communications and Technology), teachers and administrators are more likely to be tuned into *ISTE NETS* (National Educational Technology Standards for students). Like the information literacy standards, (http://www.surfline.ne.jp/janetm/big6info.htm) ISTE NETS expects students to use technology to locate and evaluate information as well as communicate it. So I have recently incorporated these standards into the matrix. Each of the Big6 skills is correlated with specific standards in both schemes and accompanied by exercises to improve the use of Internet or World Wide Web information sources.

- **Big6 Step 1. Task Definition:** ISTE NETS expects students to "use technology resources for solving problems and making informed decisions." Students (and even some adults) often need to be persuaded that information processing and problem-solving strategies are a skill they will need throughout their lives. I use examples like buying a car or choosing a college to establish the importance of learning these skills.

- **Big6 Step 2. Information Seeking Strategies:** ISTE NETS expects students to "evaluate and select new information resources . . . based on [their] appropriateness for specific tasks." Students typically think the Internet has all the answers, but may become frustrated at their inability to instantly locate pertinent information by typing a word or two into Yahoo. I encourage students to use a subject directory that arranges relevant, reliable sites hierarchically by subject. We also spend time evaluating Web sites for authority, accuracy, currency, relevance and objectivity.

- **Big6 Step 3. Location and Access:** ISTE NETS expects students to "use technology to locate, evaluate, and collect information from a variety of sources." Understanding how search engines work, and how they differ from subject directories, helps students search more efficiently and effectively. I encourage students to search using synonyms and related topics, to compare the results of the same search in different search engines, and to use Boolean logic to refine their searches.

- **Big6 Step 4. Use of Information:** ISTE NETS expects students to "practice responsible use of technology systems, information, and software." In addition to citing their sources, I encourage them to analyze sources for objectivity by identifying the sponsoring organization and comparing the information retrieved to that found in another source.

- **Big6 Step 5. Synthesis:** ISTE NETS expects students to "use a variety of media and formats to communicate information and ideas effectively to multiple audiences." I encourage teachers to consider alternatives to the traditional research paper. *PowerPoint* presentations and Web pages require students to synthesize their information by using a minimum number of words for their maximum informational impact. WebQuests can also be effective synthesizing tools when students are researching authentic, challenging tasks that may have multiple points of view and no prescribed answers.

- **Big6 Step 6. Evaluation:** ISTE NETS expects students to "use technology tools to enhance learning, increase productivity, and promote creativity." At the end of every Big6 experience, students must evaluate both their product and their process. Did the use of technology enhance their learning experience? Did they use technology to create their product?

Using a matrix that correlates the Big6 skills with national standards helps me guide my students and teachers toward achieving those standards while using the Internet for research. Future columns will focus on using each of the Big6 skills in the context of library research.

Integrating the Big6 and ISTE NETS for Students

By Evelyn Beyer, Kathleen L. Spitzer / vE2, no3

The National Educational Technology Standards (NETS), developed by the International Society for Technology in Education *(ISTE, 2000a, 2000b), define foundational technology standards for both teachers and students. ISTE is currently working with other groups to create technology standards for administrators. The ISTE NETS are available at http://cnets.iste.org/. This article focuses on the ISTE NETS for students and how these standards fit within the Big6 framework.*

ISTE NETS Categories and Standards

The ISTE NETS for students are divided into six comprehensive categories. Categories are then subdivided into the standards. Indicators at different grade levels are a further division of the standards; however these will not be examined in this article. The categories and standards are as follows:

1. Basic operations and concepts

a. Students demonstrate a sound understanding of the nature and operation of technology systems.

b. Students are proficient in the use of technology.

2. Social, ethical, and human issues

a. Students understand the ethical, cultural, and societal issues related to technology.

b. Students practice responsible use of technology systems, information, and software.

c. Students develop positive attitudes toward technology uses that support lifelong learning, collaboration, personal pursuits, and productivity.

3. Technology productivity tools

a. Students use technology tools to enhance learning, increase productivity, and promote creativity.

b. Students use productivity tools to collaborate in constructing technology-enhanced models, prepare publications, and produce other creative works.

4. Technology communications tools

a. Students use telecommunications to collaborate, publish, and interact with peers, experts, and other audiences.

b. Students use a variety of media and formats to communicate information and ideas effectively to multiple audiences.

5. Technology research tools

a. Students use technology to locate, evaluate, and collect information from a variety of sources.

b. Students use technology tools to process data and report results.

c. Students evaluate and select new information resources and technological innovations based on the appropriateness for specific tasks.

6. Technology problem-solving and decision-making tools

   a. Students use technology resources for solving problems and making informed decisions.

   b. Students employ technology in the development of strategies for solving problems in the real world.

The Big6™

The Big6™ Skills information problem-solving model developed by Eisenberg and Berkowitz consists of six stages:

- **Task Definition** - defining the problem

- **Information Seeking Strategies** - determining possible sources of information

- **Location & Access** - locating information sources and information within those sources

- **Use of Information** - reading, hearing or viewing the information and extracting relevant information

- **Synthesis** - putting together information from various sources to solve the problem

- **Evaluation** - determining if the information problem was solved and judging the efficiency of the information problem solving process

The Big6 model is being used by teachers and library media specialists to develop information literacy and technology skills in schools throughout the world. By integrating the model with existing curriculum, teachers can ensure that students achieve information and technology literacy.

ISTE NETS and the Big6™

How do the ISTE NETS for students and the Big6 fit together? What technology skills are indicated by each? Table 1 proposes an idea of how these two might be integrated.

Big6™	ISTE NETS for Students	Explanation

Entire Big6™ model	1. Basic operations and concepts
	  a. Students demonstrate a sound understanding of the nature and operation of technology systems.
	  b. Students are proficient in the use of technology.
	2. Social, ethical, and human issues
	  c. Students develop positive attitudes toward technology uses that support lifelong learning, collaboration, personal pursuits, and productivity.
		Through the Big6 model, students will use technology skills and become proficient in the use of various technologies. In so doing, students will develop positive attitudes.

1. Task Definition
  1.1 Define the problem.
  1.2 Identify the information requirements of the problem.
	4. Technology Communications Tools
	  a. Students use telecommunications to collaborate, publish, and interact with peers, experts, and other audiences.
	6. Technology Problem Solving and Decision Making Tools
	  a. Students use technology resources for solving problems and making informed decisions.
	  b. Students employ technology in the development of strategies for solving problems in the real world.
		In defining a problem, students may use telecommunications software to collaborate with others or to contact an expert. Students may also use graphic organizers or flowcharting to help define the problem and its information requirements.

2. Information Seeking Strategies
  2.1 Determine the range of possible sources.
  2.2 Evaluate the different possible sources to determine priorities.
	5. Technology research tools
	  a. Students use technology to locate, evaluate, and collect information from a variety of sources.
	  c. Students evaluate and select new information resources and technological innovations based on the appropriateness for specific tasks.
		After students have analyzed the type of information resources needed, they will determine the range of possible sources. These sources may include online databases, print or electronic books, newspapers, magazines, encyclopedias, print or electronic maps, videos or websites.

3. Location & Access
  3.1 Locate sources (intellectually and physically).
  3.2 Find information within sources.
	4. Technology communications tools
	  a. Students use telecommunications to collaborate, publish, and interact with peers, experts, and other audiences.
	5. Technology research tools
	  a. Students use technology to locate, evaluate, and collect information from a variety of sources.
	  c. Students evaluate and select new information resources and technological innovations based on the appropriateness for specific tasks.
		Students will use searching skills such as identifying keywords or concepts and Boolean logic as they seek information within databases or through search engines. Students may also use telecommunications as they seek information from others or experts in the field.

4. Use of Information
  4.1 Engage the information in a source.
  4.2 Extract information from a source.
	2. Social, ethical, and human issues
	  a. Students understand the ethical, cultural, and societal issues related to technology.
	  b. Students practice responsible use of technology systems, information, and software.
	3. Technology productivity tools
	  a. Students use technology tools to enhance learning, increase productivity, and promote creativity.
	4. Technology communications tools
	  a. Students use telecommunications to collaborate, publish, and interact with peers, experts, and other audiences.
	5. Technology research tools
	  a. Students use technology to locate, evaluate, and collect information from a variety of sources.
		Students may use word processing or presentation software to extract the information from a source. As they do so, they need to be aware of issues such as copyright and intellectual property.

5. Synthesis
  5.1 Organize information from multiple sources.
  5.2 Present information.
	2. Social, ethical, and human issues
	  a. Students understand the ethical, cultural, and societal issues related to technology.
	  b. Students practice responsible use of technology systems, information, and software.
	
	3. Technology productivity tools
	  a. Students use technology tools to enhance learning, increase productivity, and promote creativity.
	  b. Students use productivity tools to collaborate in constructing technology-enhanced models, prepare publications, and produce other creative works.
	
	4. Technology communications tools
	  a. Students use telecommunications to collaborate, publish, and interact with peers, experts, and other audiences.
	  b. Students use a variety of media and formats to communicate information and ideas effectively to multiple audiences.
	
	5. Technology research tools
	  b. Students use technology tools to process data and report results.
		In organizing and presenting information, students may use word processing or presentation software, spreadsheets, databases, interactive multimedia, or video production programs. When presenting information, students need to be aware of copyright issues and proper citation of sources.

6. Evaluation
  6.1 Judge the product (effectiveness).
  6.2 Judge the information problem-solving process (efficiency).
	1. Basic operations and concepts
	  b. Students are proficient in the use of technology.
	
	2. Technology productivity tools
	  a. Students use technology tools to enhance learning, increase productivity, and promote creativity.
	
	Note: all standards in this column are copyright ©2000, Internation Society for Technology in Education (ISTE).
		As students judge their product and process they will assess their own proficiency and productivity in using technology to solve information problems and to present information. Students may use graphic organizers or word processing software to analyze their information problem solving process.

Conclusion

As the previous chart indicates, students can achieve the ISTE National Educational Technology Standards by using the Big6 information problem-solving process in conjunction with curricular needs. To implement the standards, teachers need to analyze existing curriculum and infuse technology where appropriate. A number of sample lessons and units have been collected by ISTE and are available in print (ISTE, 2000a) or online at http://cnets.iste.org/index2ns.html. These lessons and units for grades K-12 cover five subject areas: English Language Arts, Foreign Language, Mathematics, Science, and Social Studies. As you read through the sample lessons and units, use the above chart to think them through in terms of the Big6.

Bibliography

Eisenberg, M. B., & Berkowitz, R. E. (1990). *Information problem-solving: The Big6™ skills approach to library & information skills instruction.* Stamford, CT: Ablex Publishing. ISBN: 0-89391-757-5

International Society for Technology in Education (ISTE). (2000a). *National Educational Technology Standards for Students: Connecting curriculum and technology.* Eugene, OR: Author. ISBN: 1-56484-150-2. [On-line]. http://cnets.iste.org/.

International Society for Technology in Education (ISTE). (2000a). *National Educational Technology Standards for Teachers.* Eugene, OR: Author. ISBN: 1-56484-162-6. [On-line]. http://cnets.iste.org/.

Index

C

D

E

I

J

K

Q

R

S